DR. JOYCE

What Every Ought to Love and

BROTHERS

Woman Know About Marriage

SIMON AND SCHUSTER
NEW YORK

SIMON AND SCHUSTER and colophon are registered trademarks of
Simon & Schuster, Inc.

Designed by Irving Perkins Associates

Manufactured in the United States of America

1 2 3 4 5 6 7 8 9 10

Library of Congress Cataloging in Publication Data

Brothers, Joyce
What every woman ought to know about love and marriage.
1. Marriage.   2.Mate selection.   3.Women—
Psychology.   I.Title.
HQ734.B855   1984   646.7'7   84-10584
ISBN 0-671-44159-0

*To every woman who wants to get married
and every woman who is married
and wants to stay that way*

THIS BOOK IS WRITTEN ESPECIALLY FOR YOU. IT IS AN INTENSELY PERSONAL BOOK. NOT ONLY DO I SHARE THE SECRETS OF MY OWN THIRTY-FIVE-YEAR MARRIAGE, BUT I HAVE PUT TOGETHER THE MOST SIGNIFICANT RESEARCH INTO INTIMATE RELATIONSHIPS BETWEEN MEN AND WOMEN IN WAYS THAT EVERY WOMAN CAN ADAPT TO HER OWN SITUATION, PERSONALITY AND LIFE STYLE.

THE PATH OF TRUE LOVE HAS NEVER BEEN EASY AND MARRIAGE HAS ALWAYS BEEN A DO-IT-YOURSELF PROPOSITION, BUT THIS BOOK CAN SERVE YOU AS A PSYCHOLOGICAL TOOL KIT THAT WILL HELP SMOOTH THE ROUGH SPOTS, STRENGTHEN THE WEAK ONES AND DIAGNOSE PROBLEMS BEFORE THEY BECOME SERIOUS. THIS IS YOUR BOOK, WRITTEN TO HELP YOU FIND THE LOVE AND FULFILLMENT YOU WANT.

Contents

PART ONE

THE HUSBAND GAP

And How to Bridge It

last United States census, there were 7,300,000 more women of marriageable age than men! Seven point three million more women than men!

This scarcity of husband material is due to the fragility of the male sex. Although more males than females are born (for every 100 baby girls, there are 105 baby boys), the male suffers a higher death rate during infancy, childhood and adolescence. All his life as a matter of fact. He ends up dying some eight years earlier than we do.

At age twenty-two, there are more men than women, but sometime during that year, the balance shifts, and at age twenty-three there are more women than men. From then on it is all downhill. By the time a women is forty, for instance, there are almost three hundred single women for every one hundred available men. There is no getting around these figures. They are a matter of demographic fact, there for everyone to see in all their chilling reality in the United States census reports.

This is not all the bad news. The husband gap is actually much wider than 7,300,000 men, because the pool of marriageable men is depleted by the male homosexual population. Some experts estimate that homosexuals represent about 10 percent of the male population, while others maintain that the percentage is higher. Then there are those men who, for reasons of health, economic or other obligations, personal preference or religious calling, are not husband material.

But let's stay with our 7,300,000 figure—7,300,000 too few men; 7,300,000 too many women. It is bad enough. If 7,300,000 is hard to grasp in the abstract—and not many of us deal in millions—just imagine if Austria were populated exclusively by women. Unmarried women. That is just about what it adds up to. At any time, there are enough American women who are not going to get married to populate a whole country.

Not only are there fewer men, they are more reluctant to marry these days. You can blame part of their reluctance on the pill, which has made contraception practically automatic. No fuss. No muss. And no baby. In the old days—and they were not all that long ago—sex carried the risk of pregnancy, a risk most women were unwilling to face outside of marriage. Men had little choice. Marriage was their passport to easily available sex. Today if a man is attracted to a woman, he is more likely to suggest that she move in with him than to propose marriage.

So what's wrong with that? Nothing really, if you are willing to settle for a short-term relationship. I'll talk about why the live-together life does not usually lead to marriage later on, but right now I'm talking about marriage.

Who needs to get married? Who even *wants* to get married? The answer is that most women do. And why not? Marriage is the most dependable source of happiness and security and just plain well-being there is in today's world.

I am not saying that marriage is undiluted bliss. Someone once asked if I had ever considered divorcing my husband. I replied without even having to think. "No," I said. "Murder, yes. But divorce, no." There are times when Milt drives me up the wall. And times when he would gladly toss me out one of our thirtieth-floor windows. But an hour or so later we can laugh at ourselves and love floods back.

The wonderful thing about marriage is that you are the most important person in someone else's life. If you don't come home some evening, there is someone who is going to go out looking for you.

And when the whole world seems to be rejecting you—you lost your job, someone said something nasty about you, your thirteen-year-old daughter turns hostile overnight, the vote went against you, whatever—there is someone who is not going to reject you. Someone who is going to feel sorry that you are having such a rough time. Who is going to feel almost as bad as you do. You can face up to almost everything if you know there is someone who loves you and is on your side no matter what the rest of the world is saying or thinking.

Best of all, there is someone to share happiness with. When good things happen, there is someone who is going to be happy for you and with you. Just as you are when good things happen to him.

Marriage is the salt of daily life. It makes everything just a little bit better. Yes, I know that there are women who feel that marriage is confining, that it stands in the way of their self-fulfillment, that men are just too aggravating and demanding. Perhaps so. But when they are asked, as a scientifically chosen sample of single women was asked by a team of Northwestern University researchers, more than 75 percent of them declared they would much rather be married than single.

What this all adds up to is that the woman who wants to find a man and get married and the woman who is already married and wants to stay that way are going to have to work at it. Harder than a man does. How could it be otherwise? Look at the figures. You certainly would not buy a lottery ticket offering those odds. There are more of you than there are of him, and he is not as eager for marriage as you are.

I cannot promise that you will find a husband and live happily ever after by using what you learn from this book. But I can promise that the odds will be changed in your favor, because knowledge is power. There are millions of other women out there who want the same thing you do, and 7,300,000 of them are going to be disappointed. The only way you can get an edge is to know more about how to choose your man, get your man and make him yours forever.

I can promise the woman who is married now that this book will help her change the odds to a little in her favor too. Because finding your man and marrying him is only half the battle. Keeping him is where it is at.

This is the era of the disposable wife (see Chapter 33). The divorce rate is close to one out of every three marriages, and in some areas every other marriage ends up in the divorce courts. So you can't just sit back on your marriage certificate and think you have it made. There are millions and millions of women out there who consider married men fair prey. The woman who wants to keep her marriage on the happy-ever-after track has to work at it. And I can help you with that.

We should stop complaining that we have to make the greater effort. It's not so bad. I can't think of a pleasanter line of work.

TWO

The Mr. Right myth . . . The truth about office romances . . . Twenty-two-plus ways to meet a Mr. Right . . . And three ways to meet a Mr. Wrong . . . The humiliating "seven-second encounter" . . . Why summer romances have more going for them . . . The best way to make friends and meet men in a new town

The good news is that, despite the horrendous husband gap, there are hundreds and thousands of Mr. Rights for each and every woman.

We tend to think in terms of a one and only who is somehow predestined to make us happy. No such thing. And thank goodness! Suppose there were only one Mr. Right for you and he happened to be in Tibet and here you are in Winnetka without a clue to his whereabouts. Would the two of you ever meet? It would be a miracle if you did. There may very well be a Mr. Right for you in Tibet, but there are dozens right where you are, in Winnetka or Rapid City or Hackensack or Pasadena or Montgomery.

Many women have a wildly romantic notion that some handsome stranger is going to sweep them off their feet, according to research into women's romantic fantasies carried out by a perfume company. "She wants the passionate adventurous life.

She is not going to marry the boy next door," the researchers reported.

That may be valid as far as fantasy goes, but the fact is quite different. The reassuring and marvelously comfortable truth is that most women marry a man who lives no more than a mile away and find him as sexy and exciting as the handsome stranger of their fantasies. More than half the people in Columbus, Ohio, for instance, who got married in one three-month period lived within sixteen blocks of each other.

You do not have to go to the ends of the earth to find a man with whom you can be happy. But you do have to get out of the house. While it is absolutely true that there are hundreds and thousands of Mr. Rights for you, a lot of them are Mr. Rights for other women too. Whether you are going to be the one who leaps the husband gap boils down to who gets there first.

An old recipe for alligator stew goes "First catch your alligator." The recipe for marriage is similar. First find your man. You can't just sit back and wait for Prince Charming to come knocking at your door. If you spend your evenings knitting in front of the television set and your weekends curled up with a mystery, you may never meet anyone except—just possibly—the United Parcel man or the meter reader. You have to get out of the house and meet people if you want to get married.

The man you will marry may be just around the corner this very minute. Or in the same line at the bank. Waiting for a machine to be free at the laundromat. He may be the man you see every morning at the bus stop or the one who is lifting weights while you are working out on the Nautilus machines at the health club.

Or he may be at the next desk. These days practically every unmarried woman works. And many of them get a lot more out of it than a paycheck or a promotion. When an English magazine asked two thousand women between the ages of sixteen and forty where they had met the main man in their lives, it turned out that most of them had met their boyfriend or husband at the office. It is truly a great place to meet men.

An office is like a home town in microcosm. You usually know a little bit about everyone and you have a lot in common. There is always something to talk about. The terrible coffee dispensed by the office machine...how you felt when you got stuck in the elevator that morning...why it is that the computer always seems to be "down" when you need it most. You see each other every day in a casual way. At work you have a chance to get to know each other gradually without the pressure of a dating situation when you are both intent on impressing each other.

Many people frown on office romances. Dr. Robert Quinn, an organizational management specialist, took an unromantic look at them and pronounced them undesirable—from management's point of view. Out of the 130 office romances he studied, 90 percent of them were counterproductive. They disrupted office routine or caused jealousy, resentment and gossip or interfered with job performance—or did all of the preceding.

I do not quarrel with his findings, but what I have observed is that when young people who work for the same organization fall in love, their coworkers and bosses tend to look benevolently on the romance as long as the couple do not let it interfere with their work. And there is something else. Dr. Quinn could only study those romances that were conducted in public. The smartest men and women tend to be very discreet and keep their private lives private. It is wonderful and exciting to be in love and it is natural to want to share your joy, but it is wiser to keep your feelings to yourself. Not only does this make good office sense, but discretion adds a certain titillation to the romance and brings you even closer because you share a secret that no one else suspects. And if you should break up eventually, you will be spared embarrassment since most people will not even be aware there was a romance, let alone that the romance has ended.

The office romance that creates waves is the one where one or both of the lovers is married. This is when coworkers really become resentful and jealous. "The lovers are seen as using each other for different rewards," Dr. Quinn says. "The male for sexual and ego gratification and the female for power." And the gossip can be virulent.

Management quite naturally takes a dim view of anything that affects office morale. The boss's usual way of restoring normalcy is to dismiss the lower-ranking employee. The state of sexual equality in offices being what it is, the woman is twice as likely to be dismissed as the man.

But if you are looking for the classic girl-meets-boy romance, or divorcée meets eligible male, the office can be a happy hunting ground. And there is little management can do about it. Especially if you are discreet and no one knows about your romance.

The office is not the only place where eligible men abound. Hospitals are full of male doctors and medical students, male patients and visitors. You might think about volunteering to work at your local hospital a few hours a week. You can be sure that whatever you do—making the rounds with the library cart, walking patients down the hall, pushing wheelchair patients to therapy or treatment—is useful and appreciated. You will find great reward in volunteering. Just feeling good about yourself, for instance. And having a chance to learn a little about the world of medicine. And you just might meet some interesting men.

The same goes for politics. If you are interested in politics and foursquare behind your political party, then you might consider joining your local political club. It will be a liberal education and you will have the satisfaction of knowing you are a good citizen. More than that, you can feel proud of yourself for trying to make a difference, to improve the quality of life. And the men you will meet may very well be as idealistic and ambitious as you are. But do not get involved unless you are truly interested and willing to work your head off.

Another possibility—and this is one that I have advocated for years and years—is to buy ten shares of as many companies on the New York Stock Exchange as you can comfortably afford. I would say buy just one share, but this drives brokers crazy and many of them will not do it. I advise this ploy particularly for widows, divorcées and single women who have a certain amount of discretionary money left over at the end of the month. This is not for the twenty-five-year-old who is spending every penny she earns on clothes and rent.

Buying stock offers a number of benefits. You automatically have a new interest in life. You look up your stock in the financial pages every morning to see if it has gained or lost. You read news stories about the industry that you never would have read before. The more different stocks you own, the more informed you become. All this is a big plus. Your stocks may also become a financial plus—or again they may not—but they will definitely be an educational plus.

But the big plus as far as meeting men is concerned is that owning stock entitles you to go to the annual meetings of your companies. There is often lunch involved—usually a box lunch—and you will be elbow to elbow with people, most of them male, who are interested in the same thing you are— the profit picture of Amalgamated Elbow Scuffers or whatever. You will find little difficulty in starting conversations. Most people are more than willing to share their criticisms of management when profits are down or their jubilation over a stock split.

The rule about all activities you might engage in to meet men is that they must offer something that interests you so much that they are their own reward. That way you cannot possibly lose. And if you meet a Mr. Right or two, that is the frosting on the cake.

The main thing is to do something. Swing into action. And right now. Any campaign—military or marital—takes planning if it is to succeed. The first order of business then is for you to get paper and pencil and start your own planning.

Write down ten ways you can meet men. Ten realistic ways. Down-to-earth ways that are open to you here and now, right where you live and work. Think of all the organizations and activities in your area. Consult your local newspaper. Think of your own special interests—cooking or jigsaw puzzles, photography or tennis, gardening or making dollhouse furniture, travel or folk singing. Whatever. And then before you read any further, write down ten ways in which your interests or secret desires can open the way to meeting more men.

Please do not turn the page until you have finished.

All right. You have come up with ten imaginative ways to meet men. Good work. And here are more than twice as many more ways to add to your list.

1. Make your vacations count. For instance, how about going to Florida with a girlfriend while the baseball teams are there for spring training. Find out where your favorite major league team goes for spring training and then combine a sea-and-sun vacation in Florida with watching baseball. Most of your companions in the bleachers will be male. If you have done your baseball homework, you will have no difficulty getting involved in discussions of batting averages and pulled tendons and all the rest.

2. If Florida is not feasible, you might consider a week on an old-fashioned sailing schooner that drops anchor at picturesque fishing villages and historic ports up and down the coast of Maine. These are quite reasonable and they tend to attract as many or more men than women.

3. Or how about a bridge tour? If you play bridge (and this is really for the over-forties group), such a tour might be just the ticket for you. A friend of mine conducted one of these tours last year. Over one hundred dedicated bridge players—male and female—went to Monaco on a charter flight, played bridge with European experts when they arrived, checked out the Riviera beaches and tried their luck at Monte Carlo's casino. Sounds too expensive? Not as high as you might think because of group rates. And my friend reports that two romances blossomed during the tour.

4. You might prefer to spend a week or even two of your vacation at a tennis camp. A good proportion of your fellow campers will be male. And so will most of the instructors. If nothing else, you will have a chance to improve your backhand.

Ask a travel agent for more suggestions. Level with him or her about your desire to meet men. But don't let the agent sell you on a singles cruise or resort. There is too much competition at these places. It is easy to feel depressed and unwanted. Insist on something with a small group and planned activity.

5. This is the era of self-improvement, especially physical self-improvement. Why not plan to get yourself in better shape?

Where do you do this? At your local health club or Y. And I'll tell you where the men are. They are in the machine room. Oh, you will also find them in the pool or on the track, but for an activity where you will be surrounded by males, work out on the Nautilus machines or Universal equipment or whatever your local spa or Y offers.

Please don't rule this out because your thighs are less than firm or you have a bulge where there should be a hollow. In this case you really need to get in shape. Buy yourself an exercise outfit that disguises the worst and get to work.

One young friend of mine—157 pounds of pudge—started a self-improvement program at the Y. She went four nights a week after work and worked out on the Nautilus machines, then ran a few laps around the track and finished with a few laps in the pool. The guys who worked out on the machines at the same time were very supportive of her efforts to shape up. When she had trimmed down to a curvy 120, they presented her with a gift-wrapped carton of cottage cheese.

No, none of these really nice men turned out to be Mr. Right, but one of them introduced her to his brother. And the brother was Mr. Right. So you see, you never know.

6. And while we are being physical, you might consider taking judo lessons. Once a male classmate has thrown you to the mat—or you have thrown him—the social ice is broken once and for all. Even if you don't meet the man of your dreams, you will have learned the art of self-defense, and that is one of the more practical arts these days. Many Y's offer courses. Some school systems offer judo in their adult education programs. And there are judo schools, which you can find listed in the Yellow Pages of the telephone book.

7. For the less energetic, consider the spectator sports. Support your local basketball or football team by turning up for the games. Or if you live in or near a big city, you can attend the pro games. The stands are full of men and nothing brings two people closer much faster than cheering for the same team. I suggest you go with a girlfriend. It is easier to start talking when there are two of you—and safer.

8. And there is nothing wrong with talking to strangers. No matter what your mother told you when you were a little girl. If you are on a plane or a long train or bus ride, by all means chat with your seatmate. You don't have to wait for him to start. Just don't

interrupt him while he's deep in *The Wall Street Journal* or *The Sporting News*. By the time you arrive at your destination, you may have a new friend. If not, you will have had practice in being outgoing and taking the initiative.

I know a woman who met her future husband while they were standing on line for a movie. She started talking to him as they inched their way toward the ticket office. He suggested they sit together. Afterward he suggested they have coffee together. And a fine romance was off and running.

9. Entertain on a regular schedule. This is a wonderful way to bring new people into your life. Make a habit of giving Sunday brunches or Sunday night suppers once a month. Not intimate little twosomes. Those tend to scare men off. Plan on dinner for six or eight. You can almost count on at least one invitation in return and possibly two. You will meet new people as your guests reciprocate, and little by little your circle of acquaintances will widen significantly. As you become more at ease with entertaining, you can experiment with changing the formula. Instead of Sunday brunch, have a picnic or a cookout for a change. Or a skating party. Or an after-the-movies supper.

10. If the idea of cooking for six or eight people throws you into a panic, that suggests you could benefit from a cooking course—French or Mexican or Chinese or Italian. Whatever appeals to you and is available locally.

More and more men are becoming interested in cooking and are signing up for these courses. You can make discreet inquiries about the male-female mix before you commit yourself to a class. Working together to master puff pastry or hollandaise sauce banishes all shyness and self-consciousness. Afterward, in most of these classes, everyone sits down and samples the results. Often with a bottle of wine. You will have fun, learn something new and acquire eight to ten new acquaintances.

Another plus here. If you are worried that you don't know six or seven people to ask to dinner or brunch, there is nothing wrong with asking your cooking-class classmates.

11. Cooking almost inevitably leads to wine. What are you going to serve with your crown roast of pork or your boeuf bourguignon or your broiled trout? The easiest and most inexpensive

way to become knowledgeable about wine is to take a wine-tasting course. Most of these give you a chance to sample and compare five or six wines a session and learn which are compatible with which foods. People talk a lot in these classes. There are often spirited disagreements as to how to describe or rate a wine. You get involved right from the start.

12. Join a club. It seems to me there is a club devoted to almost every subject under the sun. There are bird-watching clubs and gourmet clubs and theater clubs and music clubs and folk dance clubs and—these are the newest—computer clubs. There are doll-house-building clubs (and don't think that these don't bring out the men. Thousands of men build dollhouses as a money-making hobby).

13. Near me in the country, there is a flying club. No, not what you think. It is for people interested in building and flying model airplanes. You just know that the membership is going to be predominantly masculine. If you enjoy working with your hands, this might be something you would enjoy.

14. There are stamp collectors' clubs, and the membership does not consist of little boys. More men than women collect stamps. They look on them as a good investment. So if you are interested in meeting new people and pursuing a hobby that may prove prof-itable, think stamps.

15. Then there is photography. There must be thousands of clubs for camera buffs. One nice thing about most of these clubs is that they organize trips to special "photo opportunities." There's nothing like a trip to bring people together.

16. It might be wise, before you join that photography club, to learn something more about the subject than where to point the camera. Any photography supply store should be able to inform you about available classes.

17. Take a weekend job. Or a Saturday afternoon job. Not just any job but one where you will meet people.

Real estate is a good bet. You may have to take a course and pass an exam before you can start selling, but a course is just one more place to meet people who have something in common with you. The great thing about real estate is that you tend to meet people new to the area who need friends as well as shelter.

18. You like the idea of a part-time job, but you are not pre-

pared to invest the time and effort required by something like real estate. If you are young, how about a job scooping ice cream on Saturday afternoons at the local ice-cream parlor? Or working behind the counter at the most popular pizza joint in the area? The customers are in a weekend mood. The fellow who teases you about your ice-cream-scooping technique on Saturday afternoon may very well suggest going bowling Saturday night.

19. If you are beyond the ice-cream-scooping age, think about Saturday jobs at the local hardware store. Or the computer store. Or a sporting goods store.

20. If there is a little adventure in your soul, you might consider taking up flying. Most flying instructors are male. And practically everyone hanging out at small airfields is male. There is a wonderful atmosphere at these airports. It is like belonging to a wonderful exclusive club. And if you are learning to fly, you are automatically part of the group.

21. Buy a dog. Whether you acquire a lovable mutt (known as a mixed breed) or a thoroughbred, a dog can change your life for the better. You get more exercise, make more friends, and learn more about people and animals than you knew before you became a dog owner.

When I used to walk our old Joey (she was really Lisa's dog, but guess who walked her and fed her and took her to the vet?), I met the most interesting people out walking their dogs. We used to chat about our dogs and the weather and the traffic and the theater— and each other. We all remarked on how often single dog walkers paired off.

There is a whole dog world. There are obedience courses, handling courses, dog clubs, dog shows. Even the mixed breed is welcome at obedience courses. These are good for your dog and wonderful for you. Members of obedience classes often get together outside class to practice obedience with each other—and their dogs, of course.

If you have invested in a thoroughbred, the world of dog shows and breed clubs is fascinating. If you get involved, you will find yourself busy every weekend if you want to be.

22. Share a summer place. It is quite usual and accepted in the New York area, for instance, for a group of men and women to share a beach house for the summer. Or a ski house for the winter.

Three teachers rented a house in the Hamptons at the tip of Long Island four summers ago. They decided to sell shares in the house to three other women and six men. They advertised in a couple of newspapers and then spent a month screening the replies. They interviewed the applicants who sounded most compatible and finally settled on the other nine. Contracts were drawn up spelling out the house rules and regulations and financial arrangements.

It was a wonderful summer. All twelve house-sharers agreed they could never have had such a good time alone. Three marriages resulted from the summer. One of the men, now the father of two, said, "I don't know where else I could have met my wife. She was in publishing and I'm in broadcasting and neither of us went to singles bars. If we hadn't been sharing the house, we might never have met."

Summer romances "can lead to something very lasting," says psychiatrist Samuel Dunkell. "A summer romance has the momentum to carry much further than a more prosaic romance. It has a history, which is positive and romantic and which can be banked on when a couple starts to negotiate the realities of an ongoing relationship."

So there you are—ten ideas of your own and twenty-two of mine. If you have not met at least three new men by the end of next month, I will be very surprised. But you have to get started. And that also involves planning.

This is the time to get out your calendar and work out a schedule for the next few months. Don't plan to start more than two new projects, but do start them as soon as possible. If one or both of them does not work out, then choose two more projects until you find something that is just right for you.

Sometimes it seems that no matter how hard you try and no matter how imaginative you are about thinking up ways to meet more people, there is just nothing you can do. Perhaps you live in the suburbs where everyone is heavily married and not interested in a single woman. Or in a small town that boasts a main street and a gas station and that's it, a town where you know everyone already—and don't want to marry any of them.

In that case, my advice is to make a change. A big one. Move. To the nearest big city perhaps. Or a city on the other side of the country. Almost any place that you believe will offer the possibility of work you can do and opportunities to meet people easily. If you decide on a major change like this, please do not rush into it. It is important to do your homework before making a final decision. Write the Chamber of Commerce. Read everything you can about the area. Spend part of your vacation looking it over. When you are convinced that this is the right step, then go ahead. But not until you have saved enough money to support yourself for a while.

I am convinced that the very best way to get established in a new place is to sign up with a firm that supplies temporary office help. Going out on temporary jobs gives you a chance to find out what is available, and you will meet new people as you go from office to office and have a chance to make friends very quickly. You also build up a backlog of employers who can give you references when you settle on a job you want permanently.

Nancy, a divorcée in her thirties, was hesitant about plunging back into the business world. She signed up with an agency that sent her out on temporary jobs as a way of polishing her old skills. After six months she had worked for a dozen or more firms. Finally she found a job that she loved—executive headhunter.

"I worked for an executive recruitment firm while the manager's secretary was in the hospital," she said. "I knew a little about some of the companies they did business with because I had met executives of those companies when I used to go to conventions with my ex-husband. As I watched the recruiters at work, I realized that this was something I could do. Something I really wanted to do.

"I told my boss how much I enjoyed working there and how interested I was in the work. He agreed to give me a trial.

The salary was low—nothing more than a gesture—but I had
a chance at a job I wanted."

Nancy worked sixteen hours a day at the beginning, but it
paid off. She gradually made her own niche in the firm and
specialized in recruiting women for management jobs in high-
tech industries.

"It's a great job," she reported happily after her second
year. "And one of the greatest things about it is that I'm
meeting terrific men. Men who are attractive and vital and
successful. It's a fringe benefit I hadn't considered when I
started."

I have given you a lot of do's about how to meet men. Now
I want to give you some equally important don'ts. Some of
the most publicized ways of getting to meet men are ego destructive. Some are dangerous. And most are useless.

SINGLES BARS. I know that some women have met their
Mr. Right in a singles bar, but more women have met a Mr.
Wrong.

Not all singles bars are the sinister places that were shown
in *Looking for Mr. Goodbar*, nor are they all zoos where women
are ogled while men look for one-night stands. But even the
best of them are not very satisfactory. Women complain that
most of the men are married—or losers. Men complain that
most of the women are "dogs" and the ones who are attractive
are rude and "uppity."

The real problem with singles bars is the "seven-second
encounter." In the course of a two-month research project,
psychologists armed with stopwatches hung out in singles bars
and observed how long men spent getting to know women.
They discovered that the men judged the women they saw in
a singles bar in practically the blink of an eye. The average
encounter timed by the psychologists' stopwatches was seven
seconds. Seven seconds!

If you don't make an immediate impression, that's it. He

goes on to another woman, another seven-second snap judgment. This is enough to rule out singles bars as a place to meet
eligible men. The seven-second encounter reflects a disdain
for women. It relegates them to objects.

ADVERTISING. Both men and women have started advertising in the personals column of certain newspapers and magazines, some of them very prestigious. The ads are well read
and draw responses. But my advice is—don't.

One woman—I'll call her Lois—ran an ad to the effect that
she was twenty-nine and liked good food, long walks, jazz and
rock and would like to meet a man who shared those interests.
Lois received twelve letters, including one that seemed as if
it had been written by Mr. Perfect. She telephoned him and
they arranged to meet at a coffee bar. Before she had finished
her espresso, she knew she had made a mistake. Nothing about
him was as he had represented himself in his letter. "He was
probably the slimiest creature I have ever met," she said afterward. "But he wrote a wonderful letter."

Lois was lucky. Sylvia, who was completely charmed by a
man who responded to her ad, asked him in for a drink when
he drove her home after their first date. He led the conversation
around to his job as an appraiser for a large auction house.
He told her that a cut-glass bowl on her coffee table was worth
at least $500. She was amazed. He offered to look over the
rest of her possessions and gave her estimates on what they
were worth.

You have probably guessed what happened. Her apartment
was burglarized the next day while she was at work. The
burglar did not take the cut-glass bowl or any of the other
objects her date had told her were valuable, but her television,
her stereo, her table silver and her electric typewriter were all
stolen. When she gave the police the man's name and address,
the address turned out to be that of a motel and the man was
no longer there. The auction house said they had no record
of a man of that name ever having been on their staff.

There is also an element of physical danger in going out

with a man about whom you know absolutely nothing except what he tells you. There is also the fact that the men who answer these ads almost always believe that the woman is interested in sex.

DATING SERVICES. Most of these are perfectly legitimate and, yes, I know women have married men they met through a dating service, but by and large I consider them useless for the woman who is interested in marriage.

Women who pay the fee—and it can be high—do get dates. But when you think of how many more women of marriageable age there are than men (7,300,000 remember?), you have to wonder about the men who sign up with these services. Have they no friends? Is there no one at work who can introduce them to women? Chances are that most of them are either wimps or shoppers.

Surveys show that usually only the attractive women are asked for a second date. Now if you are attractive, why should you pay a dating service to find you a date? If you have trouble in meeting men, you would do better to explore some of the suggestions given earlier in this chapter. They are effective— and cheaper.

The less-attractive woman gets very little for her money except a feeling of inferiority. Five or ten dates with five or ten men, none of whom asks her for a second date, do nothing good for a woman's ego. There are better ways to meet and establish relationships with men.

Dating services make a great point of computer matching, but just having interests in common is not enough, as one man learned. After the computer notified him of his first date, he wrote the dating service, "Congratulations. I now have the name and address of my cousin whom I've gone through school with and worked with for the last four years." Superficial similarities are not enough. The computer cannot capture the magic that is at the base of the attraction an individual man and woman feel for each other, because it is mainly psychological. Too subtle for dating service computers to analyze.

In between the do's and don'ts, there is a maybe—the singles clubs. There are many excellent clubs, some of them with fine activity programs, sponsored by churches and synagogues. If there is one near you, by all means give it a try, but be prepared to find at least three or four women to every man. And a lot of them will be shoppers who go from singles club to singles club. But the men you do meet in these clubs are usually better bets than those who frequent the singles bars or answer advertisements. If you don't meet any men who interest you, you may meet women who do. And this can be a real plus. You will not have wasted your time if you make a new friend.

There you have it—the do's, the don'ts and a maybe. There is a common denominator to the don'ts. Neither the singles bars nor the advertisements in the personals columns nor the dating services offers anything except the possibility of meeting a man. You gain nothing else from your investment of time and money. You have not broadened your horizons. You have not learned anything that will make your life richer or easier or more amusing. You may, in fact, have become depressed and feel unworthy and rejected. And who needs to feel that way?

You should not feel there is something wrong with you because you have to make a conscious effort to meet men. There is *nothing* wrong with you. The only thing that is wrong is that there are more women who want to get married than there are men to marry them. The fact that you are making an effort says something good about you. You are not just going to sit back and hope. You are in control of your life. And you can be pretty sure that you will be one of the women who will find a Mr. Right.

How do I know that? I know it because I know that if you get busy and meet enough men, your chances of marrying will be better than most women's. I will explain just how this works in the next chapter.

THREE

How long will it take you to meet a Mr. Right? ... The five ingredients of the Intimacy Formula ... How to tell if a date will lead to a long-term relationship ... How to apply the Intimacy Formula to your own life ... Are you an Amanda or an Elise?

You know about the husband gap now. You understand that if you are to marry or remarry, you have to make an effort to get out and meet people. But how can you tell if the effort will pay off? How long will you have to keep up this campaign that you have planned so carefully?

The answer is that it all depends. On you. An ingenious psychologist has devised a formula by which you can work out your own answers to these questions. It may seem strange that something as personal as meeting a man and having lightning strike in the form of love can be reduced to a formula almost like a recipe for making pecan pie or directions for making a sweater. But it can. The reason is that despite the incredible diversity of people's likes and dislikes, values and backgrounds, there are drives and needs and reactions that are common to all of us.

The Intimacy Formula, developed by Dr. Jeffrey Young,

clinical assistant professor in the psychiatry department of the University of Pennsylvania, is based on your own personality and the mathematical laws of probability. By spending a few soul-searching minutes on this formula, you can determine how many men you will probably have to meet before you meet one with whom you would like to have a long-term intimate relationship and who would like to have one with you. You can also find out how long it will probably take you to find him.

Once you have these answers, you have a base from which to start. As you will learn, you can work to improve your chances. Most women will be able to increase their chances by as much as 50 percent. Some may increase them by 100 percent. Or 500 percent.

The Intimacy Formula consists of five items:

- Opportunity
- Selectivity
- Receptivity and Initiative
- Desirability
- Intimacy

I will use two hypothetical young women, Amanda and Elise, to show how the formula works. Amanda teaches first grade and lives at home with her parents in the suburbs. Elise has a studio apartment in the city and works for a fashion photographer. Incidentally, although Amanda and Elise are young, age is not a factor. The formula is as applicable to the woman of fifty as it is to the woman of twenty.

1. OPPORTUNITY. How many eligible men do you have the opportunity to meet in the course of a month? This does not mean that you actually meet them but that you have the opportunity of meeting them.

Amanda depends on her married girlfriends to fix her up with bachelor friends and relatives and with single men whom their husbands meet at work. She also has an opportunity to meet new people at the health club where she swims.

Amanda has an opportunity to meet two eligible men a month.

Elise works closely with the photographer's clients and models.
She is invited to a lot of parties, and she also takes a film criticism
course where she meets new people.
Elise has the opportunity to meet ten men a month.

2. SELECTIVITY. How many of the men you have an opportunity to meet do you find desirable enough to consider going out
with?
Amanda won't go out with a man who is not good looking. He
has to be taller than she is and have an annual income of at least six
figures. Only one in twenty of the men she has an opportunity of
meeting lives up to her requirements. Since she has an opportunity
of meeting only two eligible men a month, it may be a long time
before she meets a man she wants to go out with.
Amanda's selectivity score is 5 percent—one out of twenty. This
is put in decimal form, as are the rest of the scores, which makes
her selectivity score .05.

Elise is nowhere near as fussy about the people she goes out with.
She likes people. All kinds of people. Out of the ten men she has a
chance to meet each month, she would go out with half of them.
Elise's selectivity score is .50.

3. RECEPTIVITY and INITIATIVE. How many of the men you
find attractive do you actually end up meeting and letting them
know—directly or indirectly—that you would like to see more of
them?
Amanda will not approach a man even if she finds him fascinating.
She is receptive to the approaches of one out of four men who meet
her standards. Don't forget, though, that Amanda has the opportunity of meeting only two men a month and is drawn to only one
out of every twenty of these men. So even though she is receptive
to one out of four of the men she finds worthy, it is going to take
her a long, long time to meet four men who live up to her expectations.
Amanda's receptivity score is .25.

Elise is much more receptive to people and often takes the initiative in getting to know men who attract her. Out of the men she would be willing to date, she is receptive to three-quarters of them. Elise's receptivity score is .75.

4. DESIRABILITY. What percentage of the men you actually meet and are attracted to find you desirable enough to want to go out with you?

Only one out of four men whom Amanda meets and likes actually asks her out.

Amanda's desirability score is .25.

Elise rates herself low in desirability. She feels that only one in twenty of the men she meets and likes finds her desirable. This seems a very low percentage, but it is the way she sees herself.

Elise's desirability score is .05.

5. INTIMACY. How many of your dates will develop into intimate relationships that will last at least six months?

You do not have to be a mind reader or a fortune teller to answer this. Just think back over previous relationships you have had. How many of them lasted at least six months? Your past track record is a good indicator of future performance. Incidentally, intimate does not necessarily mean a sexual relationship. It can be an intimate emotional relationship. Or both.

Amanda reports that only one out of four of the men she would like to have an intimate relationship with feels the same way.

Amanda's intimacy score is .25.

Elise is more successful in developing intimate relationships. Three-quarters of the men she finds desirable and who find her desirable become intimates.

Elise's intimacy score is .75.

	AMANDA	ELISE
OPPORTUNITY	2	10
SELECTIVITY	.05	.50
RECEPTIVITY/		
INITIATIVE	.25	.75

	AMANDA	ELISE
DESIRABILITY	.25	.05
INTIMACY	.25	.75

You now have all the information necessary to find out how long it will probably take Amanda and Elise to find a Mr. Right. All you have to do is apply the Intimacy Formula.

$$\frac{.7}{\text{Opportunity} \times \text{Selectivity} \times \text{Receptivity/Initiative} \times \text{Desirability} \times \text{Intimacy}} = \text{Months}$$

In Amanda's case, multiplying 2 by .05 by .25 by .25 by .25 and then dividing the answer (.0015625) into .7 (which is Dr. Young's probability factor) equals 448 months. Divided by twelve, this comes to a little over thirty-seven years before Amanda probably meets a Mr. Right.

Elise, on the other hand, has a good chance of meeting a Mr. Right in less than five months.

The Intimacy Formula does not promise marriage. What it does do is give you the probabilities of how long it will take you to meet a man with whom you will have a long-term intimate relationship. But in my book, a long-term intimate relationship with a member of the opposite sex almost always spells marriage.

What about poor Amanda? Well, she may not have to wait the full thirty-seven years. While the formula indicates that she will meet only one man whom she will love and who will love her in the course of thirty-seven years, it is quite probable that she might meet him next year. And then not meet another man who measures up for thirty-seven years.

If I were Amanda and I really wanted to get married, I would make some changes in my life. I would try to improve those scores. Suppose she made an effort to meet more men so that she had a chance to meet four new men each month instead of two.

And if she were more realistic about the men she would go out with, just a little less picky and rigid, she could easily improve her selectivity score by 10 percent—from .05 to .15.

Let us say that she improved her Receptivity/Initiative, Desirability and Intimacy scores by 10 percent too. It is quite possible to do this.

This would mean that she would probably meet that special man in just a little more than twenty-seven months—a big improvement over thirty-seven years. And yet no drastic changes would be involved. Amanda would not have to transform her personality or act like someone she is not in order to improve her scores. In the following chapter, I will suggest ways you can improve your own scores so that you will meet a Mr. Right sooner. There is no reason for you to be an Amanda.

(If you want to know more about Dr. Young's work on loneliness and intimacy, you may be interested in reading a chapter he contributed to the book *Loneliness: A Sourcebook of Current Theory, Research and Therapy*, edited by Letitia A. Peplau and Daniel Perlman, published by John Wiley & Sons in 1982.)

FOUR

*The dream-man trap . . . Why tall men may be
disappointing . . . Are you a Melissa or a Muffy? . . . When
to take the initiative with a man . . . The dating jitters and
how to get rid of them . . . How to make a man think you
are even prettier, more charming and sexier than you
are . . . The kind of woman every man wants*

If you want to tilt the odds of meeting a Mr. Right more in
your favor, there are concrete changes you can make. The
Intimacy Formula gives a fairly accurate picture of you and
your life today. But not tomorrow. We are all capable of change.
Let's take the five ingredients of the formula one by one and
see how you might improve your score.

OPPORTUNITY

The most important change for most women is to start meeting
more people. Any of the ways I outlined in Chapter 2 will get
you off to a good start. But don't confine yourself to my
suggestions. Use your own list of ten. Or twenty. You know
more about your own special interests and needs and talents
than anyone else in the world.

SELECTIVITY

Some women are just too fussy. They set their standards unrealistically high. That mythical Amanda, the ill-starred heroine of the last chapter, should take a good look at herself and ask, "What's so special about me? Why should I only deign to go out with tall, handsome men who earn more than $100,000 a year?" By setting up unreasonable and unrealistic requirements, she cut herself off from so many eligible men that chances were it would have taken her thirty-seven years to meet just one man who was right for her.

At one time or another almost every woman dreams of marrying a tall, handsome multimillionaire. And that is fine. As a fantasy. Fantasies are a particularly delightful kind of daydream, but you should not confuse them with reality. Otherwise you fall into the dream-man trap and may never find a real man.

Height is a ridiculous standard by which to judge a man. Diana, Princess of Wales, did not let the fact that Prince Charles was shorter than she stand in the way of romance, but many women refuse to date a man who is shorter than they are.

A survey of female college students showed that they preferred their dates to be six inches taller than they were. This preference carries right through to marriage. In one group of ninety-eight married couples, the mean height of the husbands was six inches more than that of the wives.

This partiality for height is associated with a psychological phenomenon known as the halo effect. I often talk about it in my lectures because it influences most of us more than it should. The halo effect has nothing to do with saintliness but with first impressions and preconceived ideas. It can be negative or positive. Remember the "seven-second encounter"— the way men size up women in singles bars? Women do the same thing. They often make up their mind about a man on the basis of first impressions. If a man is shorter than they, some women will ignore him. We tend to believe that tall men are more competent, stronger, nobler and have more leadership qualities. This probably stems from prehistoric days when size was associated with strength and a tall man was a better protector. Today this prehistoric hangup of ours makes us consider tall men more desirable dates and husbands than short ones. We think tall men have more status.

The truth is that some tall men are great. They are intelligent, forceful, gallant, courageous and all the rest. And some tall men are wimps. They are marshmallows, often tormented by the strain of trying to live up to the exaggerated idea most people have of their abilities and strengths.

Good looks are no way to choose a man either. I will discuss the role of looks in courtship and marriage in Chapter 10, but for now let me just point out that handsome men tend to date beautiful women. If the face in your mirror is wholesome and healthy but a five compared with Brooke Shields or Christie Brinkley or Lauren Hutton, you would do better to encourage men who are fives and sixes on the masculine scale instead of waiting for a ten.

Nor is money any way to judge a man. My husband was earning practically nothing when we got married. (I am happy to say that he is doing considerably better now.) The men who make the most money often make the worst husbands, because their true love is money and the power it represents, not a woman.

If the only man who will please you is six foot two, dark haired, blue eyed, broad shouldered and with an annual income in the high six figures and an interest in tropical fish, it might be wise to be somewhat less selective, because there are not an awful lot of them around.

The qualities to look for in a man are sincerity, warmth, integrity, courage, gentleness, perseverance, sympathy, intelligence. These are far more important than height or looks or money.

RECEPTIVITY AND INITIATIVE

Just having an opportunity to meet a man will not change anything unless you take advantage of it. That knight in shining armor will never carry you off on his white charger if he does not know you are there. It is important not only to be receptive to a man's approaches but to take the initiative when it is called for.

Do not worry that a man will think you pushy or unfeminine if you indicate an interest in him. Men find assertive and moderately assertive women most appealing. It is the extremes that turn them off—the timid little mouse of a woman and the blatantly aggressive woman.

Melissa is the mousy nonassertive type.

A man she has been dying to meet is at the office Christmas party. She has watched him in the elevator and admired him striding down the hall to the Friday morning executive meetings but she has never met him. This is her big chance. And she knows it.

She makes her way over to him on the other side of the room. He is in the center of a group talking about scuba diving. This is great good luck. Melissa was a scuba instructor during college summer vacations.

But did she mention this? Did she say anything at all? No. She just stood there on the edge of the group. Listening. Listening intently is a very effective way to flatter a man, but he is never going to notice how intently you are listening unless he notices you first. Men can be extraordinarily dense about picking up body cues. A woman can walk across the room, stand next to a man, pass him an ashtray when his cigarette ash is about to drop, even brush against his arm—and he may be completely unaware of her. This would never happen with a woman if the situation was reversed. But men's brains are different, and they tend to concentrate on one thing at a time. The handsome young executive was concentrating on what he was saying. He did not notice Melissa.

There were ways she could have brought herself to his at-

tention. She could have taken his empty glass and brought
him a fresh drink, first asking him what he was drinking. She
could have asked him where he thought the best diving was.
She could have broken in during a pause with a story about
her own diving experiences. Any of these would have been
appropriate actions.

If she had said or done something to attract his attention
so that he was at least conscious of her, she would have established a basis for talking to him the next time she saw him
in the office. Perhaps saying a few words about the party or
asking when he was going on his winter vacation or telling
him that she was going to scuba dive in Jamaica during her
winter vacation.

But Melissa was a mouse. After a while she drifted away,
got her coat and went home. She had missed her opportunity.

Muffy is the assertive type.

She was eating in the company cafeteria one spring day—
reading a paperback and spooning up her yogurt. Two men
sat at her table and started talking about their weekend. They
had spent it at the beach, surf casting for striped bass.

"Excuse me," Muffy interrupted. "I couldn't help hearing
you talk about that beach. I'm looking for a place to go next
weekend. Just to get some sun and fresh air. Are there any
places to stay there that aren't expensive? Do you need a car?"

In seconds they were telling her where to stay and what to
do. The following Monday, she spotted one of the men in the
cafeteria and went over to him. "I can't thank you enough,"
she said. "I had a marvelous time. The Tide's Inn was great.
I loved those breakfasts." And so on. By the end of the lunch
hour there was a new man in Muffy's life.

The Muffys of this world know hundreds of ways to take
the initiative in getting to know a man who attracts them. But
when it comes to dating, even in this liberated day and age,
men get uneasy when women make the first move. There is
a way to get around this without alarming them. And that is
the "nondate."

You can ask a man over for Sunday night supper, for instance, as long as there are other guests. Or tell him that a bunch of you usually play softball Saturday afternoons, and would he like to join you? Keep it casual and make it seem spur of the moment. Don't ask him to the movies or a restaurant. This can make him feel crowded. But if you are asking people over to play bridge or poker or getting a group together to go Christmas caroling or picnicking, by all means ask him. The secret is to indicate an interest in him—but not a romantic interest. Not yet.

DESIRABILITY

Some women put their worst foot forward when they meet a man or go out on a date. They talk too much or too loudly. They act too sophisticated or girlish or cynical or tough. Instead of being themselves, they role-play in an attempt to impress or attract their date, but all they manage to do is turn him off.

They usually act this way because they have a case of the dating jitters. Everybody gets them once in a while. The woman who has just been divorced or separated from her longtime live-in lover may have a particularly bad case until she gets back into the swing of things.

But it is not only women. Men suffer from dating jitters even more—40 percent of men who date compared with 25 percent of women. Even college students, whom we consider very relaxed about their relationships with the opposite sex, get dating jitters. Half the students at the University of Indiana told researchers that they found dating difficult and uncomfortable, and 3,800 students at the University of Arizona reported that dating filled them with anxiety.

It does not have to be that way. Dating jitters can be cured. A psychologist at UCLA divided men and women who seldom dated and felt uncomfortable when they did into two groups. The couples in the first group dated each other and afterward wrote reports on how they liked their date. The second group of couples dated each other but wrote no reports.

After three months both groups were dating more often, even dating people outside their group. They reported they enjoyed their dates more than they used to. The members of the second group, the ones that did not have to write reports, seemed more comfortable than those in the first. When their pulse rates were taken just before they went out on a date, they were lower than those of the people in the first group—an indication that they were more relaxed.

So it seems that while practice may not make perfect, it certainly takes a lot of the anxiety out of dating. The second group was probably more relaxed because they did not have to worry about what their dates were going to write about them.

If you suffer from dating jitters, you can use these findings to cure them. First of all, go out on dates as often as you can. And second, stop worrying about what your date thinks about you and concentrate on enjoying his company and your dinner or the concert or dancing or whatever it is you are doing. These two steps are a practically surefire cure and you should find that your desirability score will start going up.

"I don't have any trouble getting dates," Jennifer said. "And I don't have dating jitters. But how do I get a man to ask me out a second time? They all drop me as if I were poison when I refuse to end the evening in bed."

"If they drop you after the first date," I said, "I suspect that it has very little to do with sex." I hesitated. "Do you really mean that no one ever asks you for a second date?"

"Oh, I was exaggerating," she said. "But a lot don't. Maybe half the men I go out with."

"In that case, I would be inclined to say that there is one reason and one reason only. The man who does not ask you out a second time simply did not find you compatible. You were not his type. That does not mean he is not interested in having sex with you. He figures the date won't be a total loss if you go to bed with him. But your refusal to hop into bed has nothing to do with your not hearing from him again."

"You think so?" Jennifer was dubious.

"I'm certain," I said. "Think back over the last three men who didn't ask you out a second time. Did you really want any of them to ask you out again? Would you have gone out with them if they had asked?"

She stared off into space. "No, I guess not," she said eventually.

"You obviously did not find them compatible either, and in that case I wouldn't lose any sleep about not being asked for dates that you don't want."

This is what dating is all about—winnowing the compatibles from the incompatibles. It is an exploratory process, a getting-to-know-you time. And a getting-to-know-oneself time. "Through dating, we can develop our sense of who we are," Dr. Stephen Josephson, a clinical psychologist, says. "We can practice different relationship skills and get feedback from a variety of people."

Half the time we are disappointed in what we get to know. Researchers who kept track of 231 dating couples over a period of two years found that 101 of them broke up. They blamed their breakups on boredom or different interests or one person wanting to be more independent.

You cannot expect that every man who asks you out is going to find you desirable, but there is a way you can encourage a man who attracts you to see you as even prettier, more charming and sexier than you are.

There is no magic involved. It happens to be a matter of psychological fact. A man is more attracted to a good-looking woman when his heart is beating faster than normal.

This has been confirmed beyond doubt by dozens of studies. One involved placing men in what they thought was physical danger. Then the element of danger was removed and a pretty woman appeared on the scene. The men were far more attracted to her than other men who had not been placed in a dangerous situation were.

Another study required men to run in place. Half of them ran for fifteen seconds, just enough to increase their heart rates slightly. The others ran for two minutes, which resulted in a significant increase of heart rate. Then both groups were shown a film of a pretty woman who talked about herself for a few minutes.

The fifteen-second men reported that they thought she was really nice, but the two-minute men thought she was terrific. They thought she was a knockout. They raved about how exciting and sexy she was and they wanted to meet her.

It is easy enough to translate these findings into your own romantic life. I do not expect you to arrange for your date to be in a car crash before he picks you up for the evening. Nor would I advise you to coax him to spend five or ten minutes on a treadmill before he sees you. What you can do, though, is suggest doing something active on your dates, at least at the beginning. Instead of having dinner and going to a movie, why not go dancing? And eat afterward? If you are sports minded, there is skating, skiing, jogging, bike riding, tennis, racquetball, a hundred activities. Or you can go for a brisk walk. If you must go to the movies, try to find a side-splitting comedy or a tension-filled film. Both laughter and tension speed up the pulse. Get his heart rate up and he will think you are the most desirable woman in the world.

Psychologists have discovered that there is an unfortunate negative side to this matter of heart throbs. "Our experiments have conclusively demonstrated that when a man's heart rate is increased, he will be more attracted to a good-looking or fairly good-looking woman," says psychologist Gregory White, assistant professor of psychology at the University of Maryland. "But at the same time, he will also be more repelled by a below-average-looking female."

That throbbing heart of his leads a man to exaggerate both positively and negatively. And this is something you should be aware of. If you feel you are not looking your best some night, it might be wiser to suggest dinner in a romantically dark restaurant instead of heading for the disco. And afterward settle for the most ho-hum movie in town. Anything to keep

his heartbeat slow and steady. Save the strenuous workouts
for when you feel you're looking great.

INTIMACY

Most women when they are dating a man who is right for them
progress naturally toward intimacy. Sexual intimacy may come
before emotional, but both are essential for total intimacy.
And total intimacy can be scary. "Intimacy is a tremendous
commitment, a commitment to become a couple instead of a
single person," says Dr. Helen Singer Kaplan. "Another person's needs, wants, desires and aspirations become part of your
own."

The intimacy decision can be a very difficult one for some
women. If you scored low on intimacy, you may be one of
them.

Do you suddenly get bored with a man when he starts
talking about vacation plans that involve the two of you or
when he invites you to travel halfway across the country at
Thanksgiving time to meet his folks? Does this kind of thing
make you feel tied down and nervous? Has this happened
before with other men?

Or is the man in your life married? This means that total
intimacy is practically impossible. While you may believe that
all of you is committed to him, all of him cannot be committed
to you as long as he is married. Some women block themselves
from intimacy by having affair after affair with married men.

If you seem to be running away from intimacy, it is time
for a little self-analysis. Do you really want an intimate relationship with this man? Do you want the two of you to be
completely involved with each other? His sorrows to be your
sorrows? His joys your joys? His frustrations yours? Are you
ready for it? Do you really want it?

Your self-analysis may result in your understanding that
you have been avoiding intimacy because it will drain you of
the energy you want to devote to your career. Or you may

realize that you have been zeroing in on married men because you are frightened of intimacy. You may discover that you want an intimate relationship but just can't seem to break through your own reserve.

If you feel that an intimate relationship will interfere with your career, you may be justified. But I suggest giving it a little more thought. Except for the three years after Lisa was born, I have juggled marriage, motherhood and career. And loved every minute of it. It has been hard work, but the rewards have been great. Are you sure that this is not just an excuse for avoiding intimacy? If it is or if you have run away from intimacy by confining yourself to married men or if you just can't seem to let yourself be intimate with another person, it might help to treat yourself to some short-term therapy. An understanding psychologist or psychiatrist can help you examine the reasons why you block yourself from intimacy. The hours and the money will be well spent.

But if you are ready for intimacy and are longing to make the final leap of commitment, I can tell you the kind of woman almost every man wants to date and marry.

He wants a woman who thinks he is the most wonderful creature who ever came down the pike. He wants a woman who is considered desirable by other men, a woman whom they find hard to get. He wants to feel he has the prize other men wanted and could not attain. And he wants to believe that you think him far superior to other men.

I did not know this when I was an undergraduate at Cornell, but it is almost exactly the way things were with me and Milt. I dated a lot in the three years before I met him. I always set a time limit on my dates. I would see one man from four to six and then I would have to rush back to the sorority house to study. I would have another date from eight to eleven, but again I would tell my date that I had to rush home at eleven because I had a paper to write or something. The result was that I never went very far physically with any of my dates.

One fraternity house at Cornell had a goldfish bowl in the

living room with a lone goldfish named Joyce. I kept asking how they had come to give such an odd name to a fish and one day a fraternity member told me.

"We call the fish Joyce," he said, "because it has one blue breast and as far as any of us know, you may have a blue breast too. None of us can prove that you don't." I laughed and thought it was a great compliment.

So when Milt came along in my senior year and I fell in love with him, all the conditions necessary for him to find me desirable and want an intimate relationship were there. I was very popular, but I was not going steady with anyone. And it was obvious from the day we met that I thought he was wonderful.

If you have succeeded in improving your other four scores in the Intimacy Formula, your intimacy score will almost automatically go up. But you can give it a little extra boost just by knowing this secret of what a man really wants in a woman with whom he has an intimate relationship. All he wants is a woman whom other men desire but who has eyes for him alone. Now that you know this, you can work at being that woman.

PART TWO

TESTING

How to Tell if He Is the Right Man for You

FIVE

Why being "in love" is no reason to get married . . .
The posthoneymoon shock of learning the truth about
each other . . . Why your heart should not rule your head
when it comes to marriage . . . How Estelle and Joyce and
Lisa met and married their husbands . . . The Five Basic
Guidelines for Mate Selection

"**I**'m in love! He's a wonderful guy!" She was in seventh
heaven. She has known him for six weeks. He is the man of
her dreams.

"Is he really right for you?" I ask. "Are you sure?"

"Oh, yes! We were made for each other. I've never been
so happy in my life. We're getting married next month."

I had this conversation with a young production assistant
at NBC. She was starry-eyed and euphoric. I smiled and wished
her well, but inside I sighed and worried about her future. I
sensed that she was looking at the world—and her lover—
through romantically rose-colored glasses. She was not seeing
reality but a fantasy made up of her own desires and excitement.

What every woman should know is that the state of being
"in love" does not have all that much to do with love. It is
Mother Nature's little way of getting a man and woman to-

gether. No matter what. In order to perpetuate the race. Mother Nature does not care about compatibility, stability or happiness. All she cares about is sex. And we go right along with Mother Nature when we are in love.

Under the spell of sexual attraction, flattery, loneliness, starlight or whatever, we often manage to convince ourselves that Mr. Wrong is Prince Charming. Much too often. Just look at the divorce rate. Infatuation—and this is probably the best definition of the state known as being "in love"—can be delicious torment, but it is not a basis for marriage. Marriage is serious. For the long run. Forever after.

No one would take a job without finding out a little about the company, without learning exactly what the job entailed, the chances of promotion, the fringe benefits, vacations, sick leave and all the rest. Nor would you buy a car without finding exactly what the warranty covered, how much gas it used and how its performance compared with other makes in the same price range.

I know women who have shopped every department store in New York City from August to October before buying a winter coat. And I know women who have married without giving half that time and thought to this major life decision.

Under the romantic spell of being in love, couples tend to believe that they think alike and want the same things from marriage. But they don't. And when they discover this, often very shortly after the honeymoon, it comes as a rude shock. They feel as if they have been deceived. And they have been. To a certain extent.

During courtship, everyone puts his and her best foot forward. We often misrepresent ourselves, trying to be like the person we believe the other wants rather than being ourselves. It is only natural. We want so much to be loved. And to love.

But how are we to get at the reality about the man we believe we love? How is someone like the NBC production assistant who is so blissfully head over heels in love going to be able to think sensibly about this major life decision?

If she were going into partnership with him to set up a
Magic Widget Company or a Carefree Catering Concern, she
would scrutinize that man inside out. She would hire account-
ants and lawyers to work out the partnership agreement. And
she would not sign her name to that agreement until she was
satisfied that she knew everything she needed to know about
her prospective partner—his financial position, his business
acumen, his reputation for integrity.

This is relatively easy to do because emotion does not enter
in. One is not infatuated with a business partner. But a prospective husband? That is different. It is almost impossible to
be objective. We rarely if ever even think of running a check
on a man to determine his suitability as a husband. We think
that love is the magic touchstone that will make everything
perfect. But the woman who wants a loving husband and a
good marriage should not let her heart rule her head. She
should give equal power to each.

In the old days there was usually a whole informal committee
of family and friends and neighbors who passed judgment on
your intended. They looked him over, observed the two of
you together, watched how he fit into the family—and made
their opinions known. Sometimes in subtle ways, sometimes
not so subtly. But today our families often do not meet the
man we intend to marry until a few days before the wedding.
Sometimes not until afterward. You are on your own.

It is possible, however, to fill this vacuum by making your
own evaluation—even though you are caught up in the delir-
ium of romantic infatuation. Psychologists have learned enough
about the marriage relationship so they can pinpoint almost
exactly the kind of background and personality your husband
should have. I have put these findings together in two psychological tests you can do by yourself to help you decide if
the man you are in love with is the man you should marry—
the Premarital Checklists in Chapter 6 and the Diagnostic Test
for Psychological Compatibility in Chapter 10.

Before I get to these tests though, I want to give you three case histories of how three women met and chose their husbands.

ESTELLE AND MORRIS

My mother and father met when they were very young. They lived in the same apartment house in Brooklyn. They started going together when they were sixteen, but they did not get married until both of them had graduated from law school. They practiced law together all their married life until my father's death in 1979.

JOYCE AND MILTON

My husband and I met at a summer boarding house, a cross between a country inn and a farm, the summer before my senior year at Cornell. I was spending a couple of weeks there with my parents and my sister, Elaine. I had a cold and was taking a nap one afternoon when Elaine burst into my room and said, "Put on some clothes and come downstairs. I've just met the man you're going to marry."

I looked at her. And sneezed. "I never heard anything so silly," I told her.

"Trust me," she said.

I looked terrible. My nose was red. My hair was a mess. But I got dressed, powdered my nose, hid my hair under a kerchief and went downstairs. Milton Brothers was tall, dark, very attractive. He was just out of the Marine Corps and about to resume his education as a junior at Cornell.

We discovered that we had grown up about fifteen miles away from each other and knew a lot of the same people. By the end of the afternoon, I had decided that Elaine was right. This was the man I wanted to marry. He was brilliant and witty. He was going to be a doctor. I was serious about him right away.

I knew that he liked me, but I did not know that he too

had felt it was serious that first day until thirty-three years later. The two of us were on a television show and the host asked him when he had first known that he wanted to marry me. "The very first day I met her," Milt said.

We dated each other at Cornell and got engaged the June I graduated. A year later, when Milt graduated, we got married. We celebrated our thirty-fifth wedding anniversary this year.

LISA AND AMIR

My daughter, Lisa, met the man she married when they were both students at Princeton. Milt and I had liked some of the boys she used to date and wondered what she could possibly see in some of the others. But when we met Amir, we liked him immediately. We agreed that he was the man for Lisa. Lisa did not seem to see it that way, however. Nor did Amir. They broke up and started dating other people.

I was sad because Amir was exactly the man I would have chosen for my daughter. Lisa is very bright, but he is a shade brighter. She can be stubborn, and he is strong enough to stand up to her. He is also an excellent negotiator, a quality that is important in marriage. They also had the same religious background, just as Milt and I and my mother and father and his mother and father had. But it seemed that this perfect mating was not to be.

When Lisa went to medical school at Tulane, she and Amir, who was at medical school in Houston, got together again. This time their courtship ended in marriage. They both specialized in ophthalmology. They are now practicing ophthalmology together in two cities in Iowa, Davenport and Muscatine, following in the footsteps of Lisa's lawyer grandmother and grandfather.

• • •

These three marriages illustrate the Five Basic Guidelines for Mate Selection for marriages that have a chance of being forever after. Very briefly, they are:

1. Know your future spouse for a significant length of time before marriage.
2. Choose a man from a similar background.
3. Choose a man who is close to you in age.
4. Don't marry a man who is far more attractive than you are.
5. Choose a man who is your psychological opposite.

The "in-a-nutshell" formula for a good marriage is that the man and woman should be socially alike and psychologically opposite. In the following chapters, I discuss each of the guidelines and the trade-offs that may be involved if your man departs from any of them. With this information, you can make your own decision, based on sound psychological know-how, as to whether the man in your life is really the man you want to live with forever after.

SIX

The case for long engagements . . . Why 10 percent of engaged couples break up . . . How well do you really know your man? . . . The four Premarital Checklists

How can you tell if the man you are in love with is right for you?

It would be marvelous if there were some kind of rabbit test that one could take to see if the marriage would be successful. Unfortunately there is not. We have to rely on our own understanding and instincts. Your best ally is time, which is why my First Guideline for Mate Selection is *Know your future spouse for a significant length of time before marriage.*

And that brings up another question. What is a significant length of time?

A sociologist who studied almost one thousand marriages found that the couples who knew each other for at least five years before the wedding had the best chance of living happily ever after. Other studies bear him out. In one study, for instance, it was found that 87 percent of the couples who had been engaged for less than six months had a hard time adjusting to marriage while 55 percent of the couples who had been engaged for two years or more had fewer problems and handled them more easily.

A 1982 survey of psychiatrists revealed that almost half of them thought that courtship—which was defined as the next step after dating—should last six months to a year before the couple decides to get married. More than a third of the psychiatrists thought the courtship should last from one to two years. Nearly 70 percent of them thought that even after a courtship period of "adequate length," there should be an engagement period.

My own feeling is that a "significant time" is one year—*plus*. There should be at least a year between the proposal and the wedding. I would make an exception if the two of you have been living together for more than a year. In this case, I do not think that a year's engagement is necessary, but I would recommend a formal engagement of at least three months. If you are more traditional, however, I recommend a full year's engagement—no matter whether it is a first marriage or a remarriage.

"But why a year?" asked twenty-six-year-old Becky. "Jason and I have been going together for almost a year already. It's not as if we had met yesterday. Or if we were teenagers. We know our own minds. Why do you say we should wait a year?"

"Because I think you want your marriage to be forever after," I said. "And you don't know Jason as well as you think you do."

"We know everything about each other!" she exclaimed. "Just because we haven't been living together doesn't mean that we haven't spent weekends together. We know sex is great with us. We know all sorts of things about each other. He knows that I spend so much money on clothes that I have trouble paying my bills sometimes. I know that his idea of a wonderful way to spend Saturday afternoon is tinkering with his car."

"That's a start," I said. "But do you know what he expects from marriage? Does he know what you expect?"

"Of course. We've talked it all out. We're going to live in the city. And we want two children. But not right off."

I shook my head. "I still think you have a lot to learn about Jason." What Becky did not realize then is that courtship is a hard-sell time, a best-foot-forward time when the man and woman go all out to win each other's love. Once that is accomplished they think they are home free. But love is not enough. You have to be sure that this man meets your needs—and that you meet his.

A formal engagement is an important milestone. The major task of the engagement period is not to plan the wedding but to get to know the man you are going to marry. I think of an engagement as the last exit on the highway before you reach the marriage tollgate. It is your last chance to decide if this is the man you really want to spend the rest of your life with.

"But he is," Becky protested. "I'd never have promised to marry him if he wasn't my dream man."

That is the core of the problem. Jason *was* her dream man. Literally. We do not fall in love with a person but with a romantic ideal—someone who may not exist except in our imagination. And while we are in the grip of the infatuation we call being in love, it is almost impossible to be objective. It is, says psychiatrist Warren J. Gadpaille of the University of Colorado, "an emotional state that is conducive to perfectly honest and good-faith self-deception and deception of each other. Each minimizes the failings of the other, reassures the other that those failings are unimportant, and each truly believes what he or she is saying." And if a glimmer of uneasiness crosses their minds about any of those failings, they happily assure themselves that the failings will disappear once they are married. But one thing you can be sure of is that marriage will not make a significant change for the better in the traits and habits you find distasteful. What you see is what you get.

Happily infatuations are not forever. Within three or four months, the first romantic fervor begins to diminish. As time passes, we are able to see the real man with all his faults and all his virtues. Sometimes the reality is a shock. Ten percent of 38,000 engaged couples who answered questionnaires about what they thought their marriages would be like discovered that they were so far apart in their expectations that they broke their engagements.

When Becky and Jason learned what each other saw as his and her roles and duties in their marriage, they were deeply upset. Despite their having talked about their future together at length, they discovered that they had quite different expectations. What opened their eyes? They had gone through my Premarital Checklists.

Every woman who is considering marriage, whether it is her first or second or fifth, should go through these checklists with her husband-to-be. I want to stress that these checklists are as valuable—possibly even more valuable—for divorcées and widows planning to remarry as for the first-time bride. The divorcée and the widow are in danger of being trapped by old patterns and concepts and may be even more blind about the new man in their lives than the woman who is preparing for her first marriage.

The Premarital Checklists provide a framework for that all-important task of the engagement period—getting to know each other. Equally important, they pinpoint differences in attitudes and values that might threaten your marriage. This early warning gives you time to try to work out your differences before the wedding.

Before we get to the checklists themselves, however, let me tell you just what Becky and Jason had expected.

Jason had thought a great deal about what he wanted from marriage and had made plans for his life with Becky. He had been positive that she would give up her job when she started their family, that she would bring up two well-behaved children who would be a credit to him, that she would use her managerial talents by involving herself in community affairs and that she would be a charming hostess when he entertained for business reasons. They would be a good team. He took these things absolutely for granted.

He had planned to rent an apartment in the city until their first child was born and then to buy a house in one of the good suburbs. When he could afford it, he would buy a place at the shore as well so that Becky and the children could spend summers there. He would join them on weekends.

Becky also knew what she wanted. She was convinced that Jason was going right to the top and that was fine because she did not want to be more successful than he was. She was doing very well as a sales representative for a pharmaceutical company, but her goal was a corner office on the twenty-fifth floor and the title of vice-president for sales. Even with time out for the two babies they planned, she hoped to reach her goal in five years. The vice-presidency would mean travel—a lot of it in Europe. Jason would be able to join her occasionally. She was sure of that. With her salary, she could hire a top-notch housekeeper so that she and Jason would be free to travel and go on vacation.

She had no doubt but that he would be as proud of her successes as she would be of his. He would gladly accompany her to the conventions that were an important part of her job just the way she was looking forward to going to his functions with him and entertaining his colleagues and business acquaintances.

The two of them were making rosy plans for their future together in the blissful conviction that they were thinking along the same lines. Then they went through the Premarital Checklists and discovered they were not.

THE PREMARITAL CHECKLISTS

These checklists will speed up the getting-to-know-him process tremendously. For some people the month that it takes to work through them can be the equivalent of six to eight months' ordinary progress toward intimacy. These checklists cover four topics—money, children, family and sex. When you finish them, you may want to add others—work, perhaps, or friends or life style or personal habits or vacations.

The most productive way to use the checklists is to take them one at a time. Set aside a block of time each week—three or four hours when you will not be interrupted—and spend it on one checklist. Both of you should answer each question. Take your time. Tell each other how you feel about each item. Be as honest and thoughtful as you can.

Do not confine yourself to the questions on each checklist. They are just to get you started. Bring up anything related to the topic that is on your mind.

When you finish your first session, make a date to talk about what you have learned. Make it at least three days later. You need that much thinking and reacting time. Spend the interval exploring just how you feel about what you have learned. Were there any surprises? Good or bad? Is there anything with which you violently disagree? Anything that makes you uncomfortable?

These are the things to talk about at your second session. If there are problems, discuss possible compromises. Are the problems really serious? Or are they something you can live with?

That is all there is to it. The next week go on to the second checklist. By the end of four weeks, you will know each other far better than you did when you started. You will be in a better position to know if this is really the man you want to marry.

THE MONEY CHECKLIST

Money is a major stress point in marriage. Husbands and wives fight more about money than anything else. One survey of divorced women showed that nearly 40 percent blamed the failure of their marriage on financial problems. Therefore it is important for the two of you to understand what money means to the other and agree on how to handle your finances before the wedding.

Will you have separate checking accounts? Why?

Will you have a joint checking account? Why?

What about savings and investments? How much do you plan to put aside each month? What form will your savings take in your first year of marriage? A savings account? A bank certificate? Stocks? A mutual fund? Other?

What are you saving for? A baby? A down payment on a house? A car? Your old age? Furniture? A vacation? Other? (Be specific.)

Do you know how much money he makes? How much she makes? Does he have any source of income besides his salary? Does she?

How will you feel if he makes less than you do? More than you do? How will he feel if you make more?

Have you worked out a budget? If not, do you have a rough idea of what your expenses will be? Do you plan to have a budget?

Do you have life insurance? Health insurance? A major medical policy? Should you make any changes in these?

If you both work, how will you handle your salaries? Who will pay what? Will you put both salaries into the common kitty? Or will each of you pay certain bills? If so, who will pay what?

If you do not plan to work after the wedding, how much money will you need to run the household?

If she (or he) is not going to work after marriage, how much money do you plan to give her (or him) to run the household?

How much money do you want every month to spend just as you please with no questions asked? Do you both agree on this?

How do you feel about borrowing money? Charge accounts? Credit cards? Buying on time?

Does either of you contribute financially to your family?

Do you think you handle money well? Do you think you are extravagant? Penny-pinching? Sensible about money?

Do you think he/she handles money well? Is he/she extravagant? Penny-pinching? Sensible?

Do you think your mother and father handle money intelligently? Would you handle yours differently?

Who will pay the bills? Balance the checkbook? Keep the financial records? Prepare the tax returns or assemble the necessary data for the accountant?

Do you have a will? If not, do you plan to make a will before the wedding? Or revise your present will?

THE CHILDREN CHECKLIST

A couple may agree that they want children, agree on the number of children, agree when they want to start their family—and still discover that they have many areas of disagreement.

Do you want children?

How many?

What sex? Will you be disappointed if the children are not the sex you prefer? Will you keep trying until you have a boy? Or a girl?

When do you want to start your family? As soon as possible? In two years? Five years? Later? Why?

How far apart do you want to space your children?

Would you ever have an abortion? What kind of problems or circumstances would lead you to seek one?

Will you be the primary caretaker? If so, what share of the child or children's care do you expect your spouse to assume? Do you plan to share fifty-fifty in their care, feeding, diaper changing and all the rest? If so, how do you plan to arrange this?

Will you, the wife, work after the baby is born? How soon after will you go back to work? How do you, the husband, feel about this?

Would you, the wife, prefer to stay home with the baby? How do you, the husband, feel about this?

If you, the wife, go back to work, what arrangements will you make for child care? Do you, the husband, agree with these arrangements?

How do you plan to raise your child? The way your parents raised you? Differently? In what ways? What about discipline?

Do you want your child to have a religious education? What kind?

THE FAMILY CHECKLIST

It is often a case of love him or her and hate them. In-laws rank high on the scale of marriage stresses. The more the two of you can talk out your feelings about your respective families before marriage and before resentments or jealousies have a chance to reach the conflagration point, the happier you will be.

Tread lightly with this checklist and keep your ears and heart open to what your intended says. You have to realize that you are not just marrying the man, you are marrying his family as well.

How do you feel about his mother? Her mother? His relationship with his mother? Hers with her mother?

How do you feel about his father? Her father? His relationship with his father? Her relationship with her father?

How do you feel about your future spouse's brothers and sisters?

How do you feel about your future spouse's attitude toward your parents? How do your future spouse's parents treat you? With warmth and acceptance? With reserve? Are they critical? Do they make you feel part of the family or as if you were on trial?

How much time do you expect to spend with his/her family after you are married? What about vacations? Holidays?

Do you plan to live with either of your families until you are better established financially? How do you think that will work out?

Will you pattern your marriage after your parents' marriage? Do you expect your husband will play the same role as your father, and you the same as your mother? Do you expect your wife to play the same role as your mother, and you as your father? If not, how do you see your roles?

FOR REMARRIERS:
THE FAMILY AND CHILDREN CHECKLIST

Remarriages are complicated because there are so many more people involved whether the previous marriage was ended by death or divorce. New in-laws. Former in-laws. Ex-wives. Ex-husbands. His children. Your children. There are infinitely more stresses in a remarriage than a first marriage. Anything you can do to defuse the stress bombs before the wedding, the better chance your marriage will have of succeeding.

How do you feel about his relationship with his former wife? Her relationship with her former husband?

How do you feel about his relationship with his former in-laws? Hers with her former in-laws?

What about his children? Her children? Will they be living with you? With the former spouse? Are they friendly to you? Hostile? Timid? How do you feel about that? How do you plan to handle it?

Will he discipline your children? Will you discipline his?

Do you plan to have children of your own? How do you think your/his children will feel about the new arrival? How do you think your/her children will feel?

Will his children be spending holidays and vacations with you? How do you feel about that?

What about the grandparents? Are there going to be difficult situations? Will they be able to accept his/her children with tenderness and warmth?

Do you expect this marriage to fall into the same pattern as your former one? If you are a widow, do you idealize your late husband?

If he pays alimony do you feel cheated? Do you think about

how much better your life would be if he did not have to give his ex-wife all that money?

If she gets alimony or child support, do you feel resentful because you think she is not getting enough?

How do you, the husband-to-be, feel about supporting her children from her first marriage?

THE SEX CHECKLIST

This is probably the least of your worries. You have been sleeping together for some time now probably and find each other wonderfully satisfactory lovers. Or do you?

Many couples discover very shortly after the wedding that they are less compatible sexually than they were before. That is rarely the truth. It is simply that during the courtship period, neither was honest with the other. She may have been excited by necking and petting and concerned to discover that the actual sexual act gave her no pleasure. Or he always came too fast and left her unsatisfied. He may have thought she was unresponsive, but sex was sex and he was getting it. Both thought things would get better—and in the meantime they assured each other that everything was wonderful. She tells him he is a great lover. He tells her she is the sexiest creature on the North American continent.

Inevitably disillusion sets in after the wedding. Now when he wants to, she doesn't. She tells him he comes in such a hurry that it does not do anything for her. He suggests that she might move a little instead of lying there like a dead alligator. Everything is just the way it used to be—but now sex is a problem. It is a problem because they have come face to face with reality.

This is your chance to talk out such problems. Sex is not that complicated a deal. If you tell each other in a loving way what is good and what leaves you cold, you will be surprised how fast things will improve. It may be difficult for you to talk specifics, but if you use the checklist to get started, you will find it easier to introduce your own questions or problems.

How often do you have an orgasm when you make love? Are you satisfied with this?

How often do you like to make love? How often do you expect to when you are married?

What about when he feels like it and you don't? Or vice versa? How will you handle this?

Do you wish you knew more about sex? Have you read any books on the subject? What did you think about them? If you have not read any, why not?

How do you feel about oral sex?

Do you like to experiment with new positions?

Do you think of sex as a duty or a pleasure?

What time of day do you like to make love best?

What kind of contraception do you use? Are you comfortable with it?

How do you feel about your body? Do you worry that you may be too fat or too thin or too something else?

Do you have herpes?

Have you ever had any venereal disease?

If he comes before you do, does he make a practice of satisfying you orally or manually? If not, why not?

This should be enough to get you started. The main thing is to get any problems that exist out in the open—and not to blame each other for the problems that do exist. As I said before, sexual problems are usually very easy to work out if you face them early on.

There you have it—The Premarital Checklists. The Big Four marriage stresses—money, children, family and sex— all wrapped up in a month's worth of getting-to-know-you discussions. If there are other subjects you want to discuss, go ahead and make your own checklist. You do not have to be a psychologist to know what questions you want to ask or problems you want to discuss.

• • •

When Becky and Jason went through the checklists, they could not believe what they were hearing.

Did Jason really expect her to stay home and be a model wife and mother and president of the Garden Club?

Did Becky honestly think that she should leave their children with a housekeeper while she jetted off to Europe on business?

Was she supposed to be stuck at the shore with the children all summer while Jason lived it up in town?

Was he expected to go to pharmaceutical conventions and act like a wife, for God's sake?

"I didn't think we'd make it," Becky told me. "We seemed to be on different tracks. Not even parallel ones. I was ready to call it off. And so was he."

"What happened?" I asked. I knew something must have happened, because they had been married almost a year when she told me this.

"We started talking," she said. "I realized that you had been right. I didn't know him as well as I thought. Didn't know how he felt about a lot of things that were important to me. But I was crazy about him. It would have been a tragedy to lose what we had. We made a lot of compromises.

"Jason decided he would rather have a happy wife with a job she loved than a rebellious one who was bored to tears with running a home and doing volunteer work. And I realized that if we had children, I really should not plan to be away from home all that much. After all, I wanted them to know I was their mother, not just some lady who breezed in and out on her way to the office or a convention. The more I thought about it realistically, the more I knew that I wanted to stay home when they were little. I wanted to enjoy every minute of their growing up.

"We decided to wait for two years before starting our family and then I would take three years off. I may never get to be a vice-president of the company—and then again I may. But children are only babies once.

"Once we got that much worked out, we decided that we would probably be able to handle any problems that came up. And so we went ahead and got married."

I too am sure they will be able to handle the inevitable problems. They solved some important ones beforehand. The problems that unhappy couples bring to marriage counselors, the ones that cause the separations and divorces, are usually ones that existed before the marriage.

"She always spent money like water," he says, or "She was always too close to her mother."

"He's always had a chip on his shoulder," she says, or "He has always been more interested in his work than his home."

If such problems can be resolved before the wedding, the marriage will not only be more harmonious, but will have a better chance of surviving. It is worth taking the time to get to know each other as you really are before you take that walk down the aisle.

Women, in particular, should do whatever they can to ensure that their marriages will last. It has been demonstrated that marriage is a far better deal for men than for women. *And so is divorce!* I will discuss this later in Chapter 33, but right now I am concerned with making your future marriage as divorce-proof as possible.

This means recognizing differences and working out problems before the ceremony. To do this you need time. Time to let the initial infatuation subside. Time to get to know each other's real attitudes and values. Time to work out any problems that may exist.

And if the problems cannot be resolved? Well, let's face it—heart-rending as it may be to break off an engagement, the emotional and financial cost of dissolving a marriage is much higher.

Especially for a woman.

SEVEN

What happy marriages have in common ... The three make-or-break issues no one ever discusses ... Why men sour on interfaith marriages ... Interracial marriage and culture shock ... Should a woman marry "down"? ... The Cinderella trade-off

My Second Guideline for Mate Selection is *Choose a man from a similar background.*

No one has yet discovered the secret of a happy marriage. Intimate human relationships are so tantalizingly complicated that it is unlikely that anyone will learn the secret in our lifetime. As the divorce rate testifies, progress has been very slow. But we have made some headway.

After more than half a century of studying the marriage relationship, researchers at the Institute of Human Development at the University of California were able to identify one common denominator in marriages that last: The husband and wife who stay together tend to come from similar backgrounds.

This covers a vast amount of territory. It includes the tremendously powerful forces that shape us. A similar background, first of all, means a similar social and economic background. As Dr. David Klimek defines it in *Beneath Mate*

Selection and Marriage, it "includes in its basic sense family history, socialization skills, occupation, wealth, attitudes, interests and general sophistication about life and the world." It also includes race and religion.

Marrying a man from a similar background makes life much easier. You know that you are going to agree on most of the important aspects of life. He may like chocolate while you prefer strawberry. He may like the mountains while you prefer the seashore. But when it comes to life style, your expectations of each other, your ideas on how to bring up children, and how and where you want to live, you are on the same wavelength.

It is not just sheer propinquity that leads so many of us to marry someone who lives less than a mile away. "There already exist within each of us certain standards that reflect our family life, background and, in some cases, ethnic or racial heritage," says Dr. John Money of Johns Hopkins. When we meet someone who measures up to these standards of what we want in a husband, we react by falling in love. And where are you more likely to meet someone with similar standards than in your own town or neighborhood?

When you have a whole early life history in common—perhaps both of you had Miss Eddington in the sixth grade and you belonged to the Girl Scouts and he to the Boy Scouts and both of you worked at the Ice Cream Scoop after school and your mother played bridge with his mother—you understand where each other is coming from.

Geography is not the key, however. One of the happiest marriages I know is that of Luisette, who grew up in a small village outside Paris, and Jeremy, who was born in Richmond, Virginia. They met when Luisette came to the United States as an exchange student in the American Field Service program. Eight or nine years later, after a lot of economy-class travel across the Atlantic, they got married.

Despite the differences in nationality and geography and language, their backgrounds are similar in important ways.

Luisette's father sells insurance. Jeremy's works for an office supplies company. Both men are frugal, hard-working and very involved with their children. Luisette's mother plays the violin in an amateur chamber music group. Jeremy's mother gives piano lessons. Both women are warm and sympathetic. Both families are Catholic.

"If it weren't for Luisette's accent," Jeremy says, "she might have been someone I grew up with. The more we told each other about our families and the way we were brought up, the more alike we discovered we were."

Another example is my own daughter, Lisa, who married a young man from Texas, which in some respects is light-years away from New York City, where she grew up. But their backgrounds are practically identical. Amir's parents are as family oriented as Milt and I are. Education has been a top priority with them, just as it has been with us. We share the same religion. Long before they met, Lisa and Amir had decided to go to Princeton. And both, quite independently, had decided on careers in medicine.

I stress family background because the family is the single most important force in our growing-up years. Even when we rebel against our families, their values and attitudes are still part of us, either negatively or positively. If you marry a man whose family background is significantly different from yours, you will face an above-average degree of adjustment. This places an above-average degree of stress on the marriage. The amount of stress depends on just how different his background is.

If he is from Miami and you are from Philadelphia, that is hardly a significant difference. But if it also turns out that his parents fled Cuba a dozen or so years ago and are Catholic and still speak English haltingly and his father is a hotel porter, while your WASP parents trace their ancestors back to the *Mayflower* and your father is a lawyer and your mother is on the board of the museum, then no matter how entranced you are with the man, there are going to be times when the two of you see things so differently that you might have come from different planets.

"Dramatic differences between the two families of origin," says Dr. R. Vance Fitzgerald of the Medical College of Ohio, "in terms of religious beliefs and values, ethnicity and socio-economic status often lead to serious difficulties in marriage." These three categories—religion, race and economic status— are somewhat less important today than they were a quarter of a century ago, but they are still make-or-break issues in marriage.

Most books and articles on love and marriage ignore the issues of race and religion and money as if they were not "nice" or proper subjects for discussion. But our race and our religious beliefs are the very fiber of our identities and philosophies. And money, more often than not, is a measure of accomplishment in today's world. It is one of the tools of power in all human relationships, whether marital, political or business. I believe that the effect of these three issues on the happiness and longevity of a marriage should be discussed and understood.

RELIGION

If you marry a man of the same religion, your chances for a long-lived happy marriage are significantly greater than if you marry a man of another faith—even if neither of you is particularly observant. The happiest marriages, according to surveys made by the National Opinion Research Center, are those of Catholics married to Catholics, Jews to Jews and Protestants to Protestants.

If you do marry a man of a different faith, religion will probably not be an issue in the early years even if your families oppose the marriage. All that family opposition usually accomplishes is to bring the couple even closer together in mutual defense.

The stress sets in after the first child is born. Especially for the husband. Studies show that men find interfaith marriages much less satisfactory than wives. Husbands evaluate the marriage negatively, says sociologist Norval D. Glenn of the University of Texas, because "it is more likely to result in a religious difference between husbands and children than between wives and children."

Wives have more influence on the children's religious beliefs, Glenn says, and disagreement over the children's religious upbringing "is likely to have a greater adverse effect on the loser." In other words, the husband and father may feel like a minority of one, an outsider in his own family.

Once the husband confronts the fact that his marriage is less than satisfactory in one respect, it is very easy for him to go on and find still more causes for dissatisfaction. The religious difference can be the thin end of the wedge that eventually breaks up the marriage.

It does not have to be that way, of course. Many interfaith marriages with children are blissfully happy, because the husband and wife were able to compromise and adapt and what started out as a stress ended up as a strength. But this is not easy. It takes work, love, and the ability—and willingness—to understand how the other feels.

Religion almost landed Anne's and Nathan's marriage on the rocks. Anne, a Protestant, had married Nathan, a Jew. They assured each other that religion would never be an issue.

"The only time I go to church," Anne said, "is when my friends get married."

"I only go to temple on the major holidays," Nathan said, "and only to please my parents."

The religious issue erupted like a volcano in the fourth year of their marriage, when Sara was three. Anne had gone all out that Christmas—trimming the tree, playing tapes of Christmas carols, talking about Santa Claus, setting up a crèche with Mary and Joseph, the Wise Men and the shepherds surrounding the infant Jesus in the manger.

Nathan's parents thought it was just too much. And said

so. Nathan himself felt outside the festivities. But Easter was even worse as far as he was concerned. There was the Easter bunny and coloring Easter eggs and Anne read Sara stories about how Christ had been crucified and risen again. Nathan tried to stay cool, but the tension grew and it surfaced in a fight on Easter Sunday that left them both shattered.

Once they calmed down, they decided that this was a problem that had to be taken care of once and for all. They spent several nights talking about it and why it had become such an emotional issue. Anne finally understood that Nathan had felt she was depriving his daughter of her Jewish heritage. And Anne explained that she felt Nathan was being unreasonable in not wanting Sara to experience the joys and wonder of Christmas and Easter.

"Why don't *you* ever talk to her about the Jewish celebrations?" she asked. Nathan admitted she had a point. This was his responsibility, not Anne's.

They arrived at a compromise that might not satisfy religious leaders but worked for them. They decided that Sara should learn about both religions and that their family would observe the major holidays of both faiths. When Sara was older, she could make up her own mind about her religious bent.

This worked for Anne and Nathan. It might not work for every couple, but their approach to the problem was ideal. Talking it out calmly. Trying to find out what the trigger point had been. Planning what they could do about it in the future.

A couple suffering from an emotional overload may find it difficult to separate facts and causes from feelings and convictions. Putting some space between the emotional explosion and the discussion, as Anne and Nathan did, helps lower the emotional temperature.

The negative effect of religious differences on marriage does not seem to be as great as it used to be. It is certainly not the barrier to marriage that it often was in times past, but it is still a serious difference.

If this is the only difference in background, I would not consider it reason not to marry. But if it is one of several differences, then it is time for some soul searching. How did you do on your Premarital Checklists? How does he measure up on the Basic Guidelines for Mate Selection? What did you find out from the Diagnostic Test for Psychological Compatibility (Chapter 10)?

Every difference represents an additional stress on the marriage. Think of marriage like a rubber band. It is extremely flexible, will stretch and stretch, but it reaches a breaking point when stretched too far. If you can reduce the stresses through mutual adaptation and compromise, your interfaith marriage may not only be happy and long lasting but sweeter than most because you have worked together to make it succeed.

RACE

It is possible also for an interracial marriage to flourish and be warmly rewarding, but there are severe strains in these marriages not present in others.

There can be family disapproval. Even more than disapproval, heartbreak. Social disapproval. In some cases, couples may be ostracized by both races. There may be the exquisitely painful stress of seeing your children mocked or penalized because of their mixed heritage. You may experience housing or job discrimination despite legislation against these evils. When you marry you automatically join a minority group—the minority of interracial couples.

When you consider marrying a man of a different race, you must understand that it is not only his race that is different but the folkways with which he has grown up. The way he was brought up as a child, the role of his mother and grandmother in the family and in the community, the role he expects you to assume, his expectations of marriage, his attitude toward fidelity, his feelings about sexual equality. Even his food

preferences. Quite often there are religious differences. All
these can add up to unexpected culture shock once the honeymoon is over. Culture shock can be anxiety provoking, de-
pressive and sometimes destructive.

The differences can be subtle, so subtle that they are mis-
understood. "Married couples from different backgrounds may
label cultural differences as badness or craziness," says Monica
McGoldrick, assistant professor of psychiatry at Rutgers Medical School. "Spouses may be perceived as being personally
offensive rather than acting out of cultural imperatives."

To understand how this works, think of an Irish husband
with an Italian wife. To the Irish, Professor McGoldrick explains, "distancing may seem to be the best move if a problem
cannot be solved," but to his Italian wife, "distancing is seen
as hostile." It infuriates and frustrates her, but her husband
cannot understand why his wife is so angry. This kind of
misunderstanding can escalate into a major crisis just because
neither partner understands the source of the other's behavior.

Husbands and wives of different ethnic backgrounds often
have very different ideas of what a family is. To the American,
the nuclear family—Mom and Dad, Tom and Jane—is the
accepted norm, even though statistics tell us that a quarter of
all households have no children and approximately one-fifth
of today's families are headed by single parents, nine out of
every ten of them women. To the Greek, on the other hand,
the family tends to be a vertical structure with the grandfather
or another elder the undisputed head of the family, controlling
the lives of his sons and daughters, their spouses and their
children to a degree unthinkable to many Americans. No matter how wonderful you consider your husband-to-be and no
matter how marvelous his family, this different family structure may take a lot of getting used to.

I know of happy interracial marriages. I also know of marriages in which the racial difference has been made the scape-
goat for every disagreement between husband and wife. And
I have known marriages where the racial differences have turned
out to be insurmountable.

This was true of Kelly's marriage. Kelly, whom I have known since she was a baby, married a Japanese. Masumi was a fine young man, well educated with a responsible position in a trading company in Seattle. Both his parents and hers tried to tell Kelly and Masumi that there were too many differences between them for a marriage to succeed. Kelly refused to listen. She told her parents they were prejudiced. Masumi assured his parents that Kelly was well aware of the differences and eager to adapt to his way of life.

Two years later they started divorce proceedings. "It was all Masumi's fault," Kelly stormed. "He thought he was still living in Osaka. I had to cook everything Japanese style. Just like his mother. *Sukiyaki* and *gyudon* and *sobordon*." She chanted the names of the Japanese dishes Masumi had demanded she cook. "And he likes raw fish! Ugh!"

It was not only food. Kelly had dreamed of mahogany and chintz. Masumi insisted on Japanese simplicity with straw mats and futons. The great dividing point, however, was that he considered himself head of the household. And one night he told Kelly he hoped that she would bear sons, not daughters. She could not believe it. This was not the man she had fallen in love with. Her sweet, thoughtful Masumi had become a macho dictator.

Masumi was equally appalled by Kelly's blithe assurance that she was an equal partner in the marriage. He was taken aback by her anger on those nights when he came home the worse for drink after the all-male business dinners that were part of his job. A Japanese woman would not consider drunkenness cause for distress, he protested.

Masumi had expected Kelly to be the kind of wife his mother had been. He was bewildered by her resistance. Kelly had expected Masumi to be the kind of husband her father had been. The cultural differences were more than either of them could cope with. Neither of them had given any real thought to what their lives would be like or what the other would expect.

If you contemplate marrying a man of a different race, I

suggest you draw up your own Racial Premarital Checklist and go over it with him. Many people hesitate to talk about racial differences. It almost seems to be taboo. But they exist. Acknowledging them is not a sign of prejudice. As Professor McGoldrick says, "Because we are all supposed to be equal, it does not mean that we are all supposed to be the same."

The first questions I would include in this checklist deal with motive.

> Why do I want to marry this man? Because we share important values, because our attitudes toward life and our goals in life are similar and I believe that my life will be richer and more fulfilling with him as my husband than without him? Or because I want to show my parents where they get off? Or because I enjoy the attention this unconventional union provokes? Because I want a husband who will be grateful to me? Because I dislike my own race?

And then go on to the points I have raised in this section and any others that have been brought up by family and friends as well as questions you have yourself, especially those you feel awkward about raising. The matter of color, perhaps. If you are white and considering marrying a black (or vice versa), how are you going to feel about the way your children look? How will your parents feel about their grandchildren? The checklist format will make it easier for you to bring up questions that you may feel are embarrassing or "not nice."

An interracial marriage is a high-risk marriage. The odds are against you. Thousands of couples have beaten the odds, however, and you may too. Just be very sure in your own mind that this is really the man and the marriage for you.

MONEY

After blockbusters like race and religion, money hardly seems like a major marital stumbling block. But it can be. Money is the root of the majority of marital fights. If the couple comes from different economic levels or there is a significant gap in earned income, the marriage is subject to more severe strains than that of a couple from the same economic level.

What about when a woman marries "down"? Now that an increasing number of women are holding executive-level positions, a "reverse" earnings gap between husband and wife is no longer all that unusual. Depending on the size of the gap, it may place little or no stress on a marriage or it may be a killer time bomb just waiting to explode.

If your plans include giving up your career, either temporarily or permanently, in favor of motherhood, your higher salary should present no problem. My suggestion in such a case would be to take your present difference in earnings and put it aside for something special—the children's education, an emergency fund, a house, your old age, a once-in-a-lifetime vacation—or a fur coat to keep you warm for the next decade.

If you plan to keep working and doubt that his earnings will ever catch up with yours, it is important for the two of you to discuss how you feel about this. Many men find it difficult to accept that their wives earn more. It puts them on the defensive. Makes them feel a little less masculine. There is an enormous potential for tension here. He may one day accuse you of throwing your weight around just because you earn more. Or you may, in anger, tell him that he can at least mow the lawn or wash the car, even if he can't earn a decent living. When you are first in love, you may protest that neither of you would ever think or say such things, but you would be surprised at the monstrous things that surface in a marital fight. They can poison a marriage. So it is absolutely essential to talk out the money question before the wedding. Be honest about how you feel. Spend extra time going through the Money Checklist. (See also Chapter 24.)

And one more thing. If you earn significantly more money than he does, you should ask yourself the following three questions:

- Why do I want to marry him?
- Why does he want to marry me?
- What are the trade-offs?

You may not be able to give honest answers to these questions in the early head-over-heels period of romance. This is reason enough not to rush into marriage. Give yourself time. Enjoy the courtship period. And think about your answers to these questions.

Are you marrying him because no other man seems interested in you? Because you want a relationship in which you are the boss? Is he marrying you for security? For your money? There are no right or wrong answers. If you decided, for instance, that you are marrying him because you need someone to be dependent on you, that is all right as long as you are sure you will not resent him later for this very reason.

The third question is the real key to whether or not this marriage can succeed. What is the trade-off? You are bringing more money to the partnership. What is he bringing to balance the scales? Whatever it is, do you think it will mean as much to you in two years as it does today? In five years? Cinderella trade-offs—no matter which sex is involved—tend to lose value rather quickly.

Women have always tended to marry "up." Unlike marrying "down," this is socially acceptable. If the economic discrepancy is not too great, these marriages have no more problems than the general run of marriages. But the Cinderella stories are something else again.

Cinderella and her prince may have lived happily ever after, but contemporary Cinderellas often have a bad time of it. There is always a trade-off when a woman in poor or moderate circumstances marries into wealth. It may be unconscious, but the woman has to bring something special to the union if a man marries beneath his economic level.

Take Walter Wealthy, for instance. He offers all the pleasures and comforts and luxuries that money can buy. What does Cinderella Churchmouse have to offer in return. In ninety-nine cases out of one hundred, one thing and one thing only. And no, it is not sex (although that may be the Cinderella trade-off in a union between Rosie Rich and Peter Poor). The primary Cinderella trade-off is her beauty for his money. Beauty is perishable, however, and men like Walter Wealthy are not noted for until-death-do-us-part devotion.

What are men like Walter Wealthy like? The best answer is probably that they are object oriented. You must understand that I am not lumping all extremely wealthy men into the Walter Wealthy category. Only those who marry Cinderellas.

The Walter Wealthies tend to operate on a less sensitive emotional level than most of us. Part of this is because they usually have been brought up by servants, people who come and go. One of the earliest lessons they learn is not to get too attached to people because they always go away. This limits their ability to love.

And part of it is because all his life, Walter Wealthy has been able to buy anything he wants. If he wants a new Rolls-Royce, he orders one. If he wants a stable of racehorses, he gets the best money can buy. If he wants a wife, he marries the most beautiful woman he can find.

He thinks of his wife much the way he thinks of his other possessions. And when her beauty fades, he will marry another beauty. The end result is that the Cinderella trade-off is short term in most cases. It self-destructs. You can read of Cinderella-and-the-prince breakups almost every day of the week in the gossip columns.

So if a forever-after happy marriage is your goal, you would be wise to look for a man whose background is not all that different from your own in most respects.

EIGHT

*A "devoted little dog" of a wife ... The daddy–daughter
marriage ... The real gamble in marrying an older
man ... The age double standard ... The trouble with
younger men ... Two reasons not to marry a younger
man ... Benjamin Franklin's advice*

You have known him for a significant length of time. His
background is similar to yours in most respects. But he is
fifteen years older than you are. Or fifteen years younger.
Either way, this is a high-risk marriage, so risky that my Third
Guideline for Mate Selection is *Choose a man who is close to
you in age.*

Close in age means approximately no more than ten years
older or five years younger, but these are only ballpark figures.
It is impossible to set arbitrary limits. A great deal depends
upon your own age. Just think how old sixteen seemed to you
when you were ten. When you reach forty, however, forty-six
does not seem all that much older. Nor does fifty-six. When
you were sixteen, you would never consider dating a ten-year-
old, but at forty-six and fifty-six, forty and fifty do not seem
very much younger.

A woman of forty who marries a man of sixty is not taking

as great a risk—all else being equal—as a woman of twenty who marries a man of forty. This does not mean that the twenty–forty marriage cannot be immensely satisfying. An age-discrepant marriage can be wonderful. And many are. But it is what psychologists call a "deviant" marriage. It does not conform to the norm. Over the last hundred or so years, the median age difference between first-time brides and grooms has ranged from two years to a little over four years. This reflects the norm. Closeness in age does not guarantee lifelong happiness, but an age-discrepant marriage definitely guarantees stresses that are not present or are less severe in other marriages.

YOUNGER WOMAN–OLDER MAN

The younger woman–older man marriage is less risky than the reverse. It has the force of tradition behind it. Marrying an older man has always been socially acceptable and often desirable.

In ancient Greece, Aristotle advised men to wait until they were thirty-six to marry and then to choose a wife half their age—young enough to be biddable. And sociologist David Mace tells of a fourteenth-century Frenchman who, on the golden side of sixty, "wrote a book of guidelines for his new fifteen-year-old wife, and for her edification used the analogy of a devoted little dog faithfully doing what her master commanded."

Not so long ago, *The New York Times* stated in its editorial columns "That gentlemen of a certain age often prefer ladies who have gone less than half their distance is a fact. That the attraction is mutual is also a fact. There is nothing more seductive than a well-nourished wallet."

No man would get away with the "devoted little dog" bit today, but there is an echo of it in most May–December marriages. The woman trades her youth for financial security, usually accompanied by a higher social status than she would have if she married a man closer to her own age. Or, in many cases, the woman has, consciously or unconsciously, been searching for an older man. A little girl's first love is her daddy. And many women never get over it. They search for a man with whom they can reestablish that old daddy–daughter relationship.

In either case, the man is proud of himself for having captured an attractive young woman. He feels young and vigorous again. He basks in her admiration and love. And she is delighted to have attracted this man who is more sophisticated and successful than men her own age, a man who will take care of her and indulge her.

These are old-fashioned marriages in the sense that it is usually taken for granted that the man is head of the household. His young wife, coddled and indulged, is more of a pet than a partner.

There is nothing wrong with this if it is what you want and need in marriage. But everything has its price, and if you are thinking of marrying an older man, here are some of the prices you may have to pay.

SEX

The two of you may have different sexual needs and expectations. You are young and full of passion. Yes, he satisfies you now. He is so much better than those fumbling young men you have known. He knows just how to drive you out of your skin with pleasure. But there are going to be times when you will be wanting sex desperately and it is just not going to be there for you.

The sexual excitation of the early days vanishes faster than you would believe. This is true of almost all marriages, and I will talk about the process of erotic desensitization in Chapter 25, but it is more acute with an older man. He will get one erection a night, not three or five. And he will get that one erection every third or fourth or fifth night, not every night.

And he may not maintain it long. With love and understanding, this need not be a great problem. There are many ways of achieving mutual sexual satisfaction if he is willing. But if he is sexually inhibited or perhaps just not interested, you may be cheated of one of the most delightful and satisfying aspects of marriage. And you may never achieve the particular closeness that good sex promotes in marriage.

LIFE STYLE

The older man has lived longer than you have. He has his own ways. His own friends. His own likes and dislikes. He probably shares more memories and attitudes with his friends than he does with you. You are the one who will have to do most of the adapting. Not he. After all, he did not marry a pretty young thing just so she could wrap him around her little finger. He expects you to fit in with his ways.

You may feel comfortable with his life style and ingrained habits, but then again you may not. You may find yourself bored with his friends, who are so much older than you are and with whom you have little in common. And he may feel the same way about your friends. You may become fed up with his Thursday night bridge club and with taking his aged mother for a ride every Sunday afternoon. And there may be times when you feel that he is comparing you with his former wife. Unfavorably.

After all, an older man has probably been married before and is either widowed or divorced. Either way, he still thinks of his first wife. And this may force you into a kind of crazy competition. You are going to show him that you are more loving, more understanding, more everything than she ever was.

He may have children who are not much younger than you are. Or even older. They may still be in school and living with you. A ready-made family presents its own problems. Resentment. Jealousy. You are suddenly a stepmother and find yourself doing the laundry and shopping and cooking for a houseful when you had dreamed of candle-lit dinners and long romantic evenings.

Even if your relationship with the children is easy and warm, there is bound to be some tension. The first year is one of the most delightful periods of marriage. You are pleased with each other and excited about the new life you are establishing together. The romantic glow has not diminished. But it is a difficult period. There are adjustments to be made. Fights to be fought. And made up. A lot of accommodations to be worked out. You need time together—alone. This is difficult to find in a household with children.

ILLNESS AND DEATH

These are facts of life. If you marry an older man, they may be the facts of your life sooner than later. He may have a serious chronic illness—the aftermath of a stroke or heart attack, kidney failure, cancer, just to mention a few—that will keep you confined to the house and his bedside. Your role will be more nurse than wife. It will be desperately hard for you to watch the man you love grow weak and die.

The chances are that he will die long before you. The average male life span is just slightly over seventy years while a woman's is over seventy-eight years. If he is in his forties now and you are in your twenties, this may seem so far off as to be in never-never land. But if he dies in his seventies, you will be in your fifties and suddenly it will be very much the here and now. If statistics are to be believed—and while they are never exact, they are usually close to the target—you face twenty-eight or more years of widowhood.

The chances of a woman in her fifties remarrying are slim. Please turn back to Chapter 3 and review the Intimacy Formula. And now ask yourself two questions.

- How many eligible men do you think you will meet in your fifties?

- How desirable do you think they will consider you when there are countless younger women available?

The answers are not pleasant to contemplate. If you are in your twenties, you may be inclined to dismiss whatever might happen in future decades as unimportant. But please do think about this. These are facts that should be faced. You may face them and accept them. That is fine. At least you are making your decision with full knowledge of the bitter as well as the sweet.

THE GROWTH FACTOR

You are divinely happy. You cannot believe how fortunate you are that this sophisticated, fascinating older man is in love with you. You admire him tremendously. You are grateful for the way he enriches and broadens your life. Your love has a lot of hero worship in it and there is nothing wrong with that. Except—you may remember that old saying that no man is a hero to his valet. Very few men are heroes to their wives either. As the years go by, you are going to develop and change. And how are you going to feel about your assigned role then? You may tire of hero worship, of being the "devoted little dog."

Now that I have pointed out some of the major stresses in a May–December union, let me repeat that these marriages can be wonderful—if necessarily shorter than most. There is no getting around the very real possibility that you will spend thirty to forty years alone, but this is one of the trade-offs. You gamble that the years you will have together will be wonderful enough to make up for the years you will be alone.

OLDER WOMAN–YOUNGER MAN

What about the other side of the coin? The older woman who marries a younger man? This raises more eyebrows. It is more deviant than the younger woman–older man marriage. People tend to suspect the young man's motives and the older woman's sanity. Katharine Hepburn gave such unions a backhanded seal of approval once, saying, "I think it's fine if the younger man is sort of a slight sap."

What is operating here is a double standard that is every bit as virulent as the old moral double standard. People tend to admire or envy a man who takes a younger woman as his wife, but when an older woman marries a young man, neither one of them gets any approval, let alone admiration.

And that is just one of the stresses in these marriages. "The mates in such a marriage carry burdens not required of people in the more conventional older man–younger woman marriage," says Dr. John F. Cuber, professor emeritus of sociology at Ohio State University.

As I wrote in my previous book, *What Every Woman Should Know About Men*:

> The younger man may have something to gain in marrying an older woman, but the woman has very little—and she has it only temporarily in most cases. As she grows older, she finds less excitement and certainly less comfort and companionship in the relationship. Usually the young man will belong to one of two groups. Either he has some very pronounced emotional problems or he is simply using the older woman as a means of support. Neither type is a good bet for the long run. There are exceptions. A young man may fall in love with an older woman because of her sophistication and competence in dealing with the world. But these exceptions are few and far between.

MONEY AND SUCCESS

The older woman is usually well established in her career. She has also achieved a certain status. The younger man, possibly only because he is younger, has not reached either her financial level or her position in the community. Because of this, there is the inevitable suspicion that he is marrying her for security—financial or emotional or both.

If he spends more money than he makes, this can be a source
of tension. It may be fine with you to carry the household
expenses, to pay the mortgage or the rent and make the car
payments, but if he is spending all his money on himself, the
time is going to come when you resent it. No matter what
your original agreement was concerning money.

Add to this the fact that the younger man may come to feel
jealous of your greater success and income. He may feel that
people respect you more and him less. And in most cases he
will be right.

EXPERIENCE

You may begin to feel uncomfortable when you refer to something that happened fifteen or twenty years ago and he draws
a blank. One television producer seriously considered marrying a man twenty-five years her junior, but as the months
went by she realized it would have been a mistake.

"When I told him I was a child of the Depression," she
said, "he thought I was talking about an emotional state. Another time I mentioned that my late husband had fought in
the Second World War. This young man was born in 1955
and he looked at me as if I had stepped out of some time warp.
It got to be unsettling. We were on the same wavelength in
one respect only—sex. And that was not enough for marriage."

JEALOUSY

This can be devastating. And cruel. "Jealousy occurs in these
marriages," Dr. Cuber says, "because the older woman often
feels insecure in the face of real or imagined competition from
younger women." There is no way around it. You are always
going to be conscious of the age gap. And no matter how much
he protests that he loves you and you only, you cannot help
but be aware of the availability of younger women.

You see your skin fading, brown spots on your hands, your

hair graying while your young husband is vital and handsome. It is easy to believe he is tempted by every attractive younger woman he meets, whether he is or not.

CHILDREN

This is a double-barreled problem. First of all, you may have children by a former marriage. The younger man may not be much older than they are. Since many young men marry an older woman in search of a mother figure, they are liable to be jealous of the children of a previous marriage.

He may consider your children rivals for your affection. He may complain that you devote too much time to them. Or spend too much money on them.

The second aspect of the problem is that he may come to want children himself. No matter what he professed earlier on. You may be past your childbearing years. Or so close to the end of them that you do not want to take the risk. A woman in her late thirties and early forties whose religion or convictions do not allow abortion has good reason to fear becoming pregnant. With every tick of the clock, the chances of bearing a healthy baby lessen.

One woman whose much younger husband decided after three years of marriage that he wanted to have children of his own suggested that they adopt a child. He refused to consider the idea. He did not want to lavish love and money on a child who was not his own.

She wanted to please him. There had been a number of magazine articles about the great increase in first-time older mothers. She would join the trend. But miscarriage followed miscarriage.

After the third, her gynecologist advised against her trying again. "Your body is giving you a message," he said. "And the message is no. I know you are disappointed, but in the long run," he told her gravely, "I think you will be better off."

She understood that he was hinting at more than he had actually said. If she had a child, she would be fifty when the child started school. Most of the other children would have grandmothers who were younger than she. And what if having a child was not enough to save her marriage? Her child would not only have an elderly mother but an absent father.

The marriage ended in divorce. Her ex-husband married another older woman—but not as much older—immediately after the divorce was final.

SEX

Some argue that it makes great sense for women to marry younger men, because it prolongs their active sex life. There is no doubt but that a woman will have a more active sex life with a younger man, but if this is the main attraction, my question is: Why bother to marry him?

Most older people seem to agree with me. Two gerontologists, Drs. Bernard D. Starr and Marcella B. Weiner, who carried out an ambitious survey on the sexual lives, opinions and desires of older men and women, reported on their findings in their book *Sex and Sexuality in the Mature Years*.

One of the questions they asked their sample of eight hundred men and women who ranged in age from sixty to ninety-one was "How do you feel about older women having younger lovers?" Four-fifths of the participants saw nothing wrong with this. In fact, most were enthusiastically in favor of the idea. Naturally there were some reservations. Most felt it would be inadvisable if the age gap was too great—"not if you're old enough to be his mother." The interesting thing was that no one suggested that a woman should marry her young lover. The few answers that included a mention of marriage warned against it.

And so do I if sex is what draws you to your young man. Enjoy him as a lover. There is no need to get married.

THE LATER YEARS

Then there are those who argue that women should marry younger men because they will spend fewer years alone as widows. This may be true, but age and disability may present problems. Your age and your disability.

Most men are uncomfortable around sick people. Some are wonderfully supportive and caring, but the majority shrink from illness. It reminds them of their own mortality. The man in his sixties may resent being tied down to an ailing eighty-year-old wife. Or the man in his fifties to a seventy-year-old wife. This, coupled with the fact that they consider themselves still desirable to the opposite sex, can make you feel insecure, jealous, even helpless. In the age of no-fault divorce, the older woman may find herself ailing—and suddenly alone.

Some older woman–younger man marriages can and do work. The needs of each partner are fulfilled and the couple thrives. "It may be that the individuals who enter into such marriages are in some way psychologically selected," speculates Dr. Paave Piepponen, a Finnish social scientist. "The men may be submissive and the women dominating. It may also be a question of conscious deviation from the behavior dictated by age-role expectations, which in turn leads to a successful marriage." In other words, if you have the guts to follow your heart despite the disapproval of the world at large, you probably have the strength to work out the problems inherent in these marriages.

I want to end this discussion of the Third Guideline with a man's opinion. Benjamin Franklin, that wise old statesman and proverb-coiner, advised young men, "You should prefer an older woman to young ones, because they have more knowledge of the world and their minds are better stored with observations." Unfortunately, he spoiled this lofty sentiment with another piece of advice. He was talking about taking a mistress, not a wife, but his words are as appropriate to the marital as to the extramarital relationship. You should choose an older woman, Franklin counseled, because "They are so grateful!!!"

NINE

How men rate women...And how one man felt about being rated like a woman...Beauty trade-offs...Why a homely woman may be a beauty in her husband's eyes...Why married couples tend to resemble each other as the years go by

The Fourth Guideline to Mate Selection is *Don't marry a man who is far more attractive than you are*. Studies have shown that marriages of plain women to attractive men are more unstable than those of couples who are closer on the looks scale.

We live in a world that rates women on the basis of looks. "She's a ten" is a superlative, while "She's a three," can be translated as "She's a dog." No man would want to be judged the way men judge women.

When Dustin Hoffman starred in *Tootsie* as an actor who pretended he was a woman in order to get a job, and then was catapulted to soap opera stardom in his role as a woman, he became aware of this in a very personal way. "I got to the point where I could fool men when I was dressed and made up as Dorothy, but I was outraged by the way they related to me." At parties, he said, no sooner would he be introduced to a man than the man would start looking around the room for a more attractive woman. At the same time Hoffman confessed, "I wouldn't ask myself out if I looked like Dorothy."

Few women consider a man's looks as important as his personality, his self-esteem, his sincerity, his warmth and a host of other qualities. A woman sees a man as a human being, not a status symbol. But women, as Dustin Hoffman discovered, are summed up and judged in a single blink of the eye. You may be charming, witty, warm and adorable, but if you are not attractive, you are going to have to work harder to make a man aware of your qualities.

Beauty is a woman's trump card. Without it she has a weaker hand. "The major negotiating asset of women, whether we condone it or not, is their appearance," state Drs. M. Ronald Mingé, George A. Giuliani and Thomas F. Bowman in their book *Mating*. "Research has shown that many men place an extremely high value on beauty and are willing to trade almost anything for that precious commodity."

And yet we all know happy couples where the husband is extremely attractive and the wife is very plain, to put it charitably. How come?

It is usually a matter of trade-offs. "To the extent that the couple is dissimilar in attractiveness, the less attractive partner must negotiate with the more attractive over the nature and quantity of resources to be exchanged to compensate for the dissimilarity in attractiveness," reports psychologist Gregory White of the University of Maryland, who has researched the role of physical attractiveness in marriage.

Marriage is one long negotiation from the word go—like any business merger. Both partners are expected to bring equal assets to the new firm. If the woman is not as good looking as the man, she has to offer other assets. The value of her assets may diminish as time goes by. If that happens, the husband may look for a better deal.

Take the case of Patty Plain and Allen Adonis. Patty was madly in love with Allen, who drove a van for her father's moving company. Allen was flattered by her almost worshipful adoration. He was not unaware that if he married Patty, he would be the logical candidate to take over his father-in-law's business in due course. He was studying accounting at night, a subject he felt would be useful in getting ahead. And so he fell in love with Patty and they were married. Her assets made him forget her dumpy figure and plain features.

They lived happily until Allen got his degree in accounting and was offered a junior executive job with a machine tool company. His father-in-law encouraged him to take it. "I can't match that kind of opportunity," he told Allen.

Allen was triumphant. "This is it," he told Patty. "I'm on the white-collar track now." Patty was equally delighted. But she lost her important asset. Allen no longer considered her father and his business necessary for his future success. And as for his wife's unstinted admiration and devotion, a lot of women found Allen attractive.

He took one of the secretaries at his new office to lunch. Invited another to have a drink after work. Started playing around. One day he met Nancy Knockout and fell madly in love with her. They were a handsome couple.

Allen told Patty he was leaving her. If she did not institute divorce proceedings, he would. And all the friends and relatives shrugged and said, "I don't know what he saw in her in the first place."

These marriages do not always end this way. In many, bonds of intimacy are created that prevent a breakup when the woman's assets diminish in value. The strongest bond is the growth of true emotional intimacy, of love. Others are children, familiarity, comfort. Even laziness. A man may feel it is just too much effort to make a change and so he stays in the marriage— discontented and somewhat resentful of being tied to his less-than-beautiful wife.

There are some looks-discrepant marriages that are as solid as the Rock of Gibraltar. The extremely handsome husband is convinced that his quite plain wife is a beauty. It is truly a case of beauty being in the eye of the beholder. And there is a reason for this, according to Dr. John Money of Johns Hopkins.

From the moment they are born, infants start forming a love map, he says. A love map is made up of "messages encoded in the brain that describe eventual likes and dislikes [including] such things as hair color, eye color, body shape" as well as temperament and personality traits. These are based on the child's perceptions of the earliest people in his life—parents, relatives, playmates. The child incorporates the looks and traits of those he likes into his love map and by the time he is eight, he has an unconscious but very precise idea of how his or her future mate should look.

The man who believes his homely wife is a beauty almost surely had a mother or doting aunt who was homely. But to the child, she was beautiful, because her love and tenderness became fused with her looks so that the message the child got was beauty.

When this man meets a woman who resembles his mother in some way—her stringy hair, perhaps, or her long nose, or her thin lips, he sees her as a beauty although the rest of the masculine world may classify her as a three or a four. She fits his love map.

So when you see a happy couple in which the husband is far more attractive than the wife, you can attribute their bliss to trade-offs or a matching love map. But these are the exceptions. Most of these looks-discrepant marriages in which the man is by far the more attractive partner are susceptible to breakup.

Most of us, however, unconsciously choose a mate who is roughly as attractive as we are. People often remark on how much elderly couples have grown to resemble each other over the years. The fact is that they probably looked very much like each other to start with. "Everybody has unconscious limits of attractiveness," says Dr. David Klimek, "with which to compare a prospective partner." And that limit of attractiveness is usually closely related to the face you see in the mirror. A study of dating couples that rated them on their looks revealed that 85 percent of them were evenly matched. Beautiful women with handsome men. So-so women with so-so men. Homely women with homely men. Most of us feel comfortable with our own looks level and that is fortunate.

Now I certainly would never decide not to marry a man simply because he was better looking than I was. But I would stop and think and get the trade-offs straight in my mind. And I would think about how the man measured up to the other guidelines. If you feel that your relationship has enough going for it for you to marry him, then go ahead. After all, there is nothing wrong with waking up to a handsome face on the next pillow.

TEN

How to have a boring marriage ... The desirable difference ... Why my husband gets annoyed with me ... And why I get annoyed with him ... Emotional magnetism, or why opposites attract ... The Diagnostic Test for Psychological Compatibility

Up to now I have been emphasizing similarities, but differences are every bit as important in assuring long-term compatibility. And so my Fifth Guideline for Mate Selection is *Choose a man who is your psychological opposite.*

If you were to marry a man whose background was similar to yours, a man who was close to you in age and all the rest—*and* was very much like you psychologically, do not think for one minute that you would have achieved the perfect marriage. No such thing. What you have there is built-in boredom. It would be like living with a carbon copy of yourself. And where is the excitement or joy in that? It is the psychological differences that add spice to a marriage. More than spice. They complete us. Help us to become more than we have been.

A word of warning. I am talking about psychological differences only. It is important not to confuse them with philosophical differences.

Edna and William were philosophical opposites. Edna was a militant feminist, an ardent conservationist and a vegetarian. Once when she took part in an antinuclear demonstration, she was dragged off to jail. William's only encounter with the police was the time he got a speeding ticket for doing sixty in a forty-five-mile-per-hour zone. He voted the straight Republican ticket, wished that women would understand that their place is in the home and was a steak and French-fried potatoes man.

You may find it difficult to imagine what could have brought these two together in the first place. It was sex. An immediate sexual attraction that was fueled by fiery disagreements over their political and philosophical beliefs. Passionate arguments led to passionate sexual encounters which led to marriage six weeks after their first meeting. The marriage was a stormy affair that ended in divorce.

Edna and William were philosophical opposites, but psychologically they were practically identical. They were both stubborn, self-righteous, humorless, and argumentative.

The man who is uncomfortably shy in social gatherings and the woman who loves having people around are psychological opposites. They complement each other. She takes some of the social pressure off of him. He feels less shy with her at his side. He helps her understand the quiet pleasures of being alone with each other, of reading, listening to music, walking in the rain. The spendthrift and the saver, the impetuous and the hesitant, the modest and the boastful can complement and gain from each other. Their lives are more rewarding and joyous because of what each contributes to the other.

This has certainly been true in my own marriage. Milt and I come from similar backgrounds and agree on most of the important issues of life, but psychologically we are as different as night and day.

Milt is outgoing. He sees people through rose-colored glasses, while I tend to be reserved and somewhat judgmental. I will say, "I don't want to get involved with this person. He spells trouble." Milt will say "nonsense" and sail right in. And there *will* be trouble later, but in the meantime Milt has usually had a great deal of pleasure.

One example that comes to my mind is the time an acquaintance asked him to invest in an art gallery. "That man has got trouble written all over him," I said. "If you put money in that gallery, it's going to be like throwing it away."

"He's a great guy," Milt assured me. "I'm sure he knows what he is doing." And he put up the money. Not very much fortunately.

I was right. The money might just as well have been flushed down the drain. But Milt was right too. He learned a great deal about contemporary art from this man and met all kinds of interesting people, some of whom are our friends today. True, he lost money, but he might have lost it in the stock market too. And true, he had a lot of aggravation, but his life had been enriched. And so had mine.

I am the one who starts new projects and Milt is the one who sees that they get finished. Take our old farm in the country, for instance. I thought it would be good to have a place to go weekends where we could lead a different kind of life. I knew exactly what I wanted—a run-down farmhouse that we could renovate. It would be something that we could do together. When I found what I considered the ideal house and location, I convinced Milt that he had to go look at it.

We drove out to see it one Sunday. "My God!" he exclaimed when we arrived. "It's Tobacco Road. You must be out of your mind!"

"Trust me," I said.

He sighed."Okay. If this is what you think you want."

We bought the place. And then we bought an armful of do-it-yourself books on just about everything from plumbing to spackling. We worked like fiends every weekend. Milt joked that he was the only one-handed carpenter in town. One-handed because the other hand was always holding the how-to book.

We pulled up layers of linoleum and found wide-board floors of pine and chestnut underneath. We broke through walls to fireplaces that had been boarded up for years. We scraped and painted and papered. It was Milt who masterminded the renovation. It was Milt who figured out how to do things. And it is Milt who feels deprived if we don't get there every weekend.

These are two of the patterns in our marriage that are a result of our psychological differences. My role is to find exciting new things to do and push him into doing them with me. His role is to find fascinating people and push me into knowing them. He is so witty and warm that he attracts a great diversity of people. And I am always coming up with something new and interesting to do or think about. We get each other into things that we would not have been involved in otherwise. And the result is that we have never been bored with each other in all our thirty-five years of married life.

This does not mean that we are always enchanted with each other. Those same differences have also been sources of stress. There are times when I wish he would not bring so many people home. And there are times when he complains that I am pushing him into things he has no time for. We can get quite annoyed with each other. But not for long. We know that the very qualities that exasperate us most in each other are the ones that drew us together in the first place. We have come to accept our differences over the years. Not only accept them but relish them. And we have learned to take the bad patches in our stride.

There is no getting around the fact that these very desirable psychological differences can just as easily destroy a marriage as make it blissful—if you do not understand how they function. Do you remember Rex Harrison delivering that wonderful line in *My Fair Lady* when as Professor Higgins he asked, "Why can't a woman be more like a man?" The truth is that the professor would have been dismayed if women were more like men. He would have discovered that was not what he wanted at all. But there it was. The differences that enchanted him—against his will—also exasperated him.

This is often a major problem in marriage. Nora and Walt discovered this the hard way. Nora was impulsive. If she saw something she liked, she bought it then and there. Walt, on the other hand, considered every purchase carefully. Did he need it? Could he get it for less money someplace else? If they ran into friends at the movies on a Sunday afternoon, Nora would impulsively ask them home for supper afterward. Or she might wake Walt early on a summer morning and say, "It's a beautiful day. Let's go down to the lake for a swim before we get ready for work." And he loved it. Life was more interesting when he never knew what to expect.

Walt was a planner. He drew up a household budget every year. He knew just when he was going to trade in their car for a new one, when they would be financially ready to move to the suburbs, when they could afford their first child. Nora was impressed by his approach to life. She felt secure with a man who thought things out beforehand. A man who was responsible.

As time passed, however, she found herself becoming impatient with his deliberate ways. "Why can't you just do something," she asked him, "instead of making a big deal about it?" And Walt blew his top when he came home from work one night and discovered Nora had accepted an invitation to go out for the third night in a row. "You might at least have consulted me," he said angrily. "Now I'll be up all night working on these reports that I brought home to do." And so it went. Their disagreements escalated. Nora didn't see why Walt could not be more impulsive, ready to act on the spur of the moment. And Walt could not see why Nora could not learn to think before she leaped. Or at least ask him how he felt before she committed him to doing things with her. For the life of him, he could not see why Nora could not be more like him.

They got their first clue to what had gone wrong in their marriage when Nora attended one of my lectures, which just happened to be on the importance of marrying your psychological opposite and the danger of trying to change him.

I told the audience that the old saying, "Opposites attract," is a scientific fact. A magnet has two poles, a north and a south pole. The like poles of the magnets repel each other; the unlike poles attract each other. A similar kind of emotional magnetism is present between men and women who are attracted to each other.

"It was just as if you had turned on a light in a dark room," Nora wrote me later. "All of a sudden, it dawned on me that if Walt changed to be like me, I probably would not like it at all." That night she told her husband what she had learned from my lecture. "We talked about it a lot," she reported in her letter, "and we promised each other to remember that the things we really loved in each other were the things we were fighting about. I loved knowing that Walt was logical and responsible. I feel safe with him. He balances my impulsiveness. And Walt said that it would be too much to have two planners in a family. He loved me just the way I was, he said, even if I did drive him up the wall occasionally."

I was delighted that my lecture had had a positive effect and helped this couple understand what was going on between them. I only wish they could have understood about emotional magnetism earlier and saved themselves some grief.

There is nothing mysterious about the way emotional magnetism works between two people. I have worked out a Diagnostic Test for Psychological Compatibility that any woman can do by herself. It will reveal more about yourself and the man you love than any other test you can take and evaluate by yourself. It not only helps pinpoint your psychological differences but alerts you to areas of potential trouble.

DIAGNOSTIC TEST FOR PSYCHOLOGICAL COMPATIBILITY

Divide a sheet of paper into quarters by drawing a line down the center and another across the middle. At the top of the first box, write your own name. In the second, write the name of the man you are considering marrying. In the third, the name of your first love, whether it was the boy you had a crush on in the third grade or someone you met later. In the last box write the name of a male friend, someone you really like but who has never been and will never be more than a good friend.

Now, without stopping to ponder over it, write down the first ten qualities that come to your mind that describe you. Then do the same for the three men. And that's it.

To show you how to evaluate what you have, I will share Celia's compatibility test with you. Celia is twenty-six. She teaches high school algebra and geometry. Jeffrey, whom she has known for nearly two years, is twenty-seven and sells mutual funds for a large brokerage firm.

"Jeffrey and I are thinking about getting married," Celia told me. "In fact, we've set the date. But I'm getting cold feet. I want to marry him more than anything else in the world. But we're so different. I don't know how we would make out."

"There is an easy way to find out," I told her. "It seems to me that you and Jeffrey are alike in all the important ways. You both grew up in small towns in the Middle West. Both of you love music. You both have responsible jobs. You have a number of friends in common. I would think that your values and attitudes are not all that different."

"But he's so charming," she said. "And so popular. He's always surrounded by people. I'm quiet. I'm great at explaining a theorem to my geometry class, but I'm not all that comfortable with people. Unless I'm with Jeffrey."

"What you are worrying about," I said, "are psychological differences. There's nothing wrong with those. I always tell people that the best marriage is the one where the bumps on your head fit the holes in his. But, to be serious, my Diagnostic Test for Psychological Compatibility can give you a pretty good idea of how compatible you are."

She was eager to try it. And here is her list of ten qualities for herself and three important men in her life.

CELIA

Perfectionist
Capable
Dependable
Worry about whether people like me
Considerate of others
Thrifty
Calm
Somewhat inhibited
Often lonely
Sensitive

JEFFREY

Sophisticated
Extravagant
Has a great deal of charm
Very persuasive
Hot tempered
Gallant
Gregarious
A little too self-centered
Aggressive
Makes the most of himself

JIM, MY FIRST LOVE

We met when we were counselors at the same summer camp.

Competent
Self-confident
Always made me feel pretty and popular
Convivial
Adventurous
A little selfish sometimes
Extremely generous
Warm

More sophisticated than other boys his age
Amusing

TOM, MY PLATONIC FRIEND

He's ten years older than I am and was my faculty adviser at college.

Work oriented
A loner
Surprisingly sentimental
Tends to intellectualize everything
I can tell him anything and be sure he'll respect my confidence.
Shrewd
A little boring
Loyal
Probably the kindest person I know
Responsible

"Now what?" Celia asked. "What does this tell me?"

"You'll find out in ten minutes. The next step is to write down the qualities that Jeffrey and Jim have in common that you and Tom do not have at all."

Celia came up with the following list:

1. Both of them like people and have a lot of friends.
2. Both put their own interests and wishes first. They are more selfish than I am.
3. They spend money much more freely than I ever would. I think of Jeffrey as being extravagant and I remember Jim as being generous, but it amounts to the same thing basically.
4. Both of them have a lot of self-esteem.
5. Both are charming. Jim always used to make me feel pretty and popular even when I felt awkward and out of it. Jeffrey has the same ability.

The similarities were striking. The two men, past and present, shared five identical or very similar qualities out of ten.

"Those five qualities," I said, "are what attract you in Jeffrey. The same ones you found so lovable in Jim when you were a teenager. Neither you nor your old friend Tom has these qualities. You are much more like Tom than like Jeffrey or Jim. That is why your relationship with him has always been and will always be platonic."

"But what do you think? With all these differences?" Celia asked.

"I think that you are made for each other," I replied. And I felt they were. Each had psychological strengths to bolster weaknesses in the other and to make the other's life more rewarding. Jeffrey's cavalier attitude toward money was going to balance Celia's thriftiness. She will learn that money is to be used to enrich life as well as to be saved. He will learn that money is not just for today's pleasures but also to provide a safeguard against what tomorrow might bring. His gregarious way of life will make her life more stimulating. And he will gain from her calmness. His self-esteem will probably be catching; she will feel more sure of herself when she is with him.

These same qualities could also present problems. I pointed out that they might find themselves disagreeing about money and that Jeffrey's busy social life and her discomfort with people might give rise to conflicts. "There will be times when he will want to go to a party or have people in and you will not feel at all like it. I can sympathize with this, because Milt and I go through the same thing quite often. But since you know beforehand that this is a potential troublemaker, you have won half the battle. The best solution to conflicts in this area is compromise."

Celia and Jeffrey found it difficult to reach a successful compromise on this. He could not understand why she would ever feel it was a problem. They finally reached a tentative solution. Jeffrey could choose what they would do three nights a week. Celia would choose what they would do another three nights. And on the seventh night, they would toss a coin to see who would choose the evening's activities.

They had no trouble in agreeing on a plan they thought

would rule out all conflict over money. They planned to set aside money every month to pay for all the necessities, including savings. Then they would divide whatever was left over evenly. If Jeffrey wanted to spend his share on opera tickets or a new pair of skis, fine. If Celia wanted to invest hers or spend it all on a wedding gift for her college roommate, fine. There would be no questions asked. No criticisms.

If all goes well, each of them will change—a little. If they change each other too much, they will lose that magic power of attraction that psychological opposites possess. But since they understand the binding strength of emotional magnetism, I do not believe there is any danger of this.

If you take this Diagnostic Test for Psychological Compatibility, I suggest that you tuck it away in some safe place after you have evaluated it. It will be easy to pinpoint the qualitites that attract you to the man involved, your psychological differences, but it may be difficult to see these differences as sources of future friction when you are in the romantic tailspin of courtship or the euphoria of looking forward to marriage.

But if a few months or even years after the wedding you find that the two of you are sniping at each other about this or that, get out your compatibility test and check it to see if you are criticizing each other for the very differences that attracted you in the first place. Just realizing what is going on may help you cool the domestic strife.

You will undoubtedly want to share your insights with your husband. I suggest that you ask him to read this chapter first, so that he will understand the role of psychological differences as well as you do.

And remember—even if some of those differences are annoying and exasperating at times, just thank your lucky stars that they exist. Without them, marriage has little spice, less enrichment and no joy.

PART THREE

THE CASE AGAINST COHABITA- TION

ELEVEN

Why you should not move in with your lover ... The mistake Maggie made ... Your chances of marrying the man you live with ... Why men are in the catbird seat ... The reason most live-togethers break up ... The myth of trial marriage ... The one exception to the "don't move in" rule ... The wedding difference

It is hard to believe that cohabitation was once known as "living in sin." Today it is as common as cocaine. And it can be just as destructive. Living together is a delightfully convenient and rewarding arrangement. For a man. But not for most women. Not for women whose goal is marriage.

Living together is for kids and for the elderly. The woman who wants to get married should not even consider moving in with the man she loves until her wedding day—with one exception that I will discuss later on.

If college students want to live together for a semester or two, fine. In most cases neither one expects the relationship to end in marriage. One researcher, who considers living together as simply another form of going steady, refers to it as "going very steady." Like going steady, it offers the late adolescent a certain security and a defense against loneliness. He has sex on tap. She does not have to worry about a date for

Saturday night. There is the very pleasant feeling of being important to another person. These relationships usually break up with a minimum of trauma.

"I was hurt when Chet told me there was someone else," said nineteen-year-old Priscilla, "but then I met Dennis and moved in with him. I see Chet every once in a while. I like him all right, but I wouldn't want to live with him again."

An increasing number of older men and women are choosing cohabitation over remarriage for several reasons, most of them financial, having to do with pensions and such. Between them these couples may boast of as much as 150 years of life experience. They know what they want and understand what they are getting into. Most find love and security and companionship in their live-together relationships.

But the woman who wants to get married has little to gain from cohabitation. And a great deal to lose. Take the case of Maggie. She belongs to that great majority of women who believe that marriage is the better way of life. Maggie loved Brendan. She wanted to share the rest of her life with him. She wanted him for her friend, her lover, her husband, the father of her children.

One blissful evening Brendan proposed. But not marriage. He proposed that they live together. "Move in with me," he urged. "I can't live without you," he said. "What does a piece of paper mean?" he asked. "Marriage is an obsolete formality. It's love that holds people together. And I will love you to the end of my life," he promised.

"Why not?" Maggie thought. "Once we're living together we're bound to get married. And if we don't—well, he's right. Living together is just another form of marriage. A higher form of marriage," she told herself. "I should follow my heart," she decided. And with stars in her eyes and love in her heart, she accepted Brendan's proposal and moved in with him.

Maggie was wrong, wrong, wrong! Moving in with Brendan was not the right thing to do. Not the bright thing to do. This is no moral judgment. Just plain old down-to-earth common sense. Maggie should have followed her brain, not her heart. Her goal was marriage. Moving in with Brendan was not going to help her achieve it. In fact, she lessened her chances of getting married by moving in with him. Not just of marrying Brendan, but of marrying any man.

It is true that many live-togethers do marry each other eventually, but many more do not. One study of 2,150 men revealed that just over a third of the unmarried men who had lived with a woman married her. In other words, nearly two-thirds of the live-together relationships did not end in marriage. They just ended. Period. According to this study, Maggie has one chance out of three of marrying Brendan.

The odds may actually be much worse. Cohabitation is such an elusive and temporary state that solid statistics are hard to come by. Another researcher, who pulled together studies of live-togethers from all over the country, found that only 9 percent had serious plans to get married. He also discovered that the average live-together relationship lasted only nine and a half months.

If Maggie had told Brendan that she loved him, but that she was not going to live with him unless they were married, he—more likely than not—would have proposed marriage. Perhaps not that night but rather soon after. After all, he was "in love" (see Chapter 5). That crazy wonderful infatuation is tremendously powerful at its peak, and there is no reason a woman should not turn it to her own advantage. But Maggie did not. Instead of using his infatuation to induce him to marry her, she became the victim of her own infatuation—and effectively lowered her chances of marriage.

One thing all women who are considering a live-together relationship should keep in mind is that nuts-and-bolts figure of 7.3 million too many women. Seven point three million more marriageable women than men.

Men are in the catbird seat today. Why should a man assume the responsibilities of marriage if he can enjoy the benefits of marriage without committing himself to marriage? There is nothing you can do about the numbers, but you can tilt circumstances a little in your favor. You don't have to give it away.

If a woman is willing to move in with a man and provide him with the equivalent of marital sex without expecting anything much except an orgasm in return, that is all she is going to get. And since most women only reach orgasm about half the time, there is no way she is going to get as much out of it as he does. When he gets bored with sex with her (and he will; 60 percent of married men admit to wishing they could change sex partners), he will drop her for someone else. After all, he is not married to her. There is nothing to hold him.

This may sound like what your grandmother used to say, but our grandmothers had a lot of shrewd common sense that we are just beginning to appreciate again. When Tom Wolfe, the writer who labeled the seventies the "Me Decade," was asked in an interview with Sheila Weller in *Self* magazine what he thought would characterize the eighties, he said, "We are going to examine the old proven systems to find their original logic. Instead of flatly saying 'What is this business of not having premarital sex? This is just a decrepit idea left over from the Victorian Age,' people (women especially) are going to realize that sex is not just fun. It is also, as people have known for centuries, a form of *power*.

"Women are going to begin to see that maybe they've been giving away a little too much. . . . The span of a woman's sexual attractiveness is still short compared to a man's. And the reason it is short is that men still have most of the power—and power is sexy. Unless we reach a point where women have every bit as much power out of bed as men do, a lot of women will be left out in the cold after a certain age."

And this comes from a sophisticated male. He makes a lot of sense. This business of being left out in the cold is chillingly true, as many women have discovered, women who have learned from experience.

But back to Maggie. If Brendan does not marry her, what then?

She has two choices. She can continue living with him. Some live-together relationships work out very well, although they are about as rare as hens' teeth. But this is not what Maggie really wants. She wants a husband. She wants children. She wants to be married. This option will not give her what she wants, except possibly children. And they would be illegitimate.

Her second option offers no guarantee of happiness, but it does give her a chance to get what she wants. This option is to move out and that is what Maggie did when she finally recognized that marriage with Brendan was not in her future. At this point she had been out of circulation for nearly three years. She had invested a lot of time in Brendan, an investment that did not pay off. In the meantime, the men she used to know had married or moved anyway or become involved with other women. She had to start all over.

It would take a significant length of time for her to find another man whom she loved—and who loved her. It would probably take her longer to meet her next Mr. Right than it did to meet Brendan. If you will turn back to Chapter 3 and flip through the Intimacy Formula, you can see just how difficult it is to start all over again to meet new people and reach the point of intimacy where marriage becomes a real possibility.

Not only are women giving it away in live-together relationships, they are usually the inferior partner. Many feminists used to be in favor of cohabitation. They saw it as two loving equals sharing their lives without the "coercion" of the marriage ceremony. But today those very same women have concluded that this business of sharing bed and board with a man they are not married to, rather than being an almost utopian union of equals, is an exploitative relationship. And the woman is the exploited partner.

Twenty percent of women under the age of twenty-five think that cohabitation has all the advantages of marriage, according to one study. But only 4 percent of women over forty consider it an acceptable alternative to marriage. The older women base their opinion on experience.

"Young people are highly romantic," explains Professor Joseph Garza, a sociologist at Georgia State University. "They believe they can have their cake and eat it too. People's attitudes change as they come to grips with the reality of real commitment. As people get older, they want more quality in a commitment, not just the quasicommitment offered in living together."

Another sociologist who interviewed live-togethers who had broken up found that the women had been more unhappy than the men. They complained that they had felt dominated by their partners. The men's wishes and convenience came first. And they felt increasingly insecure in the arrangement.

The sexual relationship reflects the power relationship. Researchers have found that the men tend to be unfaithful and the women faithful. There are exceptions, of course, but this seems to be the pattern. One couple, interviewed by Dr. E. Mansell Pattison, chairman of the department of psychiatry at the Medical College of Georgia, was typical. The man said that their sexual relationship had been completely satisfying, but, he admitted, "I wasn't totally monogamous." The woman reported that it had been only "okay" and added that she had never felt secure in the relationship.

"Sex while living together is usually more satisfying to men than to women," Pattison says, and he has found that sexual dissatisfaction is the leading cause of live-together breakups. Most sex problems are easily resolved in the early stages of a relationship, but live-togethers rarely attempt to work out their problems the way a married couple does. It is easier to find another sexual partner.

It is not only sexual problems that go unresolved in cohabitation. Discussions of money, social or emotional problems, even everyday garden-variety irritations like his leaving his socks on the floor or her playing rock music first thing in the morning are avoided like the plague. And this is why cohabitation is not a valid alternative to marriage. There is no commitment to make things work.

People who cohabit make a big deal out of insisting that a piece of paper does not mean anything, that they are bound together by love, that they are as committed to each other as if they had had a ten-bridesmaid wedding and a Bermuda honeymoon. But they are not. A man and a woman have to be committed enough to each other to work out their differences—battle them out if necessary—if they are to create a happy, intimate and lasting relationship. When people just live together, they do not make that effort.

Take money, for instance. It is one of the greatest causes of dissension in most marriages. But hardly ever in cohabitation. Cameron and Margot are a good example. Their money is strictly "his" and "hers." They share the rent and put money in a kitty for groceries, but he does not get upset if she runs up the telephone bill into three figures talking to her sister on the other side of the country, and she does not make a scene when he loses a week's salary on the horses.

"It's his money," Margot reasons. "If he's such an ass that he plays the horses, he deserves to lose it." And Cameron simply tosses the telephone bill over to Margot and says, "I'll be damned if I can figure out what you and your sister find to yak about for hours on end."

If they were married and saving for a house and children and all the rest, they would not be as cool. They would battle it out until they arrived at a set of financial priorities that both agreed on. Perhaps Margot would start writing her sister instead of telephoning. Or confine her telephoning to weekends when the rates were lower. And if Cameron really wanted to play the horses, he would keep his bets within a certain agreed-upon amount. No more going for broke. And these solutions would be palatable, because the two of them were committed to a future together.

But live-togethers do not face up to such issues. Part of the reason is that one of them—and almost always it is the woman—is afraid that she will rock the boat and he may leave her. So she never talks about the things that bother her. Neither does he. He does not want any hassles.

The result is that most live-togethers eventually create a situation where one or both are walking on eggs. They don't talk about the things that distress them, because they are afraid that the other is not committed enough to want to work them out. In time there are so many areas where they do not speak their minds that the relationship either dwindles away or the pressure builds up like steam in a tea kettle and eventually there is an explosion. That is usually the end. Too many emotions have been bottled up for too long for them to be able to fight constructively. It is too late to save the relationship.

Some people try to justify cohabitation on the grounds that it is really a trial marriage. It is not. It is nothing more than playing house. And that is for children. Marriage is for grown-ups. As the late Dr. Nathan Ackerman of the Ackerman Institute once said, "Marriage is yes or no. Not maybe."

Trial marriage is a myth. It is not for the woman who truly wants to get married. A couple can live together. Have sex together. They can put their dirty clothes in the same washing machine and share the same alarm clock. But that is not marriage. Nor is it a preparation for marriage.

Study after study makes it clear that couples who lived together before marriage face the same kinds of problems in the first years of marriage as couples who did not live together before the wedding. And both couples start from square one in working out those problems. The disagreements and differences that the live-togethers used to sweep under the rug do not stay neatly hidden away after the wedding. They have to be faced and negotiated. And the premarital live-togethers are no more skilled in negotiating them than the couples who are facing them for the first time.

As sociologists Jeffrey Jacques and Karen Chason of Florida A & M University summed up the results of their own study of live-togethers, "Premarital cohabitation may not provide types of learning experiences that significantly alter—in either a positive or negative direction—an individual's preparation for marriage."

Why not?

There is one big reason why not and that is that both partners know very well that it is a trial. They know that either of them can walk out. She does not have to put up with his morning grouchiness. He does not have to put up with her makeup crowding his shaving things off of the bathroom shelf. They are on their best behavior and tolerate traits in each other that they would not accept for one minute if they were married with a shared lifetime ahead of them. At best, trial marriage is just another form of courtship. Best-foot-forward time. It is no preparation for marriage. None of the inevitable conflicts gets worked out this way.

And please do not let yourself believe that you can have a good marriage without conflict. Marriage is one long negotiation. Some people have the romantic notion that when a man and woman truly love each other, that is all that is necessary. Everything will be wonderful because they love each other.

It won't. And the quality of their love will often be strained. The relationship between a husband and wife in a happy marriage is based on a baker's dozen of major adjustments and a vast amount of tinkering and fine tuning.

You seldom realize how many adjustments the two of you have made and continue to make until you have been married for a long time. I first realized how much Milt and I had adjusted to each other when we vacationed with another couple eight or nine years after our wedding. They were very good friends and the four of us were looking forward to our two weeks in the Green Mountains of Vermont. But we were in conflict from the word go.

They slept late, we got up early. When they wanted to play bridge, we wanted to watch the stars. When they wanted to go out for dinner, we wanted to cook at home. When they wanted to go antiquing, we wanted to go for a walk. She put the dog dish in the sink with the dinner plates. I felt it should be washed separately. Little things. But they mounted up. We were pulling in different directions all the time.

It was a surprise because we had always gotten along so well. But the real surprise was how much alike Milt and I thought. You just don't realize how many things you work through in a marriage. I knew that Milt would be bored stiff poking around in antique shops without his having to tell me. He knew that I loved having time to cook and putter around the kitchen, because most of the time we were both so busy that I rarely had a chance to do more than whip up an omelet or broil a chop. And neither of us enjoys sitting around a bridge table on a marvelous summer evening when the whole outdoors is beckoning. Time enough for bridge in the winter.

For the first time we realized that while as individuals we are temperamentally quite different, as a couple we think and act as one. It takes time and a lot of give and take to reach this comfortable point.

A trial marriage will never bring you to this happy point. When Dr. Pattison asked a group of couples who had lived together before marriage if it had prepared them for marriage, they all reported it had not.

"I thought it had," said one woman, "until I got married. I had magical fantasies about marriage. But there was no magic in marriage. Just a lot of hard work."

Nor did they find marriage anything like living together. Marriage was better. All of them agreed on this. When Pattison asked them what the difference was between cohabitation and marriage, they answered, "Having a real relationship, not a phony one.... Having someone who accepts you for what you are without pretense.... Working out a true partnership."

"It is striking that there is social intimacy and sexual intimacy in cohabitation, but not personal intimacy," Dr. Pattison said. "Couples enact the social role of living together, but they are personally apart. They live the role but hide the self."

· · ·

So there you are. If you want to get married, don't settle for living together. Spend the night with him. Spend the weekend with him. Spend your vacation with him. But don't move in with him. It will not bring you one step closer to the altar. Remember what happened to Maggie. It was all very well for Brendan to tell her that he would love her as long as he lived. The fact was that he did not love her enough to marry her.

Now for that one exception to my "don't move in" rule. If you are formally engaged and the wedding date is definitely set for the near future, I see no real reason why you should not live together. On the other hand, I see no real reason why you should. It may be convenient. It may be delightful. But since you are going to live with him for the rest of your life— at least we hope so—you ought to be able to wait a few more weeks. But if you can't, all right. Go ahead. And you have my blessing.

When I said this to a group of college students in an informal seminar, a pretty redhead said,"I don't understand. If you think it's okay to live together if you're going to get married in a couple of months, why isn't it okay to live together if you've agreed that you're going to get married sometime? Like in a couple of years? You know, when you've graduated and he's found a job.

"If the two people are intelligent and really in love and really committed to each other, why wouldn't it work out?" she asked. "I mean, what's the real difference between cohabitation and marriage if you're serious about each other?"

"There is a whole world of differences," I said, "but if you want the one big difference that sums up all the others, it is a wedding."

"A wedding! That's just a pageant. A social occasion. It's meaningless!"

I shook my head. "No, it is full of meaning. Some weddings are pageants—and usually lovely ones—but others are no-frills affairs. At City Hall or before a justice of the peace. But all of them are social occasions in the most serious sense."

The wedding is the public declaration of your commitment

to each other. You pledge your troth in front of witnesses, usually family and friends. Your vows are legally binding. Society has an important stake in marriage.

"A wedding is public business," Lance Morrow wrote in *Time*. "That is the point of it. The couple are not merely marrying one another. They are joining the enterprise of the human race. They are, at least in part, submitting themselves to the larger logics of life, to the survival of the community, to life itself."

The live-together couples who promise to love each other "forever" may argue that they also have made a solemn contract with each other and after all, they ask, who else is concerned? The answer is no one, for live-togethers do not make their promises in front of witnesses. As a contract, their promise is as intangible and ephemeral as a soap bubble. Most live-togethers are committed to a relationship of pleasure. When the pleasure stops, the commitment is over. There is nothing to hold them together. No legal, religious or social ties. And as for that promise, forget it.

"The key is the ceremony," says Professor Ned Gaylin, director of Marriage and Family Therapy Education at the University of Maryland. "Whether sacred or secular, religious or civil, the public commitment to another person in marriage makes it vastly different from living together."

"Why should I feel this way?" Elinor asked a week before her wedding. "I'm looking forward to the happiest day of my life. I'm marrying a wonderful man. Why does my face suddenly have to break out and my stomach start churning? I'm a wreck," she complained.

Most brides suffer from some degree of wedding jitters that usually surface as physical complaints. It is not unusual for a woman to develop terrible headaches a week or two before the big day because her blood pressure has shot sky high. Others are plagued by insomnia, heart flutters, flulike symptoms, you name it. Gastroenterologist Dr. Ivan Kahn calls this "wedding-

itis." Most women come to him with "premarital upper res-
piratory or lower-gastric distress," he reports. "And I see a
lot of palpitations where the bride thinks her heart is going
bananas."

He treats wedding-itis with "a lot of hand holding and talking. If that doesn't do the trick, I take more direct measures.
For palpitations, a cardiogram, so she will know she is not
having a heart attack. For spastic colons, a healthy dose of
paregoric." The best cure, however, is the wedding. All symptoms usually disappear within the next twenty-four hours.

Elinor was a "wreck" because she was facing the most important event of her life. On the life-change scale developed
by Dr. Thomas Holmes, marriage is rated at fifty stress points.
Only six life changes are considered more stressful—death of
a spouse, divorce, marital separation, detention in jail, death
of a close family member, and major personal illness or injury.
There is happy stress as well as unhappy stress and both kinds
take their toll. Our bodies often know more than our conscious
minds and Elinor's body was reflecting her stress.

I have never heard of a woman having an attack of preco-
habitation jitters. And why should she? There is not all that
much involved. On the life-change scale, the category that
most nearly approximates cohabitation is "a change in living
conditions," which is rated at a mere twenty-five points.

Women who have not suffered from wedding jitters and
believe they are taking their wedding in stride are almost always surprised by their intensely emotional reactions on the
wedding day. Faith, a Chicago accountant, had decided on a
Friday afternoon wedding at City Hall. Afterward she and
Jeb, also an accountant, would drive to Wisconsin to spend a
honeymoon weekend at a friend's lakeside cottage. And then
back to work on Monday.

"We were both so busy," she said. "It was tax season and
it was all the time we could spare. I didn't even buy a new
dress for the ceremony. I didn't take it that seriously. To me
it was just a necessary formality."

She could hardly believe it when she started crying during the brief City Hall ceremony. "When it came time for me to say 'I do,' it was all I could manage to choke out those two little words. I was absolutely swamped with emotion. I was happy and terrified at the same time. All of a sudden I understood how much it meant that we were promising to love and cherish each other forever. That we were going to share the rest of our lives."

Nobody cries when a man and woman move in together. Except possibly her mother. If she knows about it. The high-intensity emotion compounded of love, excitement, idealism and commitment is lacking.

There is more to weddings than solemn contracts and stress. They are celebrations of love and full of joy. Your wedding day becomes your own special holiday for the rest of your lives together. Year by year, your wedding anniversary becomes more meaningful as the two of you build and strengthen your marriage.

Almost every couple has its own special way of marking that day. My daughter and her husband planted four fruit trees on our farm on their wedding day. We all thought it was a good omen when the trees first bore fruit the year their son was born. Now when they visit us, they always go over to the orchard and show Micah the trees that were planted "on the day Mommy and Daddy were married." Perhaps he will plant trees on his own wedding day. But that is a long way in the future. Micah is only five.

There are very few live-togethers who establish traditions like this, who have roots in the past and a stake in the future. It is marriage that confers these blessings. Marriage is a serious commitment and it is hard work, but a good marriage is a perfectly glorious way of life.

And all marriages start with a wedding.

PART FOUR

THE SUR-VIVOR'S MANUAL
Why Women Need One

TWELVE

*Why "happily enough" is better than you
think ... Marriage as a survival mechanism ... The
married man's 2,409-day bonus ... Why marriage is
becoming like a television contract ... The new
phenomenon of the disposable wife ...
The five vulnerable stages*

You are married. And you are living happily ever after.

Or are you?

Probably not. Living happily ever after is more common in
fairy tales than in real life. Sleeping Beauty may have lived
happily ever after with the prince who awakened her with a
kiss, but real-life women, even real-life princesses, find that
marriage is not undiluted bliss.

In real life there is always a cloud on the horizon, a splinter
in your finger, a fight with your husband. But clouds pass,
splinters can be coaxed out, fights have a way of clearing the
air—and life goes on. Happily enough. And happily enough
is the best a woman can expect.

"But you are the woman who says marriage is a glorious
way of life," one woman said resentfully when I lectured on
the Myth of the Happily Ever After to a Denver audience.

"It is a glorious way of life," I said. "But even a glorious

133

way of life does not offer perpetual happiness. There is no such thing. Unless you have some unhappy times, you can never appreciate the happy times. Life would be like a diet of vanilla custard, bland and boring.

"Everyone's life is hard at times. Full of anxiety and stress. Your baby has colic. Your nine-year-old is falling behind in school. Your husband is drinking too much. Your father has a heart attack. Your son can't find a job. Your daughter is having an affair with a married man. This may sound like an outline for a soap opera, but these things happen to real people in real marriages. Yet in the long run, most of us are happy enough. We forget the pain and remember the pleasure. The strange thing about happiness is that often we do not realize how happy we are until much later. We look back at certain periods of our lives and say, 'Oh, we were so happy then!'"

I turned to the woman who had challenged me. "Tell me," I asked, "just off the top of your head without stopping to think, what were the happiest years of your marriage up to now?"

"Just after our first child was born," she said without hesitation. "My husband was transferred to another city when the baby was four weeks old. I was run off my feet what with the baby and moving. Neither of us had enough sleep, but we were terribly happy. We felt we had everything—our son, each other and a bright future."

I saw heads nod in agreement. "How many women here today would say that was one of the happiest periods of their marriages too?" I asked.

Hands shot up all over the room. It was practically unanimous. I had been sure it would be. Those early years can be hard. Almost too much to cope with. The baby cries all night. You never get enough sleep. There is never enough money. The car needs a new transmission. It is a scramble to get the rent together. Some days just getting through until bedtime is a victory of sorts. But somehow you managed, and looking back, you realize you were happy. If anybody had told you how happy you were at the time, you would have said they were crazy. But now you know that you were.

There are wonderfully happy times in marriage, but marriage and happiness are not synonymous. Happiness as a vital component of marriage is a relatively recent concept. Marriage, most anthropologists believe, evolved as a survival tool. In return for the sexual availability of the female, the prehistoric male helped feed and protect her and her infants. If primitive mothers had not had a male to help them, humans might have met the fate of the dinosaurs and the dodoes. It was a satisfying and efficient arrangement for the physical survival of the mother and children. It ensured the perpetuation of the species.

It was such a satisfactory arrangement that it survived virtually unchanged right up to just after the halfway mark of this century when the divorce rate started first to creep and then to zoom up. Marriage counselors, family therapists, psychologists, sociologists and a host of other specialists started bemoaning the sad state of marriage and predicting the disintegration of the family. Marriage has lost its validity as an institution, the experts warned.

This happens to be nonsense. Marriage is still a survival tool. No longer physical survival. We live in a different world now. It is our emotional survival that is at stake today. The psychological and emotional stresses on men and women have never been greater.

Marriage offers a refuge from stress. It gives us strength to cope with the world. It gives us someone who will share our troubles as well as our joys. This has become crucially important in an impersonal world where so many of us feel anonymous and half our mail is addressed to Occupant.

Men find even more strength and comfort in marriage than women do. According to a study by Dr. Bernard L. Cohen of the University of Pittsburgh, a married man lives 2,409 days longer on the average than a bachelor. "The safest thing for a man is to be married," says Dr. Cohen.

"It's a great stress reliever to have someone to confide in," agrees Dr. Neil Pauker, a psychiatrist at Johns Hopkins. "You can go home and pour your heart out to a spouse about your troubles at work."

The married man is also happier than anyone else, researchers have established. Even happier than his wife. And this is truly amazing, for men increasingly are the ones who are getting divorces these days. They are the ones who are walking out of marriage—and at almost every stage of marriage.

Marriage is becoming more like a television contract than a commitment for ever after. Most television performers have thirteen-week contracts. It can be nerve-racking, even terrifying, when the contract comes up for renewal four times a year. A friend of mine who is a fixture, and a popular one, on an early evening show in Los Angeles said, "I feel as if I'm on the edge of a precipice every thirteen weeks. I worry that I will wake up in the morning and have no job."

With no-fault divorce there is little more security in marriage today than there is in a television contract. It used to be that at a certain point in marriage a woman could relax. She could say to herself, "Okay, we are over the hard part. Now I am married for life." But she cannot do that today. Take a look at the statistics.

If you got married in 1983, your chances of staying married are one out of two. Almost 20 percent of 1983 marriages are expected to end in divorce before the couples reach their fifth anniversary.

An additional 15 percent of the 1983 marriages will reach the divorce court before their tenth anniversary. Most of these divorces can be chalked up to that infamous Seven-Year Itch, and you know who itches most—the husband.

Approximately 15 percent of couples married in 1983 will be divorced between their tenth and twenty-fifth anniversaries. And 2 or 3 percent of those still wed, possibly even more, will be divorced before they can celebrate their golden wedding anniversary. I know this adds up to more than 50 percent, but these late-marriage divorces seem to be changing the final statistics. When the figures are all in, it may turn out that 1983 marriages had a less-than-one-out-of-two chance of surviving.

Recent, but incomplete, figures indicate a significant jump in the divorce rate after forty and fifty years of marriage. The number of late-life divorces has more than tripled in the past few years. Men in their fifties and sixties and even seventies are breaking up their marriages. They feel time closing in on them and they panic.

"I've only got so many years left," thinks a man in his midsixties. "I'm going to kick up my heels while I can." And this staid grandfather suddenly informs his wife of many years that he wants out. The result is the brutal new phenomenon of the disposable wife (see Chapter 33).

It is off with the old wife and on with the new. For most men remarry. Even the older men have little trouble finding a woman who is younger and more attractive than the wife they discarded. After all, with those 7.3 million women who will never have a husband, they can have their pick.

It all adds up to the fact that not even the grandmothers among us can sit back and say, "I'm really married for good now. I can relax." A woman has to work at her marriage all the time if she wants that "happy enough, forever-after" union. She cannot relax.

I am convinced, however, that, despite the statistics, a woman who wants her marriage to last a lifetime can have her wish. It takes work and imagination. At almost any time during your marriage, you are going to be giving more than your husband. "A successful marriage is never really the fifty-fifty proposition that it is talked up to be," says Betty Ford, wife of former President Gerald R. Ford. "We settled for a seventy-five–twenty-five deal. Sometimes the seventy-five would come from my side. Sometimes from Jerry's."

There is no point in fretting about this. I agree that it is not fair. It is simply that marriage means more to you and so—most of the time—you have to give more. It is worth it. The rewards are enormous. You not only gain a devoted husband but a better life.

Happily married couples get much more joy out of life than most people. They are just all-around happier. They are healthier. They live longer. They are also better off financially. And they pass on these advantages to the next generation. Their children are happier, have more fulfilling marriages, are richer, healthier and live longer on the average than the offspring of unhappy marriages. But we only gain these benefits if we stay married. Happily enough married.

Before I go on I want to make something clear. I believe that it is the woman's role and responsibility to maintain and nurture her marriage. But I am not—not for one minute— saying that a woman should work to stay in a terrible marriage. There is no need to be a martyr. And there is no reward for being a martyr.

If your marriage is bad for you, physically or emotionally, and if you have done your best to make a go of it, including getting professional counseling, then you should consider a separation or divorce so that you can make a new and better life for yourself. When there are children, this takes a lot of soul searching and careful planning, but I firmly believe that what is good for you is good for your children.

For the woman who loves her husband and wants her marriage to last, the following chapters are a survivor's manual. I cover the five vulnerable stages of marriage, describe the special problems of each stage and give you psychological tools and insights to help you cope with them. The five vulnerable stages are:

- The Make-or-Break Years
- The Baby Drift
- The Seven-Year Itch
- The Doldrums
- The Twenty-Year Ditch

No matter what stage your marriage has reached, be sure to read the sections on the previous stages. Most marital problems have their roots in the past—and often the remedies of the past are effective in the present. Once you understand what you did—or did not do—you will be able to deal more efficiently with your problem. Not only that, but the techniques and attitudes I suggest for a bride in the Make-or-Break stage are usually equally valid for the woman who has reached The Doldrums.

Is marriage really worth all this trouble? Absolutely. Civilization has come up with nothing better to take its place. I will never forget what Diana Trilling, the writer and critic, said some five or six years after the death of her husband.

"The genius who invented marriage," she said, "was inventing an extraordinary institution in which each of two people is the most important person in the world to the other. And this is something even the closest friendship cannot provide."

PART FIVE

THE MAKE-
OR-BREAK
YEARS

THIRTEEN

The first rule for success in marriage... How I became disenchanted on my honeymoon... The short lifetime of romantic love... The special arithmetic of marriage... Reaching the We Point

The first three years of marriage—the Make-or-Break Years—are the most vulnerable of all. We start out with the unrealistic expectation that marriage will meet all our needs and make us happy. We think in terms of what our husband and marriage will bring to us rather than what we can give to them.

Remember those inspiring words of the late President John F. Kennedy—"Ask not what your country can do for you; ask what you can do for your country"? Substitute the word marriage for country and you have the first rule for success in marriage.

The major task of the Make-or-Break stage is achieving the We Point (more about this shortly), but first you have to adjust to each other and learn how to negotiate the petty everyday problems of life together as well as the heavier ones such as money, sex and family. You are shocked when he expects you to wash his hand-knit argyle socks by hand just the way his mother did. He is shocked when you expect to take over the checkbook and pay the bills just the way your mother did. No matter how well prepared you were for marriage, there are dozens of issues to be negotiated—and renegotiated.

This is not what we expected when we walked down the aisle. We feel cheated when reality does not live up to our expectations. The shock of reality can bring a woman down from the honeymoon high with a tremendous thud.

Marriage experts know all about this shock; their word for it is "disenchantment." In her classic book *The Future of Marriage*, sociologist Jessie Bernard described it as "the end of the romantic idealization that terminates the honeymoon. The transition to the daily life of marriage," she says, "presents its own kind of shock. So also does the change that occurs when the wife ceases to be the catered-to and becomes the caterer-to."

Disenchantment may even set in during the honeymoon. It did on mine. Milt and I spent our honeymoon at a little place called Pic de l'Aurore at the very tip of the Gaspé Peninsula in Canada. It was an idyllic place and we were blissfully happy except for the last night of our stay.

We had tried to cram everything in. We had been out all day and half the night. When we got back to our little cottage, Milt showered while I puttered about getting started on the packing. Then it was my turn. I was really looking forward to that shower. But when I turned it on, the water was freezing. Milt had used up all the hot water.

I was furious. I let him know that he was selfish and thoughtless, that he was the lowest of the low and that I was miserable. It was not the shock of the cold water so much as the shock of disappointed expectations. When we married, one of my expectations had been that Milt would coddle me just the way my father always had. What was lurking in the back of my mind that honeymoon night was that Daddy would never have used all the hot water and left me to shower with cold water.

It was a ridiculous tempest in a teapot. But suddenly this

wonderful man I had married did not seem so wonderful after all. Half an hour later, though, the old-fashioned heater had produced enough hot water for my shower. We kissed and made up rapturously, but the thin edge of disenchantment had entered our relationship.

It happens in every marriage and it usually starts with something just as childish and silly as my tantrum over the cold shower. During the courtship period, you never would have dreamed of criticizing him, but suddenly you can't stand the way he says "you know" with every other sentence or his tuneless whistle or a dozen other things about him. On top of this *he* starts criticizing *you*.

What has gone wrong?

Not a thing. It is the signal that you are entering the first vulnerable stage of marriage, the Make-or-Break Years. The first year is the most vulnerable because you face the most adjustments. There is so much to be straightened out between the two of you that it is a wonder any marriage makes it. Fortunately most do. And a lot of the credit goes to Mother Nature.

Her contribution is romantic love, that euphoric state of being "in love" that gets a man and woman together in the first place. Dr. Michael Liebowitz of the New York State Psychiatric Institute, and author of *The Chemistry of Love*, defines romantic love as a set of feelings that includes "a strong concern for the welfare of the other; a sense that one's life would be greatly diminished by the loss of the other; and an element of idealization, which involves seeing the other as more attractive, noble, intelligent or otherwise gifted than he may actually be." All this helps smooth the often rocky path of adjustment in the early years of marriage.

Not that Mother Nature is concerned whether a couple adjusts to each other or not. All she cares about is that they get together and stay together long enough so that the woman has adequate opportunity to become pregnant. Her interest is in perpetuating the species and to that end, like a fairy god-mother, she endows us with romantic love.

But romantic love starts to fade early. One behavioral scientist, Dr. Frederick Meeker of California State Polytechnic University, is convinced that the half-life of romantic love is about three months, after which you have only half the amount of romance you started out with. Dr. John Money of Johns Hopkins, author of *Love and Love Sickness*, believes romantic love stays at a peak for two to three years before starting to fade.

Whichever theory is correct, romantic love with its "element of idealization" helps countervail the posthoneymoon disenchantment until you have worked through the first major adjustments of marriage and are well on your way to—or have reached—the We Point. When you have reached the We Point, the two-of-us-against-the-world point, you have made it. You have come through the first vulnerable stage of marriage, closer and stronger than you were before.

What is this We Point? It is the sum of the special arithmetic of marriage. In marriage, one and one do not equal two. They equal three. You and I and We. And achieving that We takes time.

Each marriage partner comes from belonging to a family into a whole new situation. It is a little like the feeling a stepchild has. He wants to feel that this is his home. But it never is at the beginning.

Home is the way it used to be. Newlyweds, no matter how happy they are, often get a feeling of homesickness, the kind of feeling you may have had when you were young and went away to summer camp or to visit your grandparents. You had a great time, but it was not home. Home is the place where no matter where you have gone and no matter how great a time you have had, it is wonderful to come back to.

When you marry, you have to change your perspective. Home is no longer where you come from. Home is where you are. As the two of you begin to adjust to the fact that home is where you are now, you also begin to think of yourselves as a unit. You are still your parents' child, but first you are each other's spouse and partner.

It took me months to take the first step toward the We Point. When Milt and I got married, we had to live with my parents for financial reasons. Milt was going to medical school. I was working for my master's degree in psychology. And we did not have a penny.

I used to conspire—there is no other word for it—with my mother to get Milt to do things. He is the kind of man who always says no to something and then, when he has thought it over, usually changes the no to yes. So I used to suggest some idea or activity and he would say no. A little later my mother would suggest the same thing and nine times out of ten he would say yes.

Once, later, when I wanted us to spend the weekend with my folks in the country, I told Milt they had invited us for the next weekend.

"Impossible," he said. "I've got too much studying."

I did not argue the point. I had already arranged with Mother that she would call him. The next evening, she did. "Milt, are the two of you coming up for the weekend?" she asked. "We'd love to see you." Milt thanked her and said that of course we would come.

It was this incident that made me realize I was forming a unit with my mother instead of my husband. (I was not studying psychology for nothing.) I decided that after this if I wanted Milt to do something I would handle it myself. It made life harder in a way because we had more arguments. But even when I lost, I felt better about it, because I was no longer conspiring with my mother to manipulate my husband. I had transferred my allegiance from my parents to Milt.

I will come back to the We Point later, but first I want to chart the dangerous shoals of the Make-or-Break Years, the problems that will trigger your fights and test your love.

FOURTEEN

*What you should know about the stages of man... What
new couples fight about most... How to change his
annoying habits... Why fighting pays off... What's
wrong with prenuptial contracts...
What Pam and Burt did right*

Remember those Premarital Checklists—money, children,
family, sex? These may have seemed academic before marriage, but once the honeymoon is over you are going to have
to negotiate very real problems that revolve around exactly
these things. You can count on it.

It is the rare woman who does not have to deal with at least
three during the Make-or-Break Years as well as the problems
of adjusting to the intimacies of everyday life—mealtimes,
bedtimes, personal habits, food preferences, moods, needs for
privacy, division of labor and so on—which set off just as
many fireworks as the big three.

Before I go into these problems, though, there are certain
things you should know about your husband. In my previous
book, *What Every Woman Should Know About Men*, I described
the five stages men go through from age twenty-one to death.
It is important to be aware of these because they affect you
and your marriage.

The first male stage is the Onward-and-Upward period. This spans the tension-ridden years from age twenty-one to about thirty-five. During this time a man concentrates on establishing himself at work, marrying and starting a family. What you should know is that establishing themselves at work is as important to most men as their marriages. Even more so with some men. Part of a success-oriented man's reason for marrying is that he knows married men are more highly regarded in most areas of the business world than bachelors. They are considered more responsible. Executives relate to them more easily.

Most men are in their middle or late twenties during the Make-or-Break Years, but not all. Some marry or remarry much later.

The man in his thirties may have reached the calm period of the Consolidation stage when he pulls together the accomplishments of the Onward-and-Upward period. He hits his stride as a husband and father as well as in his business or profession. He has acquired an air of authority.

The man in his forties will be entering the Pivotal Decade. This is when he realizes he is middle-aged, and it often sends him into a psychological tizzy. This is the age when men start thinking about divorce and remarriage as a way to recapture youth. In many ways it is like a second adolescence. Most men eventually come to terms with their life and emerge from this troubled decade with more understanding of themselves—and of you.

The man in his fifties should have reached the Equilibrium stage and be at peace with himself and the world. Marriage can be very sweet at this time. But if your husband has not worked out the problems of the Pivotal Decade, he can be very difficult. He may feel cheated of success and happiness and bitterly resent the approach of age.

Finally there is the Retirement stage, from sixty-five on. It is usually a time of satisfaction and serenity when the two of you will savor life together and perhaps indulge yourselves in ways you could not afford earlier. If he is one of those who took the wrong turn in the Pivotal Decade, however, you can expect trouble. These men face their final years with deep disappointment and fear. They may make your life miserable. Or they may seek happiness with a younger woman—and make your life miserable in a different way.

Women's lives have stages too, but our lives are in such a state of flux today and our roles are so much more diverse than men's that the social and sexual revolution will have to shake down a bit more before women's lives can be analyzed and codified. And this will probably take some time, since the majority of psychological and sociological studies are still headed and controlled by men. Men are far more interested in finding out about themselves than about the women in their lives.

If you put it all together, the stages of the adult male, the as-yet uncodified stages of the adult female, and the stages of marriage, you understand that a lot is going on between the two of you in your marriage from the beginning to the end. Marriage is a process, not something that is wrapped, sealed and delivered on your wedding day, as Pam and Burt learned.

HABITS AND ROUTINES

Most quarrels in the first year of marriage are about personal habits, responsibilities and establishing routines. You may have thought you were tremendously, stupendously compatible. You thought the same way. You liked the same things. Granted he likes Beiderbecke and you like Bach, but you were beginning to appreciate each other's musical taste. And now it is almost as if you were living with a stranger.

Take Pamela and Burton. Pam woke up to the sound of Burt's electric razor buzzing away in the bathroom. She knew what she would find when she got up. The same thing she had found every morning since they got married four months ago—little black bristles all over the sink. Disgusting. A wet towel slung over the shower rack. His pajamas on the floor. What did he think she was? His maid?

"Hey, aren't you going to make coffee?" he called.

"Make it yourself," she snapped.

He stood in the door staring at her.

"I'm tired of being your slave," she said. "If you want coffee, I'm supposed to make it. If you mess up the bathroom, I'm supposed to clean it up. If you feel horny, I'm supposed to take care of that too. What I want to know is who's going to take care of me?"

Burt didn't know what hit him, but he was not going to stand there and take it. "So it's too much to ask you to make coffee! If you were the maid, you'd have been fired long ago. You never make the bed. You can't even be bothered to stack the dishwasher. The sink is full of last night's dishes. And there's stuff in the fridge that's been growing mold for weeks. Some maid!"

He was standing in front of the mirror knotting his tie when Pam dropped the bomb. "If I were getting paid for it, it might be different. But I'm not getting anything. Not even an orgasm."

That was it. Burt grabbed his attaché case and was out of the apartment in five seconds flat. Pam was furious. She threw her slipper at the door as he slammed it. She had been so sure Burt was the man for her and now look at him. Selfish. Demanding. A dud in bed.

At work that day she thought more about Burt and the scene she had made that morning than the statistics on quality control she was compiling. The whole thing was a mess and she was unhappy. She picked up the telephone to call her mother. Mom would understand. Then she put the phone down. Spilling her tale of woe to her mother was not going to help anything. She reached out for the phone again. This time she dialed Burt's office number. No matter how selfish he was, she loved him.

Everything may have been terrible, but Pam was on her way to the We Point. Deciding not to call her mother was a big step ahead.

•   •   •

This was a typical early marriage fight. It covered the waterfront from bristles in the bathroom sink to sex, an indication of the multitude of adjustments that had to be negotiated between them. It was a fight that had to be fought. And it turned out to be a breakthrough for them. It was the first time they communicated honestly about their life together.

Pam could have told Burt that sex was not great for her long weeks ago. And instead of stewing about the sprinkling of black bristles in the sink, she could have told him how she felt about it. Burt could have made it clear that unmade beds and dirty dishes bothered him. But they were captives of the courtship mode of putting the best foot forward and refraining from criticism—until Pam's simmering resentments boiled over.

When they got home from work that night, they started working out their problems. They began with the ones that were the least emotion packed—morning coffee, bed making, cleaning up the bathroom and kitchen. They were almost ludicrously easy to solve.

"About the coffee," Pam said. "You get up before I do because you have to be at work earlier. It's not really fair for you to expect me to get up early to make coffee. Why can't you make it?"

The solution they worked out was that Pam would put coffee and water in the automatic coffee maker before she went to bed. In the morning all Burt had to do was flick the switch.

As for the bristles in the bathroom sink—"I didn't know they bothered you," he said. "I'll just swish some water around and wash them down the drain. No big deal."

And so it went, one easy compromise after another until Burt said, "But what about you making the bed?"

That was something else again. Pam had never made her own bed. When she lived at home, her mother did it. When she started working and had her own apartment, the only time the bed got made was when Pam changed the sheets. It seemed a waste of time to make it in the morning only to tear it apart at night.

"Maybe it is," Burt said. "But the bedroom always looks messy. And I don't like getting into an unmade bed."

"Okay," Pam said. "If it means that much to you, I'll make it. It will probably be good for my soul."

Her first impulse had been to offer to make it weekdays if he would make it on the weekends. But she realized instantly that Burt, no matter how intellectually committed he was to equality, would never feel comfortable making a bed. "It's such a little thing," she told herself. "I can do it for him."

Pam was wise. It was one of those times when the woman has to give more if she wants a good marriage. This way she ensured that bed making would never be a friction point with them again and Burt was spared a chore he would resent.

Some couples try to work out this kind of thing before the wedding. They draw up prenuptial contracts spelling out who will do what and when. This is a terrible idea. It puts the two of you in an adversary position from the start.

Who wants to be saddled with cleaning the toilet or the stove? Who wants to scrub the kitchen floor or take the ashes out of the fireplace? Before marriage you really don't know what is going to be important in your life together. It is better to see how things evolve as you settle in with each other. You will know soon enough what the sticky points are and then you can negotiate them.

Chores and routines are relatively easy to negotiate, as Pam and Burt discovered once they got down to it. And so are the little personal habits that may be driving you up the wall. During courtship you somehow managed to ignore them, but now that you are confronted with them every day, they assume major proportions.

The only way to handle these is to speak up honestly and kindly and early on. The worst thing you can do is to tell your husband, "I can't stand that tuneless whistle of yours" after a couple of years of marriage. He is going to say, "Why didn't you say so before?" And he is going to be hurt and possibly angry. There you have been all this time hating something he does without ever telling him. He is going to wonder what else you have up your sleeve.

If he picks his nose or scratches his balls or belches and it upsets you, tell him so. But gently. Don't embarrass him. Don't make fun of him. Just tell him. These are largely unconscious actions. He probably is not aware of what he is doing. And he is probably only too willing to stop.

When he does whatever it is that is driving you crazy, give him a hug and a kiss and tell him you will love him forever if he will just not do it where you can see or hear him. And when he promises that he will try to stop, say something like, "If I see you doing it again, is it all right if I remind you?" Since these habits are largely unconscious, he probably will do it again. He can't help it. But a couple of loving reminders should be enough to make him conscious of it. Don't forget, you have all that romantic love on your side in the early days. He is not going to resent a reminder now the way he will later.

Pam and Burt were on the right track. When Pam's resentment boiled over that morning, it forced them to work out adjustments in their routines and habits that made life pleasanter for both of them. In the process they learned the necessity of communicating—not just about what had gone on at the office and what they should do over the weekend and how they felt about the World Series, but about the things in their marriage that distressed or delighted them.

This may not seem like such a great advance, but communication—or the lack of it—is the greatest problem in more than 50 percent of marriages. In fact, at one marriage clinic, 650 couples were asked what the greatest problems in their marriage were. The practically unanimous answer was sex and communication. The two are more closely linked than most people realize.

FIFTEEN

*When sex is disappointing . . . The twenty-minute turn-
on . . . Why newlyweds lose interest in sex . . . The power of
the kiss . . . How often should you make love . . . When he
wants it more than you do*

Pam and Burt spent the evening settling everything from
coffee making to bed making, but neither mentioned the one
thing they had both been stewing over all day—Pam's angry
declaration that she did not have orgasms. The subject was so
loaded with high-tension emotion that they could almost see
sparks flying. Burt had thought of nothing else. Could Pam
be telling the truth? He tried hard to be a good lover. Before
they were married, she had assured him he was marvelous.
And she always wriggled and sighed in delight when they made
love. He always knew when she was ready to come. Her rhythm
quickened and she started panting. She could not have been
faking. Or could she?

Finally the subject could not be avoided any longer. And
Pam knew she had to be the one to start. After all, she was
the one who had precipitated the whole thing.

"I've been faking," she said miserably. "I'm sorry. And I
shouldn't have thrown it at you that way."

"You're a great actress," he said bitterly. "You missed your calling."

Pam blamed Burt for not knowing how to bring her to orgasm more often. She did climax, she told him, but only half the time, if that. And he always did. Burt was angry because he felt she had been making a fool of him with her pretending. He felt betrayed. The more they talked about it the more emotional they got. This was something they could not solve by compromise like coffee making, nor, it seemed, could they settle it by discussion. The only thing they were able to agree on was that Pam would not pretend anymore.

The next day she called her gynecologist and asked him to recommend a sex therapist.

"What's going on?" her doctor asked.

She blurted it all out. "We make love five and six times a week and I'm lucky if I have two orgasms a week. Burt doesn't know anything about sex or women. He doesn't even know where my clitoris is," she said scornfully.

"Why haven't you shown him?"

"I am embarrassed."

"About what?" The doctor sounded amused but sympathetic. "You married Burt and you don't trust him enough to be able to tell him what turns you on? That doesn't make much sense, does it?"

"No," she agreed sheepishly.

"Let me ask you," the doctor said, "about your previous sexual partners. As I recall, you had two or three before you met Burt. Did you always have an orgasm with the others?"

"N-n-no," she confessed. "But I didn't mind. It was so exciting. And I loved the kissing and caressing. Sometimes I'd come just from kissing. Burt hardly ever kisses me anymore. He just gets hard and gets in."

"Have you told him how much you like to kiss?"

"No."

"Then how is he to know? Is he a mind reader?"

Pam laughed. "I guess I'm pretty stupid."

"Well, not really. You have a lot of company. Many women are too inhibited to tell their husbands what they like in bed. But I think you owe it to Burt. You just have to trust him enough to tell him what you like. He is not going to be shocked. I promise you he will be delighted to know what gives you pleasure.

"And another thing," the doctor said. "A couple of orgasms a week isn't bad at all. Most women only climax half the time and some women only climax a third of the time. If you level with Burt about what you want, you will probably find you are going to climax 90 percent of the time.

"But stop faking," he warned, "and be sure to tell Burt what I told you about the frequency of female orgasms. That way he won't feel inadequate if you don't come every time."

He made it all seem very simple, not the big tragedy she had been making it into.

"The doctor says we don't have a sex problem," Pam told Burt that night. "We have a communication problem. There are things I should tell you." And she proceeded to inform Burt of the statistics on the frequency of female orgasms and how much she needed clitoral stimulation as well as some of her sex fantasies.

"And now we don't have a communication problem any longer," she said. "Unless you've got something to say."

"Yes, I do," he said. "Let's go to bed and see if your doctor is right."

He was.

Most sex problems in the early years can be solved just this easily. Most of them result from lack of knowledge, lack of communication and inflated expectations. Novels and films lead many women to think that if the earth does not move they have been cheated. The truth is that, as Virginia Johnson of the Masters and Johnson sexual-therapy team once said, "The orgasmic experience ranges anywhere from a Fourth of July to a quiet Thanksgiving."

Some women who have a blockbuster orgasm after clitoral stimulation feel cheated because they believe they should have a vaginal orgasm. They have been told or have read that vaginal orgasms are even more terrific. This happens to be nonsense. An orgasm is an orgasm is an orgasm, to paraphrase Gertrude Stein. It is clitoral stimulation that triggers the orgasm 95 percent of the time. And an orgasm *always* involves the vagina.

Some women who do not reach orgasm even with clitoral stimulation not only feel cheated but worry that they are frigid. Again, nonsense. They should relax and enjoy. In ninety-nine cases out of a hundred, they do not climax because they do not give it enough time.

The average woman needs a good twenty minutes of clitoral stimulation to reach orgasm and some women need up to an hour, according to Dr. Mildred Hope Witkin of the Human Sexuality Teaching Program at Cornell University Medical College. "Most men do not know this," she reports, "and many women do not tell them because they fear it is an imposition." These women are cheating themselves *and* their husbands.

If you are lying there feeling guilty that it's not one-two-three-wow! with you, stop it. You are not guilty of anything. Sex is a great pleasure and there is nothing wrong with stretching it out. Take your time and relish every minute of it.

But what if you are that one woman in a hundred who cannot climax? Don't worry. You can. If you have not had an orgasm after a few weeks, don't wait and worry. Get help. Ask your gynecologist to recommend a therapist. "It is easy to teach practically any woman to have an orgasm if she wants to," says Dr. Merle Kroop, a psychiatrist at Cornell University Medical College. It usually takes one instruction session with the therapist and a few nights of practice at home. In a ten-year period, Dr. Kroop has only treated one woman who remained anorgasmic.

The cure in most cases, however, is simply better communication, letting him know what excites you. Pam had no trouble in reaching orgasm once she started letting her husband know what she wanted.

The other common sexual problems of the early years are just as easy to solve, once a couple admits they have a problem.

LOSS OF INTEREST

It seems impossible. You have lost interest in sex. And you have only been married a few months—or even a few weeks. What's wrong? Very little.

"A surprisingly large number of couples who have had satisfactory sexual relations before marriage experience an immediate onset of problems once they are married," reports Dr. Martin Goldberg, director of Marital Therapy Training and Research at The Institute of Pennsylvania Hospital. "There is a considerable loss of interest in sex by one or both partners, sometimes so marked that the frequency of sex diminishes to once a week, once a month or even zero."

The problem is usually in your head. Even in these sexually liberated times, premarital sex has the excitement of the forbidden. Once you are married, sex is no longer forbidden, it is expected. And for some people, it becomes a ho-hum chore instead of a delight.

It is a funny little psychological twist. As Dr. William S. Appleton, a psychiatrist at Harvard Medical School, points out, "A person who has enjoyed a good glass of wine for years does not suddenly view imbibing as a duty or dull simply because the drink is legal, like a spouse, rather than illegal, like a lover." But sex, once it becomes something you are expected to do, may lose its savor.

Once you understand that hundreds and thousands of couples experience this lack of interest, you can stop feeling that there is something wrong with you or him or your marriage. And once you accept the probability that your lack of interest stems from the fact that you now have a green light for sex, it will not be difficult to rekindle the fire.

The cure is simple. Refuse to let this "boredom" interfere with your sex life. Do not cut out lovemaking. Do not even cut down. Concentrate on making sex exciting and amusing and comforting. Take showers together and soap each other using your hands. Give each other a massage. Fool around a little and don't underestimate the power of the kiss. The kiss is one of the greatest turn-ons. It stimulates your pituitary and adrenal glands. It sends up your blood pressure. It makes your heart beat faster. All this adds up to sexual arousal. So if you just take the initiative, you will find that old sexual desire is going to come right back.

This raises the question of how often you should make love. The answer is that there is no "should" about making love. But there are some rough estimates of how often most people do it. In the first years of marriage, anywhere from three times a night to three times a week seems to be the range. Once things settle down a bit, the average from age twenty-five to thirty-five is two or three times a week. From thirty-five to forty-five, it drops to twice a week. There is another drop between forty-five and fifty-five to once a week. And after fifty-five—well, once a week is a high average.

But these are only *averages*. You and your twenty-eight-year-old husband may be making love three times a week. Your grandmother and your 68-year-old grandfather may also be doing it three times a week. What feels right for you is right. The problem comes when what feels right for you feels like a starvation diet for him. Or vice versa.

UNEVEN SEXUAL DESIRE

He wants to make love more often than you do. This calls for generosity on your part. Don't say no unless you have a really valid reason. Just being tired is not a valid reason. On the other hand, if you have had a rough day at the office and you're coming down with a cold and you're absolutely exhausted (as opposed to merely tired) and all you are up to is a bath and watching a TV sitcom in bed, by all means say so. But make a date for tomorrow night.

Otherwise, just be honest. Tell him you are not feeling

particularly in the mood. Or you are sort of tired. And ask him if he would rub your back first. This is the time for extended foreplay. For long slow kisses. For gentle clitoral stimulation by hand or by tongue. Don't rush things. You may not have an orgasm, but you probably will. If you don't, you will have had a loving and intimate interlude with the man you love.

What if you are the one who wants more sex? Here again I am afraid that it is up to you. If he's the one who has had a hard day at the office or who is not in the mood, he may not be able to get an erection. No matter how much he would like to please you.

You can try helping him. Sucking his penis is probably the most effective erection maker. But if that doesn't work, it is up to you to explain that penetration is not the only way of having sex and reaching orgasm. He has fingers and a tongue and most men enjoy an occasional session where they concentrate on pleasing the woman and not themselves. In the course of his giving pleasure, chances are he will have an erection and get his own share of pleasure.

But if he is really not in the mood and has brought home from the office a briefcase full of work that has to be finished before he goes to bed, you may have to settle for masturbation. There is nothing wrong with this.

The important thing to remember is that there are no "have to's," but there should be a lot of generosity. You only get out of marriage what you put into it, but it usually comes back gift wrapped. And this is particularly true of sex.

PREMATURE EJACULATION

This is his problem, but that makes it yours too. Nothing is harder on a man's pride than premature ejaculation unless it is the inability to achieve an erection, which is rare in the early years. Fortunately premature ejaculation almost always disappears as he gains experience and confidence.

The best therapy for him is you. This is no time to hide behind inhibitions. If he comes precipitously, you must let him bring you to orgasm manually or orally. You may have to suggest this. Make it clear that you love what he is doing—and love him. This way he won't feel he has failed you. And do smother any heavy injured sighs that may be welling up inside you. He feels bad enough as it is.

If it persists over time, he should consult a physician. There is a simple physical technique that can cure premature ejaculation in very short order. It requires your cooperation, which is only right since you will benefit as much as he will.

There you have the four most common sexual problems of the Make-or-Break years—failure to achieve orgasm, loss of interest in sex, uneven levels of desire and premature ejaculation. They may seem like insurmountable problems, but now you have the knowledge and the psychological tools to conquer them.

What you must understand as a woman and a wife is that when push comes to shove, you are responsible for your own sexual joy—and his too. You must let your partner know what pleases you. You must be generous in meeting his needs and sympathetic to his problems.

The more you do now to establish a rewarding sexual relationship, the better your whole relationship will be not only at present but in years to come. Good sex is perhaps the strongest of the ties that bind a man and woman together. Good sex can make other problems, like in-laws and money, seem like molehills instead of mountains.

SIXTEEN

*Why your mother-in-law is such a pain... How to handle
unwanted advice from your mother-in-law... How
tangling with his mother helps your marriage... The
Family Echo and when you should
listen to it... Guilt by association*

Each of us is an individual and marries an individual, but,
like it or not, we are surrounded and influenced by family.
You are well aware of some of the influences—your mother-
in-law's never-ending advice, for instance, or your mother's
"mistakes." (It's so easy to see where our mothers went wrong
when we are first married. Later we often revise our opinion.)
But other influences are so subtle that you may not recognize
them for years. Perhaps not until your own children are grown.
This chapter should help you spot what I call Family Echoes
early on so that you can understand how they affect your
actions and expectations. These echoes often turn into marital
booby traps.

Before you were married, in-laws were something your parents had. As a child you may have wondered why your mother
sometimes was irritated with your doting grandma. Now you
understand. You have in-laws too.

No matter how wonderful they are, you find yourself getting annoyed with your mother-in-law or your sister-in-law, even fighting about them with your husband. Your sister-in-law seems to think she can drop in whenever she feels like it. Your mother-in-law is shocked that you did not wait for the white sale to buy your sheets. And she still expects your husband to take her supermarket shopping on Thursday nights the way he did when he was single.

Your husband has his problems too. Your folks keep butting in. Your father criticizes the way he dresses. Your mother tells him you should move to a better neighborhood. But most serious in-law fights are triggered by the husband's mother (and over 20 percent of fights in the Make-or-Break years are in-law fights). It is not that your mother-in-law is any more difficult than your own mother. She may indeed be very sweet and helpful, but there is a lot of truth in the old rhyme

> *Oh, my son's my son till he gets him a wife,*
> *But my daughter's my daughter all her life.*

Now that you have married her son, your mother-in-law is no longer the first woman in his life. You have deposed her. And no matter how fond she may be of you, few people relinquish power happily. She may become officious or demanding or shower you with unwanted advice in order to prove that she is top lady on the totem pole, although deep inside she knows she is not. You have to recognize it for what it is, a bid for attention, for assurance that she still counts. Even when you understand this, however, you may resent her meddling and her invasion of your privacy.

Mother-in-law trouble was the last thing Libby expected. Libby loved Phil's mother, a widow. Before the wedding she had told her best friend, "Phil's mother is a dear, so warm and understanding. I'm lucky to have such a wonderful mother-in-law."

But one midnight, just ten months after the wedding, Libby

was whispering furiously to Phil in their bedroom. "I can't stand it," she hissed. "When is she going home? You've got to tell her to leave."

"How can I do that?" he whispered. "She's my mother."

"Either she goes or I do." Libby bounded over to her side of the bed and turned her back on Phil.

In her weekly telephone call, Phil's mother had told Libby how much she missed the two of them now that they were living four states away. "Come visit us next weekend," Libby had said impetuously. "We'd love to see you."

It was a wonderful weekend. They caught up with all the news of family and friends back in Evanston. But Monday came and Phil's mother made no move to leave. Nor did she the next day. Now it was Friday midnight and she was still there.

Libby had had all she could take. Phil's mother had directed a constant stream of advice at her all week long. She told Libby that Phil needed more roughage, was drinking too much coffee, needed more sleep. She said that their living room rug would not wear well. She told Libby she was getting too friendly with the neighbors. Libby could not face another day of it, let alone another weekend.

"Why are you so upset?" Phil asked. "She's just trying to help."

"She's just trying to keep her little boy tied to her apron strings," Libby snapped.

Saturday was awkward. Libby ws silent. Phil was nervous and had dark circles under his eyes. His mother was subdued. Sunday morning she announced that she was leaving. When Phil came back from the airport, they had the fight that had been brewing.

"She's my mother," Phil stormed. "You made her feel unwelcome. You can't treat her like that. I'm all she's got."

"I'm your wife," Libby shouted. "I asked her to come for the weekend. Not the week."

Some time later I was invited to speak to the executives and sales force of the company where Phil worked. In the course of my lecture about marital stress and how it affects job performance, I mentioned that one out of three couples had in-law problems.

At the cocktail party that followed, Libby and Phil introduced themselves and Libby asked, "How do you solve in-law problems?"

"It depends on the problem," I said, "but usually the best way to handle them is to put yourselves first."

They told me the story of the visit. "Who was right?" Libby asked. "Me or Phil?"

"You were both wrong," I said gently. "Phil, you have to realize that your wife comes first. Even before your mother. When Libby told you that your mother was driving her crazy and she couldn't take it any longer, you should have shown that you understood how she felt and done your best to help her."

"But what could I have done?" Phil asked. "I couldn't tell my mother that she had outstayed her welcome."

"Not in so many words," I agreed. "But you could have said something like 'Well, Mom, we're glad you could stay an extra day. Do you want me to make your plane reservation for tomorrow morning?'"

"I suppose so," he said, "but she would have been terribly hurt."

I turned to Libby. "He's right. The better way would have been for you to handle it yourself. On Monday when she showed no sign of leaving you could have asked her what plane she was planning to take. Of course, you would have discussed this with Phil beforehand."

"I couldn't have done that," Libby said. "If I said that, she would never forgive me. We might even have had a fight."

"That wouldn't be the end of the world," I told her. "Tangling with your in-laws is not all bad. If you have a fight with your mother-in-law, it often helps your husband separate from his family. She blames his separation on you. You become the villain. He is still her loving son. But a new distance is established. Both of you have to separate from your families if you are ever going to reach the We Point.

"And when you do reach that point, you will discover that you seldom get upset about his folks or yours any longer. You will find yourself laughing at their foibles and appreciating their good points. You will not find them as irritating. You will probably be surprised at the change in your feelings toward them. You will be more tolerant of his folks and less close to yours. There will be things that you would not dream of telling your folks, although you would have earlier. Things that are just between you and your husband and not any business of your family or his."

Libby nodded. "I understand. That makes sense. You know what really drove me up the wall was all that advice she kept giving me. How do you handle that?"

I laughed. "That's easy. Your mother-in-law cannot tell you how to run your home and your life any more than you can tell her how to run hers. But you have to listen to her advice, because she is your husband's mother and you owe her respect and courtesy. You don't have to take that advice, though. And if she asks you why you don't, all you have to do is say, 'I like my way better.'"

"That easy!" marveled Libby.

"Almost that easy," I smiled.

Libby had what I consider a run-of-the-mill mother-in-law problem, one that would work out in time. But some relationships just don't work out no matter how hard you try. It may not be your relationship with his mother, it may be your husband's with your mother.

If he says, "Your mother makes me sick," he may be telling the literal truth. "We observed that husbands often catch colds when their mothers-in-law come to visit," reported Dr. Thomas Holmes, professor of psychiatry and behavioral sciences at the University of Washington. "Patients mentioned their mothers-in-law so often we came to consider them a common cause of disease."

Dr. Holmes did not let it go at this. He conducted an experiment to find out if this was literally true. He and his associates took biopsies of the nasal membranes of men who had a history of colds that coincided with visits by their mothers-in-law. The men were in a healthy, relaxed state when the first tissue samples were taken. Then the researchers brought the conversation around to the mother-in-law. "We noticed the patients would begin to react. The tissues in their noses would get red, wet and swollen."

At that point second biopsies were made and compared with the first. "The nasal tissues had changed," he reported. "They were just like those you would find in the course of a developing cold."

Another psychiatrist, Dr. George Serban of New York University Medical Center, reported that he had seen both men and women who suffered from diarrhea and insomnia at the mere thought of a visit from their mother-in-law.

What can you do about this? Not much. If your mother makes your husband sick, it would be better for you to go see her by yourself. And if she visits you, that might be a good time for your husband to go fishing or visit his own mother. Keeping their time together at a minimum may eventually help him come to tolerate her and even see her good points. But don't count on it.

The best way to avoid in-law problems is to set up housekeeping far enough away from both your families so that visiting you becomes a major undertaking. This gives you a chance to adjust to each other and work out the problems of the Make-or-Break stage without too much family interference and static.

FAMILY ECHOES

No matter how far away you live, your family still has more influence on your marriage than you may believe. This is because of the Family Echo.

Your parents' marriage is the marriage you know best. You tend to take it as a model for your own. Oh, you may have sworn that your marriage was not going to be like theirs. Your husband is not going to spend all day Saturday on his back under the car tinkering with its innards while you do the shopping and the laundry, the way your mom and dad did. No, the two of you are going to devote your weekends to shared pleasures. And you probably will if that is what you want. But nevertheless in a hundred subtle ways your parents' marriage will influence yours. His folks' marriage will too. And you may be quite unaware of it.

The biggest fight Sherry and Rick had in the Make-or-Break stage was over Sunday night supper. When Rick was growing up, it was his favorite meal of the week. Everyone was relaxed at the end of the weekend and his mother always made a super dessert. Sherry's mother on the other hand never served supper on Sundays. She prepared a big meal in the middle of the day and that was that. If anyone was hungry later, they could make a sandwich or scramble an egg. Sherry's family enjoyed this do-as-you-please routine. Time enough for structure on Monday when everyone had to get up to go to work or school.

Sherry adopted her mother's approach. Sunday nights, she would make herself a sandwich if she was hungry. She never offered to get anything for Rick. Then one Sunday, he asked crossly, "Where's my sandwich?"

"Oh, are you hungry?" she asked innocently. "There's some cold meat loaf if..."

He interrupted her. "Why the hell can't you make me a sandwich when you're making one for yourself? Or at least ask me if I'd like one too? We live here together, remember? And I get hungry too." He worked himself into a fury.

Sherry was bewildered. What was all this about? It had never occurred to her that he would expect her to get his supper on Sundays. And what right did he have to talk to her that way anyway? She became furious too. They were both so angry that it took a while before they understood that each of them had expected married life to be just like life had been at home.

When Sherry finally grasped that Rick missed those cheerful Sunday suppers and Rick understood that Sherry was following her mother's example, the anger drained away and they began to laugh.

"I thought I knew everything about you," Sherry said, "but I never knew what Sunday supper meant to you." She promised that she would make supper from now on. "But I don't want to be in the kitchen all by myself while you're reading the paper or watching TV," she said. "The weekend's our only time to be together. How about cooking with me? It would be fun."

And she made sure that it was. Sherry was wise. She understood that this was not an issue to fight about. She made the loving gesture of giving him what he wanted. Her proposal that he help cook was equally wise. The more activities a couple enjoys together, the stronger and more rewarding their relationship. Both of them enjoyed their Sunday cooking sessions and Sunday became their special night. Something they looked forward to the rest of the week.

Family echoes don't always cause fights. But they can cause misunderstandings. He may expect to play poker with his buddies one night a week and be surprised when you object. His mother never objected to his dad's poker night. But your father never went out and left your mother alone in the evening and you don't see why your husband can't be the same.

Or you may gripe that you did not get married just to sit around doing nothing every night while he studies for his CPA exams. And he is surprised that you are making such an issue out of it. His father used to bring work home two or three nights a week and his mother never minded. She made sure that he had the peace and quiet he needed and had always seemed proud of how hard he worked.

The key here is to try to understand why you are resisting what he does. If you are perceptive, you will probably realize that it is because it is different from the way things were done in your parents' marriage. The two of you simply have two different sets of expectations based on what you observed while you were growing up. It is usually up to you to adjust. Don't fight it. Make it into a plus.

If he plays poker with the guys, you have a whole evening to do just as you please. This is a good time to catch up with your girlfriends, maybe have supper with one of them and go to a movie. Go to exercise class. Spend the evening on yourself, doing your nails and eyebrows, pampering yourself and going to bed early with a novel. Take advantage of this time to do something that will make you happier or healthier.

If he's studying for the CPA exams or brings work home from the office, he is obviously ambitious, a man who is going places. You don't want to be left behind. This is your chance to improve your French or learn how to play bridge, study philosophy, join a drama group, do some serious reading, follow up a special interest and make yourself a more interesting and valuable person.

Remember that you have a goal—a forever-after marriage. The happier he is in marriage, the better your chances of achieving your goal. It not only makes more sense for you to adjust, it is easier for you. Men do not handle change as well as women.

There are times when you will have to draw the line. If his family's idea of a great good time was to sit around smoking pot, it would be a good idea to help him find some other way to relax. Or if he expects you to iron his shirts the way his mother did and you have a full-time job, you are going to have to explain that this particular echo from the past is falling on deaf ears. In other words, you don't have to be a doormat, and you should not cooperate in anything you consider a poor idea. But for the rest of it, take the extra two or three steps to make him feel comfortable and contented and at home. You are the one who has more to gain.

GUILT BY ASSOCIATION

There is another kind of family echo that is harder to cope with. It is guilt by association. Emotional association. A woman will pin her father's shortcomings onto her husband, although he shows no evidence of sharing them. The way it works is something like this: If your father was a workaholic who never had time for you, you may accuse your husband of neglecting you, even though he is most attentive. Or if your father was irresponsible and a poor provider, you may believe that your very responsible, hard-working husband is the same.

Janice did. Her father could never keep a job. She married a man who was his very opposite, ambitious and responsible. But soon after they were married, she began accusing him of not working hard enough. She confused his personality with that of her ne'er-do-well father.

This echo is not only in women's heads. A man will accuse his wife of "pushing him around" when she asks him to do something quite reasonable, because he associates her with his mother who used to boss him unmercifully.

Guilt by association usually occurs because the wife or husband has not yet separated herself or himself from her father or his mother. When Janice accused her husband of not working hard enough, she was really accusing her father.

Unless each spouse succeeds in separating from the opposite-sex parent, they are never going to reach the We Point. Unfortunately, it is often difficult to realize that you are inflicting your father's faults upon your husband. Sometimes it takes professional counseling to understand what is behind your mental picture of your spouse. I hope that just by knowing of this version of the Family Echo, you will be able to recognize it in yourself if it occurs. If you criticize your husband by saying, "You always do such and such," let the word "always" sound an alarm in your head. It means that you have made this criticism before. Is it really justified? Would it be more justified if you applied it to your father? Think about it a little. Just being conscious of this malign kind of family echo can help you get rid of it.

As you see, your relationship with your family is more complicated than it seems. The best and most loving of families can cause misunderstandings and conflict without meaning to. Once you understand this, it will help you sort out the roots of some of your Make-or-Break-Years quarrels. And the more you understand, the easier it will be to separate yourselves from your respective families and form your own We.

SEVENTEEN

What most money fights are really about... Why you should settle money matters during the Make-or-Break years... The problems of one-account and two-account couples... The three-account solution... Why every woman should have a MOMO account... How to become financially savvy and why

Money is the root of most quarrels throughout marriage and a contributing cause to more than half of all divorces. And this is ridiculous. Money is simply a tool for living, something you should use as dispassionately as the vacuum cleaner or lawn mower.

This being so, prevention should be the best cure for money quarrels. A couple should agree on their financial commitments and priorities, draw up a budget and stick to it. When their circumstances change, they should rethink the budget and work out the necessary adjustments. That is all there is to it. Nothing to fight about.

It sounds too simple to be true. And it is. Most money fights are about power. Who is going to be boss in this outfit? But not usually in the Make-or-Break Years. And this is why you should settle on how you are going to handle money at the very beginning of your marriage. This is the time to take advantage of every bit of the good will and idealism that are present when romantic love is at its peak to establish a lifetime pattern for managing money before the issue becomes polluted by power.

DRAWING UP YOUR BUDGET

There is nothing difficult about making a budget. Sticking to one is where couples run into trouble. Drawing up a budget is as simple as one, two, three. And the one, two, three are

1. Figure out how much money you absolutely must set aside to pay for basic expenses—rent, telephone, gas and electric, food, taxes, credit card purchases, automobile payments and expenses, and so on.
2. Figure out what you are going to need for health and security—the doctor and dentist, insurance, savings, investments.
3. Finally, work out what you are going to spend on the semidiscretionary items—clothing, furniture, vacations and recreation, gifts, that sort of thing.

This last category is where the budget most often goes astray. You have to arrive at realistic figures for these items. If you allot too little, you will be tempted by (and probably succumb to) a movie that you simply must see this very night or an invitation for a weekend at the shore when you have already spent your vacation money on some impulse purchase. You have to leave yourself a little leeway.

These semidiscretionary items are also the ones on which you are most likely to disagree. He may say you are planning to spend too much on clothes. You may be flabbergasted at the amount he wants to spend on furniture. Don't lock yourself into a confrontation over issues like this. This is no time to be stubborn. Negotiate.

You believe that you need one hundred dollars a month for clothes if you are to look right on your job. He points out that if he plans to spend thirty-five dollars a month on clothing for himself, fifty dollars should be adequate for you. You argue that it is barely enough to keep you covered. He maintains that it is actually generous considering the total of your combined salaries. If his point is valid, accept it. If not, you might split the difference and settle on seventy-five dollars. When you earn more, you can up the figure.

Reaching an agreement on the sum to allot for furniture may be more difficult. The way your home looks reflects your personality, your way of life, your taste and the image you want to project to others. The important thing here is for each of you to be candid about the reasons for your differences.

You may feel that you want to know more about furniture and decorating before you spend significant money. He may expect to be entertaining business associates and want his home to do him proud.

A workable compromise might be to set aside the amount he proposes but not spend it until you both have shopped around and agreed on the look you want, the kind of furniture and a color scheme. In the meantime, you can make do with family castoffs and thrift shop finds. If he has to entertain for business, he can take his guests to a restaurant. It is a legitimate, tax-deductible expense—and much cheaper than buying furniture.

Once you have allotted money for all these categories, put it down in writing. You have your budget. It is up to you to stick to it.

Handling Your Money

Most couples have very little trouble in deciding on how they are going to handle their money. The problems appear when they put their plan into operation. There are two main ways of handling money—separate accounts and joint accounts.

THE ONE-ACCOUNT COUPLE

Linda, twenty-three, and Steve, twenty-seven, pooled their salaries in a joint checking account. They had reached the We

Point early and the joint account was a symbol of their trust in each other. To their disappointment, it became a source of friction. Several times their account was overdrawn because neither was aware of checks the other had drawn during the week. It got so that if Linda saw a lamp that was just what they needed, she would call Steve at his office and ask what checks he had written that week. Both of them were thoroughly fed up with the system, but they did not want to give it up because they were convinced that this was the proper way to handle money in a marriage—each partner taking equal responsibility and having equal rights.

THE TWO-ACCOUNT COUPLE

Luanne and William, both twenty-six, deposited their salaries in separate accounts and split all expenses from rent to Saturday night pizzas right down the middle. Each kept a little notebook in which they wrote down every expenditure and on Sunday nights they added everything up. If William had paid for more than his share, Luanne would write him a check for the difference and vice versa.

But then William got a couple of big raises. He ended up the month with twice as much money left over. Luanne did not think this was fair, but she also felt strongly that she should pay half the expenses. She began to feel trapped and resentful.

William could not understand why. "If you want anything, all you have to do is ask," he told her. "After all, I'm your husband. I'm supposed to provide for you. And I want to." He hugged her. He just could not grasp that Luanne, who had been financially independent since she was twenty-one, hated the idea of asking for money.

When she did ask for money, he made her feel like a child without realizing what he was doing. "Can you let me have sixty dollars?" she asked. "There's a sale on cashmere sweaters. They're a really good buy, but I don't have the money."

"Sixty dollars for a sweater!" he exclaimed. "My God, what were they before they were on sale? A hundred dollars?"

"As a matter of fact, they were," she said stiffly. "Never mind. If it's too much, I'll do without it."

He insisted she buy the sweater. She refused to take the money. There was a fight. She told him he was treating her like a child. He said she was treating him like a stranger.

"What's mine is yours," he told her. "What's wrong with that?"

"What's wrong is that you think you can tell me how to spend it because it's yours," she retorted.

They finally worked out a compromise. They still wrote down every expenditure in their little notebooks, but now on Sunday nights when they do their accounts, they add up what each has left over and divide the amount equally so that Luanne has as much money for her personal expenses as William does.

This works pretty well, although Luanne does not feel absolutely comfortable with it. "I don't like taking money I haven't earned," she says. She still thinks in terms of "his money" and "my money."

When you are considering the pros and cons of separate versus joint checking accounts, it may help to have a glimpse into the future. How are things going to work out four or five years down the road?

That glimpse is available. Some interesting research has been done on the effect of separate and joint accounts on two-income marriages. Northwestern University sociologist Rosanna Hertz studied a group of two-income couples. The men and women in her sample were quite affluent. Their median joint income was just over ninety thousand dollars a year, but her findings are applicable to lower-income couples.

She found that in couples who put their salaries into a joint account, the men make most of the financial decisions. These marriages tend to follow the traditional pattern with the wife being responsible for the home and children and the husband deciding on how their money is spent.

The wives were not happy with the arrangement, even though

they had agreed to it in the beginning. Some of them had even suggested it. The women reported that they had liked the idea of joint accounts because they believed marriage should be based on sharing, that "ours" was the operative word, not "his" and "mine." Some of the women also felt that their husbands would feel uncomfortable ("emasculated" is the word one woman used) if the wife handled her own money and paid her own expenses.

These wives were disillusioned because pooling their salaries had not resulted in equality. They handed over their paychecks and had little or nothing to say about how the money was to be spent.

The couples who kept their earnings in separate accounts seemed more satisfied with their marriages, especially the women. The marriages were more equal in that the men shared in the domestic chores to a certain degree. And, as sociologist Hertz pointed out, "There is usually less arguing and fewer tensions over money in these marriages since both husband and wife have control over it."

You can see how power inevitably becomes part of any money arrangement. If the women who had pooled their incomes in a joint account had taken an active part in drawing up the family budget, they would not have felt quite so powerless. Their lack of participation put them in the position of a woman dental technician (not part of the study) who put her money into a joint account and told me, "I always feel as if I have to ask my husband if I can buy a new dress. But he never asks me if he can buy a raincoat or a new tennis racket. It's not fair. I earn the money and he tells me how I can spend it."

The separate-account couples seemed to have achieved more equality, but there is always a danger when husband and wife have their own accounts and share expenses on a predetermined basis that one of them will always feel faintly resentful because the other earns more. And the resentment may be more than faint if it is the wife who earns more and the husband who has less money to call his own.

• • •

There is a way of avoiding the disadvantages of the separate-account and joint-account systems and having the best of all possible marital financial worlds. And that is to combine both methods of handling your money, as Isabelle and Judd did.

THE THREE-ACCOUNT COUPLE

Isabelle, twenty-five, and Judd, thirty, had started off like Luanne and William. And Isabelle, just like Luanne, resented it when Judd started making more money than she did and had more left over at the end of the month. But she was adamant about paying half their expenses. She felt uncomfortable when Judd spent his money on her. She should be able to buy her own winter coat, she thought, without Judd giving her the money. Then one day after they had been married a year and a half, the whole arrangement suddenly struck her as silly.

"I had been thinking in terms of 'my money' and 'his money,' and it wasn't either one. It was our money," she said. "All of a sudden I felt as if we were one, as if we had meshed as a unit." What had happened was that they had reached the We Point and Isabelle was no longer thinking "I" but "We."

She and Judd worked out what I consider an ideal arrangement. They kept their separate accounts and opened a third, a joint checking account into which they deposited their salaries. All expenses and obligations were paid from the joint checking account. Each of them also drew a check for everyday expenses—carfare, lunches, groceries, the cleaners and such. What was left over at the end of the month was discretionary money. They divided it equally and deposited it in their MOMO accounts, their individual checking accounts.

What is a MOMO account? Everyone should have one. MOMO is short for Money of My Own. It is yours. No strings attached. No questions asked. You can save it for a fur coat, buy theater tickets, put it toward a break-the-bank vacation,

buy your husband a pair of gold cuff links for his birthday,
invest it, take scuba-diving lessons, anything that your heart
desires.

I always advise couples to establish MOMO accounts. No
matter how little money you have, you should have a certain
sum of personal money, even if it is only five dollars, that you
can spend as you please. It makes life pleasanter and more
interesting. You can buy a music tape without feeling madly
extravagant if you have the money in your MOMO account.
He can buy a new lens for his camera without feeling guilty
if it's his MOMO money.

Milt and I have always had our own MOMO funds, although
when we were first married, we could only give ourselves fifty
cents apiece. I spent most of mine on chocolate bars. Now
that we are in our top earning years, we spend our MOMO
money on somewhat larger items. For instance, last year I
bought Milt a bright red sports car for his birthday. His surprised delight was worth every penny the car cost. I still dip
into my MOMO account every now and then for a box of
chocolates. Somehow I don't think I should spend the household money on something so sinfully fattening.

THE HOUSEWIFE

Some women are ashamed of this title. Or self-conscious. I
hear so many women say, "I'm just a housewife." There is no
"just" about it. A housewife has chosen her own career and
it is at least as worthy of respect as that of a computer operator,
receptionist, bus driver, teacher or astronaut. Sometimes I
think it takes a little extra dash of courage for a woman to
decide that her career is going to be her home and children.

The housewife needs to have as much of a voice in money
management as does the working wife. And, of course, the
discretionary money left after all obligations have been met
should also be split equally between her and her husband for
their MOMO accounts.

Too many stay-home wives make the mistake of feeling that since they do not bring in a paycheck, they are not entitled to any more money than they need to run the house. They are quite wrong. This puts them in the position of having to ask permission every time they want to buy a new dress or whatever. "It is infantile and dehumanizing for a woman to have to account for her expenditures," says clinical psychologist Roy Nisenson. "It is essential for the wife to have money that is hers alone. If not, she may see herself as another child in the family."

Either that or she may resort to deception, as many of our mothers and grandmothers used to do. And some still do. They never had any money they could call their own and, as a result, they used to squeeze out a nickel here and a quarter there, an occasional dollar from the food money and tuck it away in an old sugar bowl or coffee can. They felt better for having this money of their own.

It is a mistake to think of your husband's salary as his money. It is yours too. You are contributing to the family. "Marriage is a trade arrangement," points out economist Fredrika Pickford Santos of New York University. The husband supplies the money, she says, while the housewife supplies services that could be sold outside the home but instead are contributed to the family.

Just take a look in the help-wanted section of the newspaper and see the salaries that are being offered for a cook, dietitian, housekeeper, window washer, chauffeur, gardener, nursemaid, laundress, dress maker, hostess, and so on. Estimates of the monetary value of the tasks a housewife and mother performs range all the way from $25,000 to $40,000 a year. Your husband is getting a bargain.

One of the large British insurance companies made a study of what English housewives and mothers would earn if they were paid at going rates. Most of them would make more than their husbands. The housewife who works an average seven-day week would make as much as a bishop in the Anglican church or a sergeant-major in the army.

It is as important for the housewife as for the working wife to share in financial planning and decisions. Women who have left money matters to their husbands find it difficult to make their voices and needs heard later on. (And women who have not participated in the family financial decisions who become divorced or widowed experience a greater degree of stress when they are least able to cope with it.) Money is power, and most men do not want to give up even the tiniest portion of whatever power they have. Who can blame them? You do not want to relinquish power either.

The stay-home wife will be wise to involve herself in drawing up the family budget and handling the family money just like her working sister.

ACQUIRING FINANCIAL SAVVY

I am often surprised as I go around the country to meet intelligent women who know next to nothing about money. They do not know the difference between a money market fund and a savings account or the pros and cons of buying stocks versus a mutual fund. I must have met hundreds of such women. And each time I am shocked. Money is a tool and you should know how to use it.

If you lack basic financial savvy, I strongly urge you to acquire it. There are excellent books on money management and family finances that are available at most public libraries. Many of the women's magazines now run a regular column on money matters as well as articles dealing with investments and mortgages and taxes. There is at least one popular magazine solely devoted to money matters.

Many YMCAs give courses on investments and money management. So do brokerage houses. Your local high school may have an adult-education program that offers a course on finance.

And don't forget the daily newspaper. If you read the business and financial pages regularly, you will be able to discuss bank certificates, mutual funds, interest rates, mortgage options, tax shelters, and the pros and cons of renting versus buying with informed assurance. In fact, if you really buckle down to it for a couple of months, you will probably know more about such things than your husband. There is nothing all that mysterious or arcane about family finances.

I stress the importance of acquiring financial savvy because if you are going to be an equal partner in marriage, you must play an equal role in financial decisions. And you can't do this without knowing what you are talking about. If you leave it all up to your husband, you are abdicating your share of power to him. And the time may come when you will regret it. Remember what I said earlier—most money quarrels are really about power. Power should be shared, not abdicated, if you want a good marriage.

PART SIX

THE BABY DRIFT

EIGHTEEN

How children affect marriage . . . The Baby Drift . . . When is the best time to start your family? . . . Why so many women postpone motherhood until the last moment . . . How much will your baby cost per pound? . . . The four big don'ts

"IN VIEW OF THE ACCUMULATING EVIDENCE THAT IN AMER-ICAN SOCIETY CHILDREN TEND TO LOWER THEIR PARENTS' MARITAL AND GLOBAL HAPPINESS AS LONG AS THEY LIVE IN THE PARENTAL HOME AND IN VIEW OF RECENT TENTATIVE EVIDENCE THAT THE EFFECTS CONTINUE TO BE ON BALANCE NEGATIVE AFTER THE OFFSPRING LEAVE HOME AND WHEN THE PARENTS ARE LATE MIDDLE-AGED AND ELDERLY, IT IS IRONIC THAT MOST AMERICANS WANT TO HAVE CHILDREN AND DO HAVE CHILDREN,"

say Norval D. Glenn of the University of Texas and Sara McLanahan of the University of Wisconsin.

These two sociologists are right in step with the rest of the social science and mental health community in their estimation of the destructive effect children have on marriage. And yet most couples want children. Eighty-eight percent of a group of college students reported they wanted to have children when they were married. And most of them do.

Most of them also find that baby dear has stood their marriage on its metaphorical ear. The baby that was supposed to be the symbol of their love and commitment to the future is wrecking their marriage.

Most women feel that children affect the quality of their marriage for the worse. When 46,000 *Redbook* magazine readers responded to a questionnaire on motherhood, 84 percent reported they had had to sacrifice things that were important to them for their children. Other studies confirm that women are less satisfied with their marriages after the first baby arrives than before. One study, which was based on data accumulated over a six-year period, made it very clear that the negative effects of children on marriage far outweigh the positive effects.

In a study of the very youngest mothers, women aged twenty-one and under, almost three-quarters of them reported that their children had lowered the quality of their lives. Another study—this one carried out in Australia, which shows that it is not just American women who find life after motherhood less than glorious—revealed that at least half the participating mothers did not like being mothers.

You must have the idea by now. Babies are not the little bundles of joy we have always believed. Quite the opposite. "Children are a major strain on marriage," warns Dr. Laura Singer, the marriage therapist. "They have an impact on marriage like nothing else." If you think in terms of an earthquake or a hurricane, you will have a glimmering of the kind of impact she is talking about.

What is going on here? We all know couples who are happily married and have children to whom they are absolutely devoted. In fact, one survey of 200,000 people showed that, if they had it to do all over again, 78 percent of them would have the same number of children. This seems to directly contradict the findings of studies that show children have a negative effect on marriage.

What is this all about? What *do* children do to a marriage?

What this is all about is the Baby Drift, the second vulnerable stage of marriage. As for what children do to a marriage, let me quote Dr. William S. Appleton, a psychiatrist at Harvard Medical School and father of three. "Tranquillity departs after an infant arrives," he reports. "With their privacy gone, their romance interrupted, their sleep disturbed, their chores multiplied, their spontaneous comings and goings stymied in a search for baby sitters, the once happy partners may succumb to weariness and quarreling."

And weariness and quarreling do not tend to bring a couple closer. Quite the opposite. A certain amount of drifting apart is inevitable in the first weeks and months after baby arrives. Many couples, in fact, start drifting well before the baby makes its appearance.

Those men and women whose marriage was better before baby are victims of Baby Drift. And many of those women are going to find themselves victims of the Twenty-Year Ditch (Chapter 33), which is where the Baby Drift leads if it is not reversed.

Forewarned is forearmed. The time to prevent serious Baby Drift is when baby is nothing more than a gleam in his eye and a dream in your head. How far a couple drifts and how long it takes them to get back together—or whether they manage to get back together—depends to a great degree on how successfully they weathered the Make-or-Break Stage.

I am always very concerned when a baby arrives during the first or second year of marriage. This invariably spells trouble. It means that most of these couples never reach the We Point. They become Mom and Dad before they have a chance to work into their roles as husband and wife and establish themselves as a marital unit.

"Couples need time to form their separate marriage unit and build a foundation that will stand the stress of the child," says Sandra Rodman Mann, who teaches child development and parent skills at Fordham University. "It is better to be ready for a child than have that child too early and be resentful."

I advise most couples not to stop using contraception until their third wedding anniversary. By the time your second anniversary rolls around, you should have reached the We Point and your marriage should be on a fairly even keel with the major adjustment problems behind you. The task of the third year is to consolidate all that you have achieved and enjoy life.

The third year can be a golden year. Your marriage is still

a love affair—just the two of you. This is the time to indulge yourselves. A time for leisurely uninterrupted hours of love-making. A time to live for yourselves. Travel a little. Accumulate shared experiences. Enjoy the new friends you are making as a couple. This is the time when you can decide to eat out or go to a movie or for a walk in the rain without it becoming a big deal involving a baby sitter.

Once you start your family, it will be sixteen to twenty years before you will be as carefree again. Possibly even longer. You will not only be bound by the time and energy a child or children demand, you will be carrying a heavy financial burden. Children have become luxury items.

If you give birth to an eight-pound baby, you can figure that he or she is going to cost you something more than $10,000 a pound to raise to age eighteen—if there is no inflation. If you allow for an 8 percent annual inflation rate, that baby will cost you more than $13,500 a pound. You can't really equate a baby with a roast of beef, but price per pound does dramatize the high cost of bringing up baby today.

I base these figures on a report put out by the Department of Agriculture, which states that it will take $80,926 on the average to raise a baby born in 1982 to the age of eighteen. In some parts of the country, it could cost as much as $89,720. This comes to a little under $5,000 a year. Important money. No wonder more than half the married women with children work outside the home.

The staggering expense of bringing up children is another good reason to postpone starting your family until you are financially ready to meet your child's needs. Many women, in fact, are putting off having children until later. Much later. The number of women who gave birth to their first child in their thirties increased by an astonishing 94 percent in the five years between 1975 and 1980. And the number will probably increase by at least half as much again when the figures are in for the 1980–1985 period.

"Most couples would like to postpone childbearing as long

as physically possible," says psychotherapist Leah Potts of
Berkeley, California. "If they could count on reliably fertilizing
the last healthy egg produced, that would be their goal."

These women are not postponing motherhood solely on the
basis of expense but because most women today have so many
sources of fulfillment. A recent survey showed that 83 percent
of women no longer consider motherhood as the chief means
of fulfillment for a woman. This is a tremendous change from
yesteryear—yesteryear being just a little more than a generation ago. For some women today, their professional lives come
first. For others, the chance to be free to explore their interests
is more important than a child in the early years of marriage.
For many working wives, the ease of a two-income life opens
up so many options for travel, education, enrichment of all
sorts—including simply living the good life with the man they
love—that they postpone motherhood as long as possible. And
many postpone it forever.

Whether a couple decides to start a family early or late,
most men and women who have children today have them
because they want them and have planned for them. And yet
these responsible loving couples suffer from Baby Drift. They
may have waited three or four years or longer to start their
family. They may have enough of a financial backlog to tide
them over most emergencies. But they are still prime candi-
dates for serious Baby Drift. In some cases, Baby Drift starts
before the baby is even conceived.

The particular poison that operates in most of the early cases
is ambivalence—almost always male ambivalence. Women are
rarely ambivalent about having a baby. A woman wants a child
or she doesn't want one, and she knows her own mind. But
it is different for a man. Most men, given their druthers, would
like to have a child or two, a boy for him and a girl for you,
but only if it would not be too much bother.

If you have worked out your Make-or-Break-stage problems
and settled down as a couple and are enjoying life, your husband is undoubtedly very happy. He has it all. A wonderful

wife. A wonderful life. A baby would be nice, but he worries that he or she is going to upset his comfortable apple cart. And he is right. Baby will. Most husbands want a child, but they also think life as a twosome is just about perfect. On top of that, they are not at all sure they want to share your love with anyone else. Not even a baby.

Then there is the man who has been married before and who already has children. He knows very well what children do to a marriage. He has been through the sleepless nights, the diapers, the feedings, the pediatrician's bills, the whole bit. He does not really much want to repeat the fuss and fatigue of fatherhood. But he loves you and if you want a baby, he is not going to say no. But he *is* going to be ambivalent.

Husbands usually keep their ambivalence to themselves after the baby is conceived. After all, it is less than graceful for a man to tell his pregnant wife that he would just as soon not have a child. But the ambivalence is still there. We all have conflicting feelings. Much as you yourself want the baby, absolutely hunger for it, there will be times during your pregnancy when you will wish you had never gotten yourself into that state—or that shape. And there will be times after the baby is born when you would be just as happy to give it away as keep it. Not really, but you do get to feeling that way.

So before you take the big step, do be sure that everything that can be in your favor is in your favor. Observe the four big don'ts.

1. Don't get pregnant until you have finished the Make-or-Break stage.
2. Don't get pregnant until you can afford it.
3. Don't get pregnant if your husband does not want a child.
4. Last and very important: Don't get pregnant because you think it will help your marriage.

It won't. Having a child for this reason is madness. A tragedy for all three people involved but especially for the child. If a child has a negative effect on a good and loving marriage, think what it will do to a bad one. It will wreak havoc. So don't try to fool yourself that a baby can accomplish what two adults cannot. Instead of having to cope with the Baby Drift, you will be coping with divorce.

So there you are. If you have observed the four big don'ts and if both of you are ready to make the transition from couple to family, then go ahead. Don't let the Baby Drift frighten you. All you really need to cope with it is understanding and love—tons and tons of love.

NINETEEN

Life before baby... Your husband's difficult pregnancy... How to postpone the Baby Drift... When sex becomes a sometime thing... The mistakes Madeline made... How to bond your husband to his unborn child

The laboratory report is in. It confirms what you were sure of all along. You are pregnant. It is a dizzyingly joyful moment, one of the great watersheds of life. Your life will never be the same again. And neither will your marriage. Starting from this very moment.

Few women are prepared for the psychological changes of pregnancy. No one ever tells you about them. Not even your wonderful obstetrician. Pregnancy is not simply the nine-month period the fetus needs to develop into a baby that can flourish outside your body. It is a time when both you and your husband go through significant psychological changes, all of which affect your marriage.

At first the two of you are in a state of happy shock. Your husband becomes endearingly proud. There is something about siring a child that seems to be a final affirmation of manhood. And in the early weeks when you are suffering from morning sickness or just feeling vaguely rotten, he becomes the nurturing partner. It is almost as if he were the father and you the child. For him, it is a minirehearsal for fatherhood.

Then there is a switch. All of a sudden he is helpless. He will ask, "Do I have any clean underwear?" before he even looks in the drawer. He will stand in front of the refrigerator and ask, "Where do you hide the cheese?" when it is right in front of him. He will grouse that you never buy butter pecan ice cream the day after he asked you to get chocolate almond for a change. And to listen to him you would think he was a physical wreck. His back is bothering him. He can't sleep. His stomach is upset. He is worried about his blood pressure. It is enough to drive you crazy if you do not understand why he is acting this way.

The helpless act reflects his need to be reassured that he still comes first and that you will love him just as much when the baby comes. His physical symptoms are also a normal male reaction to pregnancy. We have learned that most first-time fathers-to-be suffer significant physical and emotional reactions to their wife's pregnancy. "We're just beginning to appreciate what an overwhelming experience it is to become a father," says Dr. Morris A. Wessel of Yale. "We are learning that the men also need attention during pregnancy."

Many expectant fathers experience cramps, nausea, all kinds of aches and pains, nervous stomachs, insomnia, symptoms they did not have before the pregnancy and that disappear when the baby arrives. Such symptoms, Dr. Wessel says, are a psychosomatic response to anxiety.

Some men get really scared when they think they are going to be the sole support of three people in the very near future. They lie awake nights worrying about what would happen if they got fired or fell ill. Others, while they are delighted about the prospective baby on the one hand, feel tied down and resentful on the other. Some men have a difficult time adjusting to change. It makes them feel insecure. And some suffer from sheer empathy—one man I know had morning sickness, craved pickles and ice cream just as his wife did and gained as much weight as she. "I was eating for two. Just the way she was," he said. "When she felt sick, I felt sick. It was the worst nine months of my life."

The anxiety and the conflicting feelings are not unusual, "but because so little attention is given to the expectant father, he sits on his feelings and frequently they come out in ways that are self-destructive," says Professor Sue Rosenberg Zlak, a psychologist who has counseled expectant fathers. "Sometimes they come out in ways that are destructive to the marriage," she warns.

Dr. Jack Heinowitz, a psychologist and author of the book *Expectant Fathers*, agrees. "A lot of men are very frustrated," he says. "They feel left out and they are jealous. Too many divorces take place soon after the birth of a child. I'm sure it is because of all that has been going on in the mind of the man during his wife's pregnancy."

There is no doubt but that a child disrupts marriage, even the eagerly awaited and desired first child. "Rather than bringing couples together, children can drive them apart," says Dr. Avodah Offit, a Manhattan psychiatrist. "In my practice I have observed that a husband's first affair often occurs around the birth of his first child. Often he cannot sustain being set aside within his home, even if he has wanted the child all along."

How can it be that this unborn living being can have such a devastating effect on your husband and your marriage? This life that was so desired by the two of you? That was the result of one of those tender nights when you held each other close after lovemaking and wondered, "Did we? Was this the night?" This wish come true should bring you closer, not drive you apart. But it does.

What causes the Baby Drift? To a very large extent you do. If you are like 99 percent of first mothers-to-be, the whole focus of your life changed the moment your pregnancy was confirmed. Now everything revolves around the life you are carrying. Your physical self is devoted to the task of nourishing and protecting the embryo. You stop drinking and smoking, change your diet, sleep more. All these things affect your husband too. He misses those relaxed evenings sitting at the table over wine and cheese. It's not the same when you are drinking tomato juice or milk. Some of the romance has gone out of it.

And your emotional self is concerned with the future rather than the present. As the weeks go by, you increasingly tend to be lost in dreams of what life with baby will be like. Everything else seems secondary to the miracle of creativity you are involved in. Even your husband.

"Pregnant women tend to be very self-centered," says Dr. Wende Donziger, a psychologist who works with expectant parents. "Wives should be more attentive to what husbands are going through," she advises. She is absolutely correct. This is the only way to keep the Baby Drift within bounds.

There is going to be a certain degree of drift once the baby arrives. It is inevitable. But there need not be any drift during pregnancy if you will follow two simple guidelines. These two Antidrift Guidelines should stop it during pregnancy and keep it to a minimum after birth.

The first guideline is designed to cure your husband's physical aches and ills and banish his helpless behavior.

1. ADMINISTER MONSTER DOSES OF LASA. LASA is composed of equal portions of Love, Attention, Sympathy and Appreciation. You cannot give him too much. Coddle him when he complains of feeling poorly. Cuddle him when he acts helpless. Above all, do not criticize him. This is your chance to practice being maternal, just as your dependency during the first few weeks gave him a chance to rehearse the paternal role.

The second Antidrift Guideline not only reinforces your husband's position and banishes his feelings of insecurity, it sets the pattern for the rest of your life as parents.

2. PUT YOUR HUSBAND FIRST. Let him know that he is first in your heart and always will be. By words and deeds and attitudes. Start your campaign of love and reassurance early in pregnancy so that he will not have a chance to feel insecure or jealous of the coming baby.

• • •

It is also important to maintain an active sex life during pregnancy. It is easier than you might think to get out of the habit of sex while you are waiting for the baby. You feel queasy or you feel sleepy or you are not in the mood, so you say no. And pretty soon he stops asking. This is a mistake, because sex is not only a joy, it is a wonderful emotional adhesive. It mends all the little cracks and splits. The sexually satisfied husband is not going to drift far.

Some doctors forbid sex during the first three months if a woman has spotting or certain other problems. Madeline and Craig had always had what they considered a fabulous love life. Unfortunately it came to an end shortly after she became pregnant. Her obstetrician advised her to avoid orgasm until after the third month. She had had some suspicious spotting and he said the contractions of orgasm just might trigger a miscarriage. Once she got through the first trimester, the doctor said, she and her husband could resume their normal sex life.

Madeline went the doctor one better. Six months better to be exact. She told Craig that the doctor said they could not have sex during her whole pregnancy. She was really frightened of losing the baby. If abstaining from sex for three months was good, she reasoned, abstaining for the whole nine months would be better. If she had asked the doctor if this was true, he would have set her mind at ease and corrected her misapprehension. But she did not ask him. The fact was that pregnancy seemed to have dampened her sexual desire (this is not at all unusual), and she was just as happy to go without.

She had also exaggerated the doctor's advice. All he had said was to avoid orgasm. He had not meant that they should not have sex. Not by any means. In cases like this, fellatio, bringing the man to orgasm by stimulating his penis with your mouth and tongue, is literally just what the doctor would order. Or at least suggest. Fellatio and cunnilingus are absolutely marvelous for the last months of pregnancy also, when penetration may be uncomfortable or even dangerous.

• • •

Sometimes it is the man who loses sexual desire during pregnancy. It is not all that common, but it happens. He may fear that he will hurt you or harm the fetus with his thrusting. Or he may believe—with or without reason—that you are not interested and so, out of a combination of consideration and resentment, he suppresses his sexual desire. Some men are simply turned off by the changes in their wife's body. Others may suffer from what psychoanalysts describe as a manifestation of the Oedipus conflict: The husband now sees his wife as mother—and that makes her sexually taboo.

How do you handle this? First of all by talking about it. Tell him that you miss him as a sexual partner and that you want to be physically and emotionally close to him during these important months. Second, by increasing the LASA dose and making him feel utterly beloved and important to you.

If neither of these works, I would suggest you consult your obstetrician. He or she will usually be happy to talk with your husband. Often the reason is that the husband is scared stiff of doing harm and once the doctor reassures him that everything is all right, that old desire will come right back. If there is a more serious problem, the obstetrician may suggest a therapist. Whatever the problem, don't let a sexual gulf develop between you now. You will regret it later.

When the baby, a little girl, was born, Madeline had to have an episiotomy and was quite uncomfortable for several weeks. On top of that, the baby took all her time and energy. Craig had to shift for himself.

It was four months before she and Craig made love, the first time in more than a year. They never regained their previous intimacy, either emotionally or sexually. Their fabulous love life was a thing of the past.

Craig had had several meaningless short-term affairs during Madeline's pregnancy, and he continued his independent sex life after the baby was born. Madeline was always so tired that when they did make love, it was a brief, lackluster affair. Often as not, it was cut short by the baby's crying.

Craig found the baby more of a nuisance than a delight. Nothing was the way it used to be. His wife was more interested in the baby than she was in him. She seemed to have lost all her former interest in cooking and she was unwilling to leave the baby with a sitter to go out for meals. Craig felt like an outsider in his own family.

Three years later, he asked Madeline for a divorce. She was absolutely shocked. She had thought their marriage was satisfactory despite their diminished sexual and emotional intimacy. She had thought this was a normal development in marriage after a child was born.

Even with the mistakes Madeline had made by cutting off sex and putting the baby ahead of her husband, she might have been able to halt the Baby Drift short of divorce if she had shared the baby with Craig from the beginning. It takes time to turn a husband into a parent, but once a man becomes bonded to his child, he is much more reluctant to break up his marriage. And if it is a male child, he is even more reluctant. For some reason fathers of sons are less likely to divorce than fathers of daughters. Sons seem to bind a man more to his wife.

It is important, right from the beginning, to talk with him about the baby and start planning together. Read Brazelton and Spock and White and other books on child care and development together. Discuss how you want to raise your child. Keep your husband involved all the way.

You may be planning to enroll in a childbirth class. Suggest that he join you. This is a marvelous way to get him involved, as the father-to-be has an important role as coach in the classes. He also gets to know other expectant fathers and this helps because he does not feel as if he is the only man in the world whose wife falls asleep at nine in the evening or wakes up at midnight with a craving for Roquefort on rye. Sharing his experiences and feelings with the other men makes him feel part of a group. And working with you makes him feel closer and more involved with the birth. Most husbands who attend these classes choose to be present during delivery, supervising their wife's breathing and helping her relax between contractions, putting to use what they learned in class.

Mitch, the husband of one of my daughter's friends, said he felt much closer to his second child than to his first because he had been present at her birth. "The first time I saw Kimberly was through the window of the hospital nursery," he said. "She was just one red-faced baby out of a dozen. But I was in the delivery room when Priscilla was born. I felt an immediate outpouring of love for her."

A father who feels like this will never be jealous of his child. There may be moments when he resents the chaos and fatigue that seem to be part and parcel of life with baby, but he will not worry that you love baby more than you love him if he is truly bonded to his child.

The bonding may occur even earlier. The baby becomes more real to both of you during the second trimester when the fetus quickens and you can feel it moving. The first time your husband puts his hand on your belly and feels his child move is a very special time, a very emotional time. For many men it is like a thunderbolt of reality. That is his child! He is going to be a father! It hits him all of a sudden for the first time. He may come up with a pet name for the baby. This is when many parents begin to speculate whom the baby will take after. And it is a lovely time of making silly jokes about the baby. Milt always used to insist that Lisa was trying out for the Prenatal Football Team because she kicked so hard. I think he was a little surprised when his young footballer turned out to be a girl, but he doted on her just the same.

The aware wife can prevent Baby Drift practically up to the moment of delivery if she uses all the loving tools at her disposal. If she lets her husband know that she still finds him sexually exciting, if she administers those huge doses of LASA, if she makes it clear that, much as she is looking forward to motherhood, he is always first in her heart, if she shares the pleasures as well as the miseries of pregnancy and in every way makes it clear that he is going to be as important to the baby as she is, her husband is not going to drift. Or if he does, he won't drift far.

TWENTY

Life after birth ... The nurturing need ... Why your husband may be disappointed in the baby ... The sexual bonus of childbirth ... Dividing the pie of life ... The thirtieth hour

You are no longer just a married couple. The nine months of pregnancy have produced not only this wonderful baby but also the psychological reality of a new family unit. Baby makes three and this is the true eternal triangle.

The baby pushes its way between you and your husband immediately. You may have been able to avoid Baby Drift up to this point, but now you cannot fight Mother Nature.

THE NURTURING NEED

What happens is that the nurturing instinct takes over. The nurturing need is different from one person to another. Some women have very strong nurturing needs. My mother is one of them. She is the kind of woman who peeks into baby carriages and coos at every baby she sees in the supermarket. I have never cooed at strange babies. Or very rarely. But when Lisa was an infant, my nurturing need was very strong indeed. Taking care of her took precedence over everything. Not only was it my duty to care for her, it was what I wanted to do more than anything else in the world. And yet, two hours before she was born, I had almost panicked at the thought.

They were wheeling me down the corridor to the delivery room when I had a kind of reality shock. All of a sudden, in between contractions, the full implication of having a baby became clear. For the rest of my life, I was going to be responsible for this new human being. There would never be a moment when I did not have the responsibility for this baby that was pushing and kicking its way out into the world. I remember thinking wildly, "It's too much. I can't." But there was nothing I could do about it then. Two hours later, I was embracing the responsibility.

It was a difficult birth. I developed an infection and a fever and was quite ill for several days. This meant I could not hold my baby, nor feed her, nor even see her. And all I wanted to do was hold that baby girl, feed her and care for her. I felt like a lioness deprived of her cub. And, in truth, I was very much like one.

The nurturing need is deep within us. We share it with most other mammals. I remember in graduate school repeating a classic experiment that illustrated the strength of the nurturing need. It consisted of putting a rat in a cage that was separated from another cage by an electric grid. The grid was wired so the researcher could administer shocks of varying strength when the rat crossed from one cage to another.

In the experiment, the researcher eliminates everything from the rat in the cage and determines how strong a shock the rat will take to gratify a need. The strongest of all needs is air. A rat, deprived of air, will take incredibly strong shocks to get to the cage with air.

The second strongest need is the nurturing need. It is not consistent. It ranges from very strong to very weak. If a rat has just given birth, she will suffer extremely strong shocks to get to the cage where her pups are. But as the pups get older, her willingness to suffer shock decreases daily. Finally when the pups are almost grown, she refuses to cross the grid to get to them if she experiences a shock.

The same nurturing need can be produced in a male rat by

injecting it with female hormones. Since injecting your husband with female hormones is not only undesirable but out of the question, he will not feel the same nurturing need you do. He may be committed to sharing in the care of the baby, but he is probably not going to understand the strength of your need. He will not have the same compulsive reaction to baby's every cry and move.

He may also be somewhat disappointed in his new son or daughter. Studies of expectant fathers reveal that when men think of having a baby, the picture in their minds is usually that of a child somewhere between three and ten years old, not of an infant.

The traditional joke about new fathers running out to buy the baby a baseball mitt or a football are based on emotional truth. And it is not a joke. I know one man who bought roller skates for his week-old daughter. They stayed on the top shelf of the hall closet for eight years.

When the father is confronted with the reality of infancy, there is often a letdown. The new-father blues are the male equivalent of a woman's postpartum depression, but they are rarely deep or long lasting. The sooner you can include your husband in your life with baby, the sooner he is going to bounce back from his letdown.

What about your own case of blues? Well, not all women suffer postpartum depression. Most have only a mild case. And either way, the best way to overcome it is to face your feelings and then remind yourself that they are temporary and go about life as best you can. Don't make a big deal of it. When you cry, blow your nose and wipe away your tears and tell yourself that you will feel better next week. Demand a little special cuddling. Your husband is going to feel good knowing that you need him, that you look to him to help you. It may even help him put his blues behind him.

You should guard against letting your nurturing need blind you to the importance of bonding your husband to his child. The stronger the bond, the slighter the Baby Drift. Let him help with baby. Not just changing diapers, but doing the fun things like feeding and bathing. Let him hold the baby when you are busy around the house. Most fathers will happily sit and rock the baby in their arms for half an hour at a time.

If you just give your baby enough time with his or her father, baby will take care of the bonding. An infant is born with the ability to elicit love. As the famous baby doctor T. Berry Brazelton says, "If you give him a human face to look at, his eyes will widen, and he'll get more intense and he'll follow you. As he follows, his face gets more and more alert and more and more involved, and you can feel yourself getting more and more involved back.

"This kind of visual involvement is more than just looking. You've got another component from the baby, which says to the person doing this, 'You're terribly important.' And the person is bound to feel important. What I'm getting at," says Dr. Brazelton, "is that the baby's competence will call up competence from parents." And while calling up that competence, the baby also calls up love.

"My blues disappeared the first time my daughter looked at me. She just looked and looked," a new father said. "All of a sudden I was ready to slay dragons for her."

PUTTING SEX BACK INTO YOUR LIFE

The sooner you can resume your sex life, the better for your marriage. "The advent of a child often causes some degree of sexual estrangement," reports Dr. Martin Goldberg of the University of Pennsylvania medical school. "Couples find it difficult to integrate being parents and lovers."

"Difficult!" sputtered one new mother. "It's impossible. I'm drag-around tired. Every time I lie down, the baby cries and I have to get up. My stitches still bother me and my breasts drip. I feel fat and stupid. And I haven't had a good night's sleep since I left the hospital."

You may feel like something the cat dragged in, but your husband has probably felt like an outsider for weeks while you have been devoting yourself to baby even if he has given her an occasional bottle or bath. It may be fine being a father, but he wants to be a husband too. First and foremost. So as soon as the doctor gives you the green light for sex—usually four to six weeks after birth—by all means take advantage of it.

Now is the time to start reconstructing your life together and sex is a wonderful way to reinforce your relationship. You are facing another period of adjustment. Baby has irrevocably changed your lives. The adjustment will be easier once your sexual life is back on track.

Many, many women report that they have sex less often after baby—and enjoy it less. This is a shame. Not only a shame but wrong. They are shortchanging themselves. There is a terrific bonus after childbirth. You become more orgasmic. What happens is that you have a larger supply of blood to the pelvic area, which makes you more sexually responsive.

Dr. Lonnie Barbach, a sex researcher, and Susan Lichtendorf, a medical writer, interviewed hundreds of women and found that many women who had been unable to reach orgasm before childbirth became orgasmic—and often multiply orgasmic—afterward.

Many women miss out on this bonus, partly because sex after baby is often uncomfortable the first time or two or three. You are still tender and perhaps sore. On top of that, you may not be in the mood. Masters and Johnson, the sex researchers, did a study of sex and pregnancy that revealed that 47 out of 101 women had no interest in sex for the first three postpartum months. This is usually because your hormonal system is still adjusting from pregnant to not pregnant, which means that your libido is at an all time low because your estrogen level is way down. This also means that you don't lubricate. No wonder sex does not seem all that great.

But just you wait. Once you start menstruating, your estrogen level is going to get right back up there. It can take anywhere from three to twelve weeks. If you have turned sour on sex because it was not great the first few times, you will miss out on the bonus. It seems to be one of those things that if you don't use it, you lose it. So don't let yourself be dis-

couraged if there are no shooting stars or rockets the first time
you have sex after baby. There will be pretty soon.

There is another obstacle to good sex. Baby. It is uncanny.
You are next door to orgasm—and the baby cries. You lose
it. He loses his erection. And that is usually that. If, after you
have changed and comforted the little pest and tucked him or
her in again, you are still in the mood and your husband has
not fallen asleep, you may try again. And baby may cry again.
An eight-week-old baby cries anywhere from two to four hours
a day. But one of these nights, baby will sleep through to dawn
without a whimper. You can count on it. And in the meantime,
if you can laugh when baby ruins your big moment, that may
help. A little.

DIVIDING UP THE PIE

Sex is not enough, however. It will create an atmosphere that
makes the adjustments to live with baby easier, but they are
still going to take work and patience and love.

If you are worried that you and your husband are not as
close as you used to be, you can take some comfort from the
fact that this seems to be a normal state of affairs. "This is
probably the most difficult transition period an adult will have
to make in his or her whole life," says Dr. Philip Cowan,
director of the psychology clinic at the University of California,
Berkeley. "Becoming a parent and at the same time changing
your intimate relationship from that of a couple to that of a
family is psychologically tumultuous."

Dr. Cowan and his wife, Carolyn Pape Cowan, a teacher,
headed a study of couples during the sixteen-month period
before and after the birth of a child. In the course of the study,
they worked out a do-it-yourself exercise to help couples work
together on the adjustments that are part of the transition from
couple to family. They call their exercise "The Pie."

I have made a few very slight changes in it, and I think you
will find The Pie a useful addition to your psychological tool-
box. All you need to start with is two pieces of paper, pencils

and an hour with your husband. This is how it goes:

1. Each of you should draw two circles four to six inches in diameter on a piece of paper.

2. Then each of you should divide your first circle into pielike segments, each segment representing a role you are playing in life at this period. The more time your role requires, the larger the segment should be. The pie slice you label "daughter," for instance, will probably be a sliver compared with the one labeled "mother." The slice he labels "work" will undoubtedly be larger than the one labeled "lover."

3. Spend five minutes looking at your divided pie. Does this represent your present existence fairly accurately? If, after consideration, you want to change the size of the slices or make new ones, this is the time to do it.

4. Now divide the second circle into slices. This time the segments should represent the roles you want to play and the time you want to devote to each. You have more roles in this circle. Or fewer. You may have different roles.

5. Spend another five minutes thinking about the way you have divided the second circle. Would you be happier if your life was like this? Again, if you have second thoughts, go ahead and make the changes.

6. Exchange your papers. Take another five minutes to study each other's pies. You may be surprised at the way your husband sees his life. Or at the changes he would like to make. Or both. And he is probably going to feel the same way.

7. Start talking. How can you change your lives so they will be closer to your ideals? Don't spend all night talking about this unless you are both bubbling over with ideas. I suggest that you spend no more than an hour on the whole exercise at this time.

8. At the end of the hour, tape your papers on the refrigerator or a kitchen cabinet or the bathroom wall, someplace where you will see them several times a day. This is going to spark the thinking process and at this point thinking is usually more productive than talking.

9. The following week, set an hour aside to discuss changes you think can be made in your lives. Some men find it next to impossible to discuss such things. If your husband is one of them,

don't push him. Concentrate on your own changes. And if you make
a little progress in revamping your life roles, share it with him. He
may not talk, but you may be sure he will be listening.

10. After your talk, tuck the papers away in some safe place
for six months. Then look at them together and see just how much
your lives have changed. You may have come a long way or just a
little way. You may discover that you have new ideas about your
roles in life. I think you will also discover that the two of you are
much closer now than you were six months ago. Just working together toward a goal represents an increase in intimacy.

THE THIRTIETH HOUR

It is not only sex and determination that hold a marriage together and guard against Baby Drift. There is another much
more powerful marital glue. It is love, of course. Don't let a
day go by without following the two Antidrift Guidelines. Your
husband needs that monster dose of LASA even more now
than during pregnancy. And he needs to know that he truly
comes first. Putting your husband first does not mean loving
baby less. The truth is that love is inexhaustible. You have
more than enough for both of them.

Beverly Sills, the opera star, impresario and mother of two,
has a wonderful prescription for the stressful days of early
motherhood. "Ooze love from every pore," she says. "Love
your husband and your child, not just to hear their needs, but
to fill their needs.

"And," she emphasizes, "you must reserve that thirtieth
hour of the day when he has you all alone to himself for your
husband. If you wonder when you'll get time to rest, well,
you can sleep in your old age."

TWENTY-ONE

A second child? ... The eleven relationships of the two-child family ... Why do you want a second child? ... Can you cope with another child? ... The working wife's dilemma ... Avoiding the termite effect

Should you or shouldn't you? This is a decision only you and your husband can make. And before you make it, you should consider the impact a second child may have on your marriage.

In most cases the second child makes life more complicated and is even harder on the marriage than the first child. If there was a certain amount of Baby Drift when your first child was born, you can count on an increased drift with your second.

According to a five-year study carried out by the Wellesley College Center for Research on Women, the great majority of parents feel that the time after the birth of their second child is the most difficult time of their marriage.

"First children are born to couples," says Dr. Kathy Weingarten, one of the authors of the study. "Second children are born to families. The qualitative difference, the density and texture of family life is very different with two children. The number of potential groups in a three-person family is four, but in a four-person family, it is eleven."

This puts an emotional strain on you that did not exist with your first child. Now you have to juggle those eleven relationships. A look at the following list will show you the complicated emotional network that springs into being once a second child is added to the family.

1. Husband and wife
2. Husband and wife and two children
3. Husband and wife and first child
4. Husband and wife and second child
5. Husband and first child
6. Husband and second child
7. Husband and first and second child
8. Wife and first child
9. Wife and second child
10. Wife and first and second child
11. First child and second child.

Not only are you, the mother, the one responsible for maintaining and encouraging these relationships, but as one mother complained, "I have twice as much work and only half the time." A grandmother, looking back to the days when her second child was a baby, said, "With the first baby, I was always able to keep up with the ironing. When the second baby came, I never saw the bottom of my ironing basket until the first one was old enough to help me."

Given this fairly discouraging picture of the impact of a second child, it seems amazing that anyone would have more than one child. And yet hundreds of thousands of couples do. Joyfully. Eagerly. The majority of couples feel that children are an important part of marriage. And whether they belong to "the more the merrier" school or "a boy for you and a girl for me" school, they take the fatigue and responsibility and the financial burden in stride. To them it seems a small price to pay for the joy of children and family life.

Then there is the ecstasy of motherhood. Many women find it the peak experience of their lives. "The baby is an extension of ourself," explains Dr. Priscilla Kauff, a psychiatrist and a mother. "For a period of time there is no complete boundary between yourself and your baby. That feeling is extremely pleasurable and many mothers want to repeat it—not only a second time, but often more times than that."

Caroline Seebohm, a writer who had her first baby at age thirty-seven and did not plan on having a second, was astonished to find herself eager for another child. "For me," she wrote, "the desire to repeat what was an astonishingly pleasurable experience drove all other reasoning out of the window."

So there you are, caught between the knowledge that a second child may have a shattering effect on your marriage and a yearning to have that child. How do you make up your mind?

One way is to draw up your own balance sheet. And a word of advice—the woman who wants her marriage to last should put her marriage first when she evaluates her personal pros and cons on the second-baby question.

WHY DO I WANT A SECOND CHILD?

1. Is it because you and your husband have always wanted a family? Are you agreed on the desirability of two or three or four or more children?

2. Are you having a second child because your first was a girl and your husband wants a boy (or vice versa)? What if the second is another girl? How will you feel about her? Will you decide to try a third time for a boy?

3. Do you think a little brother or sister will be good for your first child?

The most common reason couples give for having a second child is to prevent the first from being an only child. Studies show that these parents are not doing their firstborn any great favor by giving him or her a little brother or sister. The Center for Population Research of the National Institute of Child Health and Human Care has concluded on the basis of the findings of scores of studies that only children are not all that different from other children, but they do have some advantages. They tend to be brighter, to achieve more and to get along better with grown-ups. And when only children marry, they tend to want fewer children than those who have been raised in larger families. In fact, one child usually suits them just fine, a reflection of their satisfaction with their own childhood.

4. Do you want another child because you think it will prop up your marriage?

It won't. If you are having problems, a second child will only exacerbate them.

CAN WE COPE WITH A SECOND CHILD?

1. Can we afford another child? Do we really want to double our financial burden for the next eighteen to twenty years?
2. Do I have the physical stamina to take care of two children and cope with the rest of my life?
3. Do I have the emotional resilience?
4. Does my husband have the emotional resilience?

THE WORKING WIFE'S DILEMMA

The working wife must ask herself one more question: Do I plan to go back to work after this baby is born?

The woman who loves her job and is ambitious to advance in her field should ponder her priorities very carefully. Unless your husband has already shown himself to be one of those rare men who cheerfully assume significant responsibility for child care, you will be sentencing yourself to an energy-draining treadmill life for the next two or three years. "You feel that you're always running, that the machine is always in high gear," says Dr. Carol Galligan, a psychologist. "Time is the enemy. You live by lists and you're constantly preoccupied. It is a strain on a marriage and on a woman's system. She finds herself unable to think straight."

Most fathers will "help" with the children. If you ask, your husband will do the grocery shopping on Saturday while you are cleaning house. If you ask, he will take the baby out for an hour or feed or dress him or her. But you have to ask. He is doing you a favor. Helping you. Most men do not consider themselves responsible for sharing child care or housework.

Even in societies where the concept of equality is deeper rooted than in ours, fathers are seldom fifty-fifty parents. In Sweden, for instance, where nine-month paternity leaves have been available to all fathers for years, less than 10 percent of Swedish fathers take them, although there is no penalty attached. The father gets 90 percent of his regular salary while he is on leave and his job is held for him. Nevertheless, few fathers jump at the chance, and the ones who do only take six-week leaves on the average. Only a handful take the full nine months.

When an American father arranges for paternity leave— and it is not easy—or decides to become a house husband for a few months or years, this is often reported in the press along the lines of a man-bites-dog story. I keep hearing that younger men are taking more responsibility for the care of their children, but I see no signs of this becoming a trend that will sweep the country in the near future.

Be honest with yourself in answering these questions. You know what your answers signify. And before you make your final decision, stop and think about the Baby Drift.

You are going to be wrapped up in this second child just as you were in the first. You are going to be amazed all over again at the perfection of tiny fingernails and shell-like ears, the softness of baby skin. But this time, you are going to have to make room for your first child and give him or her extra reassurance and love and help him cope with his feelings toward this usurper of his parents' attention.

And you are going to have to find the time and energy to give your husband that outpouring of love and attention he is going to need. Finding that thirtieth hour is not going to be easy.

The woman with a demanding and fulfilling job might do well to content herself with one child. She will be able to give more time and energy to that child than she will to two children. Her marriage will be subject to less strain. And she will have a better chance of staying on the fast track at work.

In the end, however, each couple must make its decision on what seems right for them. Some women can juggle a job, six children and a marriage without blinking. Others are stressed to near burnout with one child. If you do have more than one child, however, beware of the Termite Effect.

THE TERMITE EFFECT

The second child often ushers in a different kind of Baby Drift, more insidious and thus more dangerous. It starts with a couple's idealistic decision to put the family first.

You want to be the best of parents. "We're going to do things as a family," you tell each other. And so you do. You eat together, play together, vacation together. If you can't take the children, you don't go. You tend to lose some friends this way. You spend your evenings and weekends with the children, and after they are tucked into bed you spend the rest of the evening talking about them. Your family is a strong and loving unit.

But what about the marriage? Putting the family first can undermine your husband-and-wife intimacy so gradually and so imperceptibly that you may never quite understand what happened. It is like termites eating away at the foundation of a house. You never know they are there until the floor caves in.

It starts when the children are small. You may start by calling each other Mommy and Daddy. It seems cozy, but it means that you are drifting away from seeing each other as husband and wife. Little by little you lose your special identity as a couple, as a We. You are the children's parents. And that's it.

Then one day the children grow up and leave home. You

suddenly perceive your marriage as hollow. The family has been nourished but not the marriage. Your husband will look around and see the whole world out there. He will realize that he is still an attractive man with a lot to offer. And there will be women eager to confirm him in this belief.

You, on the other hand, will look backward and wonder how your life got away from you. Even the working wife who has considered her life full and rewarding, divided between job and family, suddenly confronts an emptiness. She may also confront the fact that her husband is leaving her. The fact that her marriage is over. And belatedly she may realize that it has been over for a long, long time. Ever since she and her husband started putting the children first instead of each other. This is the ultimate Baby Drift. You are washed up in the fifth vulnerable stage of marriage—The Twenty-Year Ditch.

It does not have to be this way. You have the power to change the scenario once you understand the danger. All you have to do is follow the two Antidrift Guidelines. Put yourself and your husband first. Children are precious, but they are ours for a very short time. If you do your job right, they leave you to lead their own lives and form their own families. And what do you have left?

You have that wonderful man you chose to spend your life with. If you have nurtured your marriage as well as your children, he will be your friend and your lover as well as your husband forever.

PART SEVEN

THE SEVEN-YEAR ITCH

TWENTY-TWO

The "unavoidable restlessness"... What 6.8 means in marriage... What happened when Chrissie's marriage became too comfortable

You have been married four, five, six years. Your marriage is going along swimmingly. Most of the kinks have been worked out. Your sex problems are worked through. Your family is started. Or you have decided to postpone the baby decision. Every day is filled to the brim. You look forward to life. Today was fine and tomorrow is going to be even better. You and your husband have got it made. It is clear sailing from here on out you tell yourself.

Wrong!

There is never a time in marriage when you can afford to sit back and relax. What you are experiencing now is the delightful calm before the storm. Right around the corner waiting to surprise you tomorrow or next year or the year after that is the Seven-Year Itch, the most vulnerable stage of married life. It is not funny and it is no myth. It attacks marriage anywhere from the fourth to the tenth year.

"The restlessness is almost inescapable," says Dr. Barbara DeFrank-Lynch, professor of family counseling at Southern

219

Connecticut State College. "At this time marriages go through a period of dissatisfaction. Grave doubts about mate choice come into sharp focus. The potential for extramarital affairs increases."

The unhappy truth is that half of all the marriages that are going to end in divorce will have ended by the seventh wedding anniversary. The median length of such marriages in this country is 6.8 years, proof that the Seven-Year Itch is not just the title of a wonderful old movie with Marilyn Monroe.

Chris Evert Lloyd, the tennis star, described how the Seven-Year Itch affected her marriage to fellow tennis player John Lloyd. There had been rumors of unhappiness at one time and gossip linking her with other men. There had been corresponding gossip about her husband.

"We got so comfortable with each other," Chrissie said, "that we stopped stimulating each other mentally and emotionally."

John Lloyd agreed. "We went through a period where we took each other for granted and didn't work at our marriage."

"It's important to be comfortable with each other. And John and I always have been," Chrissie said, "but I also think it's important to stimulate each other. That's probably where we have to work at it more. I have to watch out that I don't get too ambitious in my tennis and want to go to too many tournaments and be away from John too long. You have to work at a marriage the way you have to work at a career."

The strains on the Lloyd marriage were twofold—Chrissie's concentration on her career, and boredom, which in their case stemmed from their taking each other for granted. This dual stress on a marriage is characteristic of the Seven-Year Itch. It affects your self-esteem, your sex life, your health. It can destroy your marriage, as it seems to have destroyed Chrissie's.

Like it or not, the Seven-Year Itch is in your marital future. It can be triggered by your job—or his. But its chief symptom is a marriage killer—boredom.

TWENTY-THREE

*Living happily ever after with a workaholic . . . The Baby
Boom time bomb . . . Why 90 percent of the men under
forty are redefining their ideas of success . . . What to do if
your husband suffers from avoidance anxiety . . . Why
Baby Boom men may turn out to
be the best husbands of all*

Most men are ambitious. And some are very ambitious. They
may not want to be President, but they certainly would like
to be on the executive floor, preferably in the executive suite.

Their career orientation begins to get on the stay-home
wife's nerves very acutely between the fifth and eighth years
of marriage when she realizes that what she had thought was
a temporary way of life is the way her marriage is always going
to be. Her husband is always going to be more interested in
getting ahead than in his wife and family, even though he will
profess to love them dearly. The working wife seldom has any
trouble in adjusting to life with a workaholic husband, but the
stay-home wife often begins to complain and nag and act injured. This can spell death to the marriage. It is not what the
ambitious man wants in a wife. If she keeps it up, he will tell
himself that "she is not growing with me" or that "I made a
mistake in marrying so young," or some other nonsense. He
will also remind himself that sex has become routine. The old
zing has gone out of it. And in that he will probably be right.
Suddenly he is ready to start looking for a more suitable wife.

The wife herself may decide that she has had enough of this and wants out. But if you really love your husband—or have even a few tag-end remnants of the love you once had—think twice. And then think again. He will almost certainly marry again. You may not. You may join the ranks of those 7.3 million leftover women.

You would do better to remind yourself about his good and lovable qualities (see Chapter 25 for help on this), stop complaining, and reorganize your own life to provide rewards and satisfactions independent of your husband, as Lily did.

"Will you be home for supper tonight?" Lily asked as Bill left.

"Don't know. I'll call you if I can make it. Don't wait up for me." He kissed her, got in the car and pulled out of the driveway.

Lily sat down at the kitchen table and cried. Her marriage was falling apart. When Bill was home, he shut himself up in the dining room and worked. When she would suggest they go to a movie or have another couple over for dinner, he would stare at her as if she had suggested they move to Moscow. Last night when she had said something about never seeing him, he had been really nasty. "For God's sake, will you get off my back," he had barked.

She could not believe this was the man she had married. When they were courting, Bill had made her feel that she was the center of his world. He had been tender, loving, considerate, amusing, attentive. And now?

"He doesn't love me anymore," she told me.

"I don't believe that" was my answer. I had known Lily ever since her mother and I used to wheel her and Lisa along the paths in Central Park in their baby carriages. And I had known Bill since he was a teenager.

"He doesn't," she insisted. "He's never home. When he is, he's either working or sleeping. Sometimes the twins don't see their father from Saturday to Saturday."

"Men like Bill live for their work," I told her. "Marriage

is important to them, but it has a lower priority on a day-to-day basis. Of course Bill was wonderful when he was courting you. He loved you and wanted to marry you. He's a man who knows how to get what he wants. Once he had you, he turned his attention to his burning interest in life—getting ahead. This doesn't mean he doesn't love you."

"But what about me? Don't I matter?"

"Of course you do. But if you want your marriage to last, you must start making a life for yourself, not depend on him for stimulation and companionship."

Lily stared at me. "But he's my husband!"

"Exactly. Not your father or your nursemaid. He doesn't want a dependent child-woman sitting at home waiting for him to brighten her life. He needs you as a support system, someone who loves him just as he is, someone he can relax with. Men like Bill expect very definite things of a wife. She should always be well groomed. She should see that his suits get to the cleaners and that the laundry does right by his shirts. She should be a good hostess. The house should be clean and attractive. The children well behaved. And his wife should not nag."

"What you're telling me is that my job is to be a housekeeper and mother. I'll never be able to hold up my head as a feminist."

"That's nonsense. You made a contract—of equal partners. He works to earn the money. You work to make your home attractive and bring up happy, healthy children. When you were engaged, Lily, I remember your saying that you wanted a large family and you thought that bringing up children and making a happy home was as creative as painting a picture and more important.

"You are fortunate. You can afford a large family. And with the twins you have a good start. You can also do almost anything else you want. Bill wants a wife he can be proud of. Someone who has her own area of competency whether it is her golf game or her knowledge of Etruscan art, or gourmet cooking, politics, ecology, you name it. The more you are involved in, the more interesting a woman you will be, the more valuable a person. And that's important. Not just for you but for your marriage."

"Don't forget, Bill compares you with the wives of his bosses and colleagues. You are important to his success. You have to be able to handle yourself and others as well as the wife of the president of the company does. After all, that's where you may be one day."

While Lily was thinking this over, I went to my files. I had clipped an article from *The Wall Street Journal* that I wanted to show her. The newspaper, in conjunction with the Gallup Organization, had asked the wives of 476 top American executives: "What advice would you give to a young woman about to marry an executive who is likely to be successful?" I felt that the advice these women had given—extremely sensible, sensitive and imaginative—was as suitable for a married woman as a bride-to-be. I underlined three answers for Lily to read.

The first was from a woman in her fifties who had urged: "Identify a personal interest of your own—music, art, continuing education, career, whatever—and pursue it attentively through child raising and all else. It will sustain you as the latest bulletin from the executive suite may not."

The second was from a wife in her forties who had advised: "Learn the facts about your husband's career and become familiar with what the steps are to his rise to power. Plan your own future the same way he plans his so that you will be experiencing self-fulfillment apart from marriage fulfillment. Become your own source of happiness and do not seek to fill your life with him or you will be greatly disappointed."

And the third piece of advice I had underlined was from a woman in her thirties who had answered: "Make the home a refuge from the pressures of the business world, a place he is anxious to go and does so every chance he gets, a place where he will not be hassled or nagged at or where expectations are heaped on him. Find time to sit with him and talk every time he gets home. Make sure the entire family understands that with you, he comes first—even before the children."

These were wise suggestions from wise women. Lily read them attentively. "It sounds as if they've really been where I am now," she said when she finished. "Instead of making demands on Bill, I guess I had better start making demands on myself."

Lily was quick to understand that if she did not want her marriage to founder during this vulnerable period (or later), she would have to adapt to Bill's career-centered life. Her marriage was not going to be like those of her friends with less ambitious husbands. It is not only the corporate striver who follows this pattern, incidentally—it may be a politician, a scientist, a writer, a doctor—anyone who puts work first. What their wives lose in some areas they gain in others.

The rewards of being married to a successful man can be very satisfying. You will have the good things in life that money will buy. You can travel. You can give your children all the cultural and educational advantages. And if you are your own woman, growing along with him and becoming a person of status in your own right, he is going to want to hang onto you forever and ever.

It may not work out this way, however. Success is not guaranteed in this world. There is a very strong possibility that your upward striver will never reach the top of the ladder. Sometime around their seventh wedding anniversary 90 percent of the ambitious men under forty are going to discover that, great as they are, there is not going to be room for them at the top. Not ever. Perhaps not even halfway to the top. A delayed time bomb hits them and shatters their expectations and changes their lives.

More than 64 million members of the Baby Boom generation, those men and women born between 1946 and 1961, are competing with each other for jobs on every level. "They are so numerous," *Newsweek* reported, that "they will face intense competition for promotions and top salaries throughout their working lives."

A corporation is like a pyramid. There are a lot of people starting at the bottom in the mailroom and as secretaries, receptionists, and assistants when they are young. In time, a certain number are promoted on merit to middle management. And, in normal times, a certain number of these employees are eventually pulled out of middle management and moved up to executive level. But these are not normal times.

Today middle management is full of terrific people in their late twenties and thirties. They are college educated, bright, hard working and ambitious. Most of them enjoyed the great suburban childhood of the 1950s and 1960s. They were given all the advantages and brought up to believe that getting ahead in life means a better position, a better title and more money. Hard work, long hours and commitment were the way to reach their goal, just as they had been for their fathers. But it does not work that way any longer. "The career ladders for many of the Baby Boomers will be blocked," reports Sandra Shaber of Chase Econometrics. This is something the majority of Baby Boomers have not yet grasped.

A recent survey of people aged twenty to thirty-five found that 85 percent of them believed that hard work paid off and 86 percent of them believed that they could control their own destiny. Hard work, of course, pays off. But it is not going to pay off for the male Baby Boomers the way it did for their fathers. They are going to have to work just as hard for smaller rewards. "From now until 1990, nearly one-quarter of the Baby-Boom college graduates will be overeducated for the jobs they get—secretaries, store clerks, cab drivers and factory workers," according to *Newsweek*. And as these men discover that they are not in control of their lives, it hits them hard.

Just as it hit Bill.

Bill had risen remarkably rapidly to the top ranks of middle management. He confidently expected to be tapped for the next opening on the executive level. But he wasn't. The man in the office across the hall was. And Bill was devastated.

"He's impossible," Lily said to me in a later conversation. "I try to tell him that it's no tragedy, that he still has a very good job and a very good salary. But he acts as if the world has come to an end. He sits and stares at nothing. And he's not sleeping well. He tosses and turns all night. This morning he shouted at the twins, told them to shut their 'goddamned traps.' That's not like him at all. Saturday night he just sat in front of the television and drank. He had a terrible hangover the next day.

"I don't know what's wrong with him," she concluded.

"It's hard on you," I sympathized, "but it's even harder on him. He has just discovered that the rules he has been living by don't apply anymore. He's having to readjust his whole way of thinking."

"But I don't believe he's even thinking. It's like he's in shock."

"He is in a kind of shock. He knew what he wanted out of life and he believed that he could get it. He is certainly qualified, as far as intelligence and appearance and personality go, to go right to the top. And now he has learned that he has gone as far as he can go. He is in a state of high anxiety. He suddenly realizes that he is no longer in control of his life, that hard work and good results do not guarantee promotion. He probably is worrying that they do not even guarantee security in this day and age when so many firms are merging or folding or being forced to let people go as economic and technological realities catch up with them. Anxiety does strange things to people," I told her.

I knew about anxiety. I have followed anxiety research very carefully ever since my student days. My doctoral thesis at Columbia had been based on a study I did on avoidance anxiety. I had been surprised by the results.

I divided the volunteer participants in my project into three groups. I warned all of them ahead of time that the experiment would involve their getting an unpleasant but harmless shock on the hand. They would hear a tone and then they would get a shock. Each of them would be wired up so that I could measure their physiological response on my equipment.

The members of the first group were told that after they heard the tone, they could avoid the shock if they pressed a button on the table at the right moment. The problem was to determine just what the right moment was. This was the Avoidance Group.

The second group was told that they would feel the shock, but as soon as it started, they could press the button and it would stop. This was the Escape Group.

The third group was told that they just had to sit there and take it. There was no way of avoiding the shock. This was the Anxiety Group.

The tension level of the Avoidance Group went way up as each person took his or her turn, but then as they started to try to find the right moment to press the button, their tension went down. The fact that there was something they could do to help themselves lowered their anxiety level.

The Escape Group had an even higher tension level at the beginning, but again the tension dropped when they discovered that, just as I had promised, they could stop the shock by pressing the button when it began.

The Anxiety Group had the highest level of tension. It went way, way up. Then, when the shocks began, it dropped way, way down—even below their relaxed or resting level, which I had ascertained earlier. I could not understand this drop. At first I thought my equipment had gone bananas and was not registering the tension levels correctly. I tested everything over and over and everything tested out in good working condition. This precipitous drop in tension was a very real phenomenon, one I had not expected.

When I talked with the members of the Anxiety Group afterward, they told me that after a while it got so that their arm just did not seem to belong to their body. What I was picking up on my electronic equipment was that dissociation. If the arm did not belong to the body, then the hand that was getting the shock did not either. These subjects had simply removed themselves emotionally from the unpleasant situation.

The fascinating thing was that the members of the first group, the Avoidance Group, had suffered almost as many shocks as the people in the Anxiety Group. Most of the time they did not press the button at the correct moment to avoid the shock. But even though they were experiencing the shocks, their anxiety level stayed down. This was because they did not feel helpless. There was something they could do to relieve themselves, even if they did not succeed every time. The Anxiety Group on the other hand had simply given up. They had removed themselves emotionally.

"Like Bill," Lily said. "That's exactly what he's doing."

"It is not psychologically healthy," I warned. "If he keeps it up, he'll be walking around like a zombie, no good to himself or anyone else."

"What should I do? Do you think he needs to see someone? A therapist?"

"Right now," I told her, "I suspect the best medicine for him is you. You can help him realize that he can find satisfaction and rewards in other places besides the executive suite. Excitement too.

"You know," I added, "this might be the very best thing that could have happened to your marriage."

Lily raised her eyebrows in disbelief.

"I mean it. Bill is not an isolated case. Roughly 90 percent of his age group is in the same boat in one way or other. They are discovering that they cannot control the course of their lives in the business world. After they recover from the initial shock, many of them are turning to that part of their life they can control—their families. I don't mean control in the sense of bossing the wife and kids around, but that they can order their life to find happiness and satisfaction in the family. These men are going to be better friends with their wives. They will spend more time with their children and enjoy them as they grow up. In some way it might be the best thing that ever happened, because when men—and women—no longer identify themselves by their jobs but by their relationships and interests, they are going to lead warmer and more loving lives. That just has to be good.

"It does not mean they suddenly scorn the work ethic or neglect their jobs. Quite the contrary. What they do is change their approach and decide to make the very most of what they have. Bill still has his very good and challenging job. What he should do is to try to make it even better. Instead of aiming for promotion, which he has been told is not in the cards, he should find a challenge in discovering ways to improve his performance even more."

"Oh, I wish you'd tell Bill all this," Lily said.

"It is better that you tell him and explain how other men are beginning to redefine their ideas of success and turning their disappointment into triumph. Don't lecture. Be tactful. Tell him perhaps that you and I were talking about how the Baby Boom has turned into a time bomb. Let him ask questions. Don't you volunteer. Right now he needs to feel appreciated and loved and important to someone, much more than he needs a lecture on looking at the silver lining of his particular cloud."

"What I get from what you're telling me is that I won't have to be like those wives of top executives and pursue my own interests so that it doesn't matter whether my husband is around or not," Lily said with a smile.

"Not quite. I'm telling you that you have a chance to create the kind of emotionally close and sharing marriage that you have always wanted. But you still have to pursue new interests and new talents. When Bill pulls himself out of this slump, he is going to keep changing and growing. It is important that he continues to see you as an exciting and stimulating woman."

"No problem," she laughed. "Since we talked last year, I've gotten into so many activities and made so many interesting new friends that Bill may be surprised when he finds out what my nine-to-five life is like. He's not going to have a chance to be bored."

I was sure she was right.

TWENTY-FOUR

*The working wife ... The statistics that threaten
men ... Who's the happiest of them all? ... If you earn
more than he does ... Who comes first, your job or your
child? Wrong! ... Why competition has no place in
marriage ... When he's jealous of your job
... The big payoff*

The working wife is a juggler who has to keep four or five
balls in the air at all times. She has to cope with her home,
her children if she has any, her job, her husband and her
husband's attitude toward her job. Unless her husband is highly
work oriented (the kind of super-striver that makes the stay-
home wife feel neglected) or has both a healthy ego and an
honest pride in her abilities, her job or career usually represents a threat, actually a series of threats. To his manhood,
his self-esteem, his health, his comfort, his status. He may
even see it as a threat to his survival.

Job strain becomes particularly acute during the Seven-
Year-Itch stage. The strains may have been there from the day
you got back from your honeymoon, but there is so much
going on in the early years that most marriages are not significantly affected until around the fifth or sixth year, when
the domestic routine is established and the early giddy excitement has simmered down. The couple now begins to assess

what they are getting out of marriage. And the strains begin to escalate.

When Milt and I were first married, one of the men in our circle of newlywed friends used to boast that he had the most wonderful wife in the world. What were this paragon's virtues? She met him at the door every night with a kiss and an ice-cold martini!

Today the working wife's husband may get the kiss as she breezes in half an hour late with an armload of groceries, but if he wants that ice-cold martini, he is probably going to have to make it for himself—and one for her too. On top of that he finds himself helping with the shopping and cleaning. The day has gone when a man could count on coming home at night to find his slippers, his pipe, his faithful dog, his smiling wife—and a perfectly cooked dinner on the table. These days he is probably going to have to walk the dog before settling down with his pipe and slippers or the contemporary equivalent. And dinner is most likely to be something out of the freezer by way of the microwave oven.

Liberated and fair thinking as a man may be, you cannot expect him not to regret the loss of the traditional masculine perquisites and comforts. Like it or not, however, most husbands in their twenties and thirties know that their friends are in the same boat. And, in itself, this sharing of the domestic tasks is not all that much of a threat to the marriage. After all, if there are no children, a two-income family has the money to buy most of the services and comforts usually provided by the stay-home wife.

THE THREATENING STATISTICS

The real threat is far more serious. It is unprecedented, unique to our time and one that men are totally unprepared for. If your husband is in his twenties or thirties, he is part of the Baby Boom generation and the props are being knocked out from under him left and right. In the last chapter I explained how the glut of highly qualified, ambitious men meant that the majority were never going to reach the career heights they have a right to expect on the basis of ability and performance. There is just too much competition.

There is another dimension to this, something even more shattering to the male ego and expectations. It is reflected in some rather somber statistics issued by the Bureau of Labor Statistics in the late summer of 1983. The number of women in the labor force, the BLS reported, increased by 3.1 million in three short years—from 38.3 million women at the end of 1979 to 41.4 million at the end of 1982—an 8 percent increase.

The employment picture for men was nowhere near as rosy. The number of men in the labor force increased by only 200,000 in the same period, an increase of less than half of 1 percent.

"Women in the hundreds of thousands are moving rapidly into virtually every area of the labor force despite the recession," said Samuel Ehrenhalt of the BLS. True, most of the new female workers held traditionally feminine, low-paying jobs in offices, retail stores and food services. But a significant minority entered the business world on the managerial level. The number of self-employed women, for instance, increased by 600,000 against an increase of 400,000 for men. And the number of women in managerial and administrative positions increased by 300,000 against a mere 55,000 for men. On top of this, the Labor Department predicts that two-thirds of all new jobs created between now and 1995 will be held by women. In sum, you and your sister working women may soon have the lion's share of paid employment. Or should it be the lioness's share?

Not only are women moving into the labor force in enormous numbers; it is good for them—physically, emotionally and psychologically. Not too long ago, 52,000 readers of *Psychology Today* cooperated in a survey on happiness. Among the findings was: "The women with the best of all possible worlds are those who are married and employed outside the home."

A job makes a woman feel better about herself. She becomes more independent. She is more likely to have charge accounts and credit cards than the stay-home wife. She has more say-so on how and when to spend the family income. And as the gap between her earnings and those of her husband decreases, her say-so increases.

Working is not only good for her self-esteem, it is good for her health. Stay-home wives suffer more from a broad range of ailments including headaches, insomnia, constipation and ulcers than the working wife. They are also lonelier and often more depressed.

If You Earn More than He Does

The flip side of this happy picture is the fact that, with each thousand dollars the working wife earns, her chances of divorcing increase by about 2 percent.

The employment statistics that I just gave underlie men's attitudes toward their working wives today and may tend to increase that 2-percent chance to 3 or 4 percent. A man may not be aware of the exact statistics, but he sees women taking jobs away from men. He sees women being hired while men are out of work. He sees women getting promotions that formerly would have gone to men. At best, this causes a certain amount of subliminal resentment—and insecurity. At worst? It can cause open hostility. Even if a man's wife is in a totally different field of work and not competing with him in any way, a certain amount of hostility and resentment may spill over into their home life. I say "may," not "will." It depends upon the man and the marriage. And upon you. And if you earn more than your husband, it can be disastrous. He will feel less of a man.

There are individual exceptions to this, of course, but the only significant group of exceptions is composed of men of the upper middle class who are secure in their own careers. It is quite common for such men to ask each other, "What does your wife do?" It is practically taken for granted by men of the Baby Boom generation that the wife is indeed doing something outside the home—whether paid or volunteer.

As far as these husbands are concerned, the more interesting the wife's work, the more she earns and the higher her status, the better. He sees her and her career as another status symbol like his Mercedes, his handmade English shoes, club memberships and showplace home. But this attitude is largely confined to the one class. It is a phenomenon that shows no sign of spreading.

Actually these men are no different from the great majority. Their status is not affected by their wife's status or earnings. She is a status symbol, not a status setter. By and large a woman's status in private life is still governed by that of her husband. "A man may sweep along a wife as he goes up the occupational ladder," writes sociologist Cynthia Epstein in *Women in Law*, "but there is no comparable image of a wife sweeping along her husband. Most people feel sorry for such a husband and consider him eclipsed, although were he the more successful one, they would congratulate the woman on his achievement and assume she was enhanced by it. A woman, by cultural definition, improves in image with her husband's success; a man may well be diminished by his wife's success."

Most men are. Not only psychologically but physically. Researchers at the University of Michigan's Institute for Social Research asked men if they agreed with the statement "I am a person of worth." More husbands of stay-home wives agreed with the statement than husbands of working wives. In another survey husbands whose wives earned more than they did reported that they loved their wives more than they thought their wives loved them. These men worried more about money than most men. And the majority reported that their sex lives had run out of steam. Like stay-home wives, these men complain of insomnia, constipation, stomach upsets and other minor ills. They are prone to heart disease. Premature death from heart disease is eleven times more frequent than normal among men whose wives earn more.

Even when the wife's higher income permits the husband

to enjoy a more relaxed life style and the kind of financial security that is hard to achieve in a one-income family, he resists acknowledging it. Professor Marta Mooney of Fordham University analyzed the lives of three-hundred men with better-than-average jobs and incomes and found that when their wives had good jobs and incomes, these men tended to take life much easier.

They no longer worked as hard, cutting down their working hours by a whopping 12 to 15 percent—almost surreptitiously. They put in as much time at the office, but stopped taking work home at night and working on weekends. "When I confront men with the results of my analysis," Professor Mooney reported, "they tend to deny it." Yet it is as if they feel guilty for enjoying the benefits conferred by a working wife.

It all comes down to power in the end. Money represents power and men have always had the power—up to now. (You might just take a few minutes here to turn back to Chapter 17 and review the material on money and power.) Study after study bears out the fact that it is a severe blow to a man's self-esteem to have a wife who out-earns him.

The wife who brings home a larger paycheck is a very recent phenomenon but more common than you might think. The wife is the high earner today in one out of every ten marriages in which both partners work full time. Such women are still the exception of course. Despite the fact that hundreds of thousands of women are entering the labor force at the managerial level, if you take a man and a woman of the same age with comparable educational backgrounds and abilities, the man will earn twice as much over his lifetime as the woman. That is a statistical fact.

On the average, a woman makes only fifty-nine cents for every dollar a man makes. And if you think that the woman's movement has made great strides, you will understand just how much further women are going to have to travel before they attain equality when I tell you that in 1939, almost fifty years ago, the working woman was making—you guessed it—fifty-nine cents to a man's dollar.

WHAT IS A WOMAN TO DO?

The one thing not to do is give up your job. You love your husband dearly, but work is challenging and stimulating. And, yes, it is fun. It is a whole world of your own with its own routines and friends and satisfactions. I know that I keep preaching one sermon—Put Your Husband First—but I don't mean that you should put him ahead of yourself. You should put him ahead of your friends, your parents, your children, but that's it. In your life, you come first. This is not selfish; it is self-preservation.

You would never consider telling your husband to quit his job because he comes dragging home bone tired, too pooped to talk night after night. Nor would he consider quitting it. Nor should you if you have a job you love that pays what you deserve—or almost what you deserve. If you should give it up, you are not going to get any gratitude. Not for more than two minutes. And you would be compromising your future. What if your husband dies unexpectedly? What if, heaven forbid, your marriage does not turn out to be forever? If you have a job at least one part of your life will be solid and sustaining. It will not make your sorrow or your hurt any easier, but it will give you an anchor for your days and nights as well as financial stability.

There is nothing you can do about the economic state of the country or employment statistics. These are a fact. They affect you as much as they affect him. The difference is that you have always known that you faced competition from both men and women. He, on the other hand, never dreamed he would have to compete with women in the marketplace. He sees this as a betrayal and a kind of enormous insult. There is nothing you can do about this either.

"You just have to be sensitive to the unspoken terror," advises psychiatrist Helen Singer Kaplan, head of the Human Sexuality Teaching Program at The New York Hospital–Cornell Medical Center.

The man whose wife earns more than he does "is going to

act up," she warns. "He is going to provoke. And he is going to be a son of a bitch. He is going to assume that if he doesn't cut the mustard in money, she'll think he is a jerk."

You can afford to overlook most of this. You can be more giving and loving. He needs lots of strokes. And you must be sensitive to his psychological raw spots. For instance, women with good jobs who earn good money get used to being catered to. You don't want to carry that expectation home from the office. At home you are the wife, not the department head.

The most important thing you can do is let him know how very much you need him and how much he means to you. Don't put your job ahead of him. Don't rub his nose in your success. By all means talk about your work if he is interested, but if you detect the slightest sign of envy or irritation or boredom, clam up. Share your triumphs and your problems with a woman friend. Just tell your husband enough about what's going on at work so he feels part of your life.

A New York television producer had the worst fight of her marriage after a cocktail party where one of her colleagues greeted her husband with, "Well, you certainly must be proud of your wife," and he didn't know what she was talking about. The show she produced had just been nominated for an Emmy award. She had not told her husband about it because he was not doing very well on his job and she did not want to make him feel bad. The result of her poor judgment was that she made him feel terrible. And angry.

Love and sensitivity will do more than anything else to keep your job from weakening or wrecking your marriage. This Seven-Year-Itch period is a particularly difficult one. Your marriage faces more problems than the strains stemming from your job, so you should try to minimize the work-related problems. They are truly not the most important, but they tend to be exacerbated when other problems exist.

Always keep in mind that your goal is a forever-after happy marriage. It is worth working for. And it can be achieved— even if you earn more than he does. One of the most disparate couples I know are Phil, a construction worker, and Arlene, an assistant professor of chemistry at a Sun Belt college.

Phil finished high school. Arlene finished college and five years of graduate study. Phil earns excellent money when he works, but construction has been slow lately. On a yearly basis she brings home significantly more money. None of this seems to bother them.

Phil has a very healthy self-esteem. He sees himself as a highly skilled worker and intelligent enough to attract a woman like Arlene. She admires his competence and his take-charge approach to his work. "When I see him on one of those big construction jobs," she told me, "I always think of him as an artist. And when I see the completed building, I know he is."

Phil is proud of Arlene's education and very much interested in her teaching and research. He has an excellent grasp of what she does and she keeps him abreast of the progress of her research projects.

They also have several strong interests in common. They are devoted gardeners. They belong to a choral society and to an amateur chamber music group. Phil taught Arlene how to play poker and for years there has been a standing Wednesday night poker game with Phil's construction friends and their wives. These two have made their lives mesh happily. Neither money nor status interferes with their enjoyment of being with each other.

IF YOU HAVE CHILDREN

Before I go into specifics, let me just say that if you married a man whose mother worked—as I did—you have a little something extra going for you. His parents' marriage serves as a model that helps him take his own marriage to a working wife and the upset and tension that accompany juggling a job and a family in stride.

You don't need me to tell you that when he works and you work and you have a child or children that life is going to be a rat race. You are running from morning to night. And most husbands don't help all that much. If your husband puts in one-fourth of the time you do caring for the children and doing household chores, you should consider yourself fortunate. Most husbands put in considerably less.

One study that was carried out recently in Connecticut of fathers whose wives went back to work after the birth of their first child discovered that the men who really pitched in and helped with the laundry and child care, shopping and cooking said they had good marriages. The husbands who resisted doing "women's work" reported that they and their wives argued a lot, that they had unsatisfactory sex lives—and did not find their marriages satisfactory either. Of course, with results like this, you wonder if it is a question of which came first—the chicken or the egg? If the wives are always nagging at their husbands to help them out, that might account for the arguments, the disappointing sex life and the unsatisfactory marriage.

Money helps. The more you have, the more help you can afford. Unfortunately, no matter how good your help is, it is impossible to hire anyone who will do all the work a wife does for love. You are always going to face a mountain of chores when you get home at night.

When Lisa was born, I stopped all my teaching and research to stay home for three years. At that time it was believed that a child needed his or her mother's care for the first three years to enjoy optimum psychological and emotional development.

I enjoyed much of my time at home with Lisa, but at the end of two and a half years, I confess I was practically climbing the walls. Lisa was adorable, funny and bright, but I needed more stimulation than she was providing. When the chance came along for me to get out of the house and rejoin the big world, I never looked back. I do not regret one minute of those years, but I was glad when they were over.

Today the experts are divided about the importance of the mother staying with her child for the first three years. Some believe that it is not as vital as we used to think. They cite studies of children in child-care centers who are vigorous and blossoming. But others still feel that the mother's presence is vital. Burton L. White, author of *The First Three Years of Life*, which has become a classic in its field, says, "My ideal pattern is this: No substitute care for six months, with the exception of an occasional night out; part-time substitute care with parents equally sharing child care the rest of the time. My opinion," he says, "is based on a lifetime of doing research on what is best for babies. I am not in the business of making life easier for young couples."

I bring this up because your guilt can be an added strain on the marriage during this third vulnerable stage. Are you depriving your child by continuing to work? Should you give it all up for three years and then try to pick up where you left off? There is no one right answer. You have to really think about your priorities and then act on them. Either way, you are going to lose something—the joy of watching your child's day-by-day development or your steady climb up the career ladder. Whichever you choose, leave guilt behind. You are doing what you think best. And don't for a moment feel sorry for yourself either. Many women have no choice. They have to work—baby or no baby—to help their husband pay the rent and put food on the table. If you have a choice, you are one of the fortunate ones.

With guilt off your back and your acceptance of the fact that the bulk of the housework and child care is probably going to fall on your shoulders (you can take consolation in the knowledge that the worst of it will be over in three years), it is time to face up to the chief threat to your marriage— forgetting or neglecting to put your husband first. There are so many demands on your time and energy that it is usually the squeaky wheels that get the grease. And the squeakiest wheels are the child and the job. You tell yourself that your husband understands the pressures on you. He probably does. He will also understand that you are putting your job and the child ahead of him.

Don't let yourself fall into this trap. Make sure he knows he is first. No working mother is ever so busy that she cannot spare five minutes every now and then for a hug, and squeeze out that important thirtieth hour every blessed day. Remember what Beverly Sills said—you can always sleep when you're older. This special hour that is just for the two of you should be the most blissful part of your day. No matter how tired you are, an hour alone with your husband has to be relaxing and revitalizing, fun, loving and rewarding. It is your special time with the man you love. Don't let yourself be cheated out of the thirtieth hour.

The woman who cannot make time for the hugs and the togetherness is asking for trouble. You know what the Seven-Year Itch is all about. If you do not put your husband first, he may scratch it.

IF YOU DON'T HAVE CHILDREN

You do not make more money than your husband, you do not have children, but your problems—with one exception—are essentially the same as those of women who do. They differ only in degree. The exception is competition. The working couple who does not have children tends to compete more. This is a mistake. Competition has no role in marriage. There should not be a winner and a loser in a marriage—only two winners. If you are hellbent on getting promoted sooner or faster than he does or earning more than he does, stop it right now. And take some time to ponder your answer to a very important question: What am I trying to prove? Are you trying to prove that you are smarter or more competent than he is? Suppose you prove it, what then? Does success at work mean more than success in marriage? Do you want your husband to acknowledge that he is the inferior partner? Whatever your motivation, you are weakening the marital relationship at one of the most vulnerable stages of marriage.

I do not for one minute mean to suggest that you do less than your best on the job or that you do not compete as keenly as ever with your colleagues for raises and promotions. Just do not compete with your husband. Work and money are so tied up with the masculine ego and identification that the competitive wife puts maximum stress on a marriage.

If it works out that you get promoted faster than he does, that is fine. And he will be happy for you if he does not feel that you are inwardly crowing, "Yah, yah, yah, I'm better than you are!" Do better than the others in your office or profession, but keep competition out of your marriage. There is no need to hold back because you might do better than he does as long as doing better is not your goal.

I wish I had always been this wise. When Milt and I were first married, I worked for my Ph.D. in psychology while he was going to medical school. I had considered going to medical school myself and becoming a psychiatrist. I decided against it because I thought it would make us too competitive. I had visions of the two of us in medical school at the same time comparing our marks. What if I did better in something? It was too much of a risk to take.

I was a product of the era when you just did not compete with your husband. A wife's role was to bolster his confidence and provide the support system that would allow him to achieve. Today I think I made a mistake. I should have gone to medical school, gone the psychiatry route rather than the psychology route, because so many of the breakthroughs today are in the biochemical realm. I keep up with the new research by reading professional journals and talking with the top experts, but I have limitations that I would not have if I were a psychiatrist. For instance, if I were ever to go into private practice, I could not prescribe one of the new antidepressants or even a mild tranquilizer for a patient. You have to have a medical degree to prescribe medication.

I realize now that Milt and I would not have been competitive. His specialty is not psychiatry. Our goals were different and so are our temperaments. I think that if both of us had gone to medical school at the same time, the experience would have been enhanced and enriched for us. We would have brought two perspectives to bear on what we were learning.

There are times these days when I seriously consider stopping my lecturing and all the rest for a couple of years and going to medical school to get the degree I should have gotten thirty-five years ago. It is not too late.

I did fall into the competition trap once. And once was enough. It was unwitting. I was not really competing with Milt, but I was trapped into a situation in which he felt very much the second fiddle. It was more than twenty-five years ago, and it still nags at him every now and then.

It was after I had won "The $64,000 Question." It was a big deal. In those days "The Sixty-Four," as we called it, was *the* most popular program. Everybody watched it on Tuesday nights. And the winners were instant celebrities. In fact, just being on the program guaranteed you a certain amount of fame.

When I won, I received invitations from all over the country to make personal appearances, to be on television, even to open a county fair. One night when I had a date to appear on television before a live audience in New Jersey, Milt went with me. It went off very well. Everybody seemed pleased. I had put on my coat ready to leave with Milt when members of the audience started coming up and asking for my autograph. I signed a few and then the producer of the show said, "You better take off your coat. It's hot in here." He helped me off with my coat—and handed it to Milt to hold. Milt never blinked an eye. He stood there patiently holding my coat until I signed the last autograph. I knew he was mentally gritting his teeth. He did not enjoy being the coat-holding husband of a celebrity wife.

It stuck in his craw. Once in a while he makes a joke about it even now. But I know he did not really think it was funny or he would have forgotten the episode long, long ago. I learned from that night. I decided I would never again put Milt in a position where he would be playing second fiddle. Fortunately he is extremely successful in his own field of medicine. We have never had a problem of who has more status or who earns more money. We both have status in our respective fields and we both earn above-average incomes. We are happy equals.

• • •

The husband of a working wife in a childless marriage tends to be as jealous of her job as the husband whose wife earns more than he does. The jealousy is an amalgam of sex and competitiveness.

A couple of years ago in Ottawa, I was interviewed by a young and very attractive reporter. The interview went well. I was impressed by the questions she asked. Finally she put her notebook away and said, "I have one personal question. My husband is jealous of my job. He's a reporter too. When we were first married, I was a secretary and I did some reporting on the side. Last year I was promoted to reporter.

"My husband never minded my job before, but now he's always making cracks. I'd love to tell him about meeting you, but I won't. He'll just shrug his shoulders and say, 'Big deal.' What can I do? We've been married six years, but I'm not sure he wants to be married to me anymore. Not if I keep this job. But I don't want to give it up."

Her voice was shaking as she concluded.

"I don't think you should give up your job," I told her. "I suspect that you can wipe out his feelings of jealousy once you understand why he's jealous. There could be several reasons. First of all, now that you are a reporter, you represent competition, even if you are not trying to compete with him. You have a byline just like him. Perhaps your byline appears more often than his does some weeks. He is going to have to come to terms with that himself, but you can help matters by taking a real interest in what he writes. Praising it. Asking how he got someone to tell him this or that.

"There may be sexual jealousy at work here too. A secretary stays in the office, but a reporter goes out and meet interesting people. He may worry that you will meet someone you find more interesting or attractive.

"You also may be giving him a message that he's not as important to you as he used to be. You may be so anxious to do a good job that you are more absorbed in your work than in him. Is that possible?"

"Ummm," she answered. "I do think about it a lot. Like last night, I was preparing for this interview. I read everything in the morgue about you and then I started thinking of the best questions to ask you."

"What was your husband doing while you were doing your homework?"

She shook her head. "I don't know exactly. He watched television for a while. Then I heard him talking on the telephone. I don't really know. He was asleep when I got to bed."

"Do you spend many evenings like that?"

"I'm afraid so," she said. "I hadn't looked at it that way, but I can see why his nose is out of joint. He never brings his work home."

"That's probably the major cause of his jealousy. You've put your job ahead of him. If you want to get back to the happy relationship you used to have, you're going to have to reverse your priorities. He has to know that he means more to you than an interview with Joyce Brothers does. If you are going to spend your evenings on your job, he is going to look someplace else for the comfort and attention and fun that he's not getting at home."

But what if the two of you are competitive types? If you thrive on competition? Love it? Then you have to find another arena besides marriage for your competitiveness. Compete against someone else. Do your winning and losing outside your marriage.

I cannot emphasize too strongly the dangers of putting your job first. Jobs are a little like children. You do the best you can by them and enjoy the rewards they provide, but at sixty-five they are going to leave you high and dry. And what are you going to have left in your life then? If you put your job first, you may not have a husband with whom you can share and enjoy your leisure years.

Tammy faces this prospect. She and Al had been married

for seven years. Tammy worked for a large New York bank, where she had just been promoted to head of personnel. Al was a free-lance writer whose byline appeared in many popular magazines. Tammy often talked personnel problems over with him. And he used to show her the first drafts of his articles. They enjoyed feeling helpful to each other.

Tammy was in the middle of a big shake-up and reorganization of the personnel department when Al had an idea for a novel. He spent three weeks preparing an outline and then asked Tammy to read it. "I'd really like to know what you think," he told her. "It's a first for me and I'm nervous about it. Maybe it's not such a hot idea."

A couple of days passed. Tammy did not mention the outline. Finally after a week, Al asked her what she thought.

"I'm sorry, darling," she said. "I just haven't had a moment. I've been so busy with the reorganization."

Al was hurt. Perhaps beyond reason. He could hardly believe that she had not been able to find a half-hour to read his outline. How could she put her job ahead of this? She knew he was very nervous and unsure.

Three years later, talking about his divorce, Al cited that moment as the beginning of the end. "I can't tell you how hurt I was," he confessed. "It was like a slap in the face. I had always thought we came first with each other. This was my first clue that her job came ahead of me. There were other similar incidents. And then I met Lois. From the very beginning, she made it clear that I came ahead of everything and everybody. We sneaked around seeing each other secretly for a few months and then I decided to make the break. As soon as the divorce came through, Lois and I got married." As of now, Tammy has not remarried.

This is a typical Seven-Year-Itch case history. Tammy was finding more excitement in her job than at home. When Al realized this, he was hurt and then angry. He started looking outside his marriage. He still loved Tammy in a way, but the initial passion was long gone and Tammy had not nurtured that deeper, stronger love that can hold a couple together through thick and thin, sickness and health and all the rest. She had not put him first.

One man summed up the male attitude when he insisted that his wife's job was responsible for their divorce. "I didn't mind her working," he said, "but I minded like hell playing second fiddle to her job."

What a wife must understand is that the second fiddle may leave the orchestra during the Seven-Year Itch. This extremely vulnerable stage of marriage is the most likely time that his hurt and anger will boil up. He will either continue in the marriage, but seek—and find—comfort, consolation and attention on the side (see Chapter 27), or walk out and try his luck with a second marriage.

THE BIG PAYOFF

With all this discussion of the strains your job can impose on your marriage, let us not forget the very real plus that the working wife has going for her. It is not the salary she earns. It is not even the satisfactions she finds in her job. It is the stimulation it adds to her marriage. Studies have shown that the husbands of working wives complain a lot about having to help around the house and the fact that their domestic life may not run as smoothly and comfortably as that of their friends with stay-home wives, but they have fewer divorces. When a wife works, she brings more to the marriage—a spark, a stimulation. More interest and excitement is generated between husband and wife. The husband may be less comfortable, but he usually has a lot more fun. Boredom is at a minimum in these marriages.

It really is true that the working wife can have the best of all possible worlds.

TWENTY-FIVE

*Living life by sevens... Why sex turns boring... What
you can learn about men from monkeys... The almost
irresistible seduction power of admiration... The husband
you don't know... The Widow Game*

You may have minimized the stresses and strains involved in
juggling your job and your marriage, but you still have to face
the Seven-Year Itch, the stage when the grass looks a lot green-
er on the other side of the marital fence.

It is a dangerous time. Everything was going along so
smoothly. The two of you had never been happier and then—
you don't know quite how it happened or when—you were
suddenly out of your skin with boredom. Nothing has changed,
but you just can't stand it. Sex is one big ho-hum. And so is
your husband.

If this is where you are right now, you may be interested
to know that your husband had probably been feeling this way
longer than you have. Men get bored faster. What you both
need is a change. One marriage and family counselor, Monette
Thatcher of Eugene, Oregon, has an intriguing theory that we
live our lives by sevens or approximations thereof. As children
we start school around the age of six and start applying ourselves seriously to mastering reading and writing and arithmetic at seven. It is the end of carefree childhood, the beginning

of no longer being able to do what we want when we want.

Seven years later, at fourteen, we are in high school. We start dating and see ourselves as responsible. Seven years after that we are through school and on our own. We start to work. We may get married.

Seven years after that we still have the job and we are still married. Isn't it time for a change? We have had a change every seven years. Why should this be different? And, of course, it isn't. We start to suffer from the Seven-Year-Itch. Boredom is the poison that seeps into marriage and triggers the Seven-Year Itch. If this psychological itch is not treated promptly and effectively, it can lead to infidelity and often divorce.

Much of the boredom is because you locked yourselves into the patterns and habits you created in the Make-or-Break Years. This was the time when you learned to adjust to each other, when you worked out ways of getting along, worked out your sexual problems, learned how to deal with your families and all the rest. When you reached the We Point and everything settled down, you were blissfully happy and decided that this was the way things should be. But the only constant in marriage, the only thing that you can count on not to change, is change.

"If you think you have it all worked out, just wait," warns Dr. Patricia Light, chief psychologist of the counseling service at Harvard Business School. "You will have to work it all out again."

WHY SEX TURNS BORING

Not only do husband and wife change mentally and emotionally; they become desensitized to things that used to give them great pleasure. Especially sexual pleasure. The man who used to have an instant erection when he saw his wife naked does not even look up from his book now as she undoes her bra and peels off her pantyhose. The woman who used to adore having her breasts caressed as part of the lengthy foreplay ritual developed in early marriage now finds herself lying there passively as her husband, thinking he is giving her pleasure, caresses her breasts the same way he has for years. She now finds sex about as exciting as doing the dishes and wishes he would hurry up and get on with it.

What every woman should know is that marriages reach a point where both partners suffer from acute stimulation deprivation and this can cause erotic desensitization. We all have certain basic needs. Water and air and food. A place to live. A certain amount of security. We also need change. No matter how great a delight we take in a certain sexual caress, the taste of chocolate ice cream, the fragrance of lilac blossoms, the view from the front porch, we eventually become desensitized and lose our keen sense of pleasure in whatever it is.

Let me explain how this works. You are married. You wear a wedding ring. For the first few weeks after the wedding, you are acutely conscious of that ring. You look at it. You twist it. You are aware that it is on your finger. Little by little, you become desensitized and finally you don't even feel the ring on your finger. If you wear glasses all the time, you are not conscious of those glasses on your nose, except when you get a new pair and then for a few days you may be aware of them because they are heavier or lighter than the previous pair. In the same way, a sexual caress or position that used to drive you crazy with delight no longer does anything for you. You have become erotically desensitized.

Our eyes crave stimulation too. One of the most effective window displays I ever saw was of a piece of costume jewelry, a single earring with clusters of small rhinestones dangling from it. It was suspended on an invisible wire against a black velvet background. It looked like a million dollars. Everyone stopped to look. If the display artist had filled the window with a dozen pairs of the earrings, no one would have taken a second glance.

We become desensitized to smell. We are rarely conscious of our own body odor. If you wear the same perfume every day, you tend to apply more and more as time goes by because you need more to be aware that you are wearing it. When people complain that the formula of their favorite perfume must have been changed because it no longer has the same staying power, the truth is that the formula is the same. The wearer's sense of smell has become desensitized.

And, as I said, we become desensitized to sex as well. A fascinating experiment carried out with male rhesus monkeys seems to indicate that—contrary to the common belief that males can never get too much sex—the male actually may not have the ability to enjoy sex over the long term as much as the female.

The experiment probably made the male rhesus monkeys feel they had found a sexual paradise at the beginning. The sex life of the male monkey is restricted to the two to two-and-a-half months a year when the female is in heat. But not those of the four male rhesus monkeys at Emory University, where psychiatric researchers injected four female monkeys with drugs to make them sexually receptive all year round and put them in a cage with the four males.

The males embarked on a sexual orgy that lasted for months and months. They seemed insatiable. But then something unexpected happened. The males began to lose interest. Not the females. They wanted more, but the males had had it. It got so that when a female came near a male, he ran away.

At this point the researchers tested the males' potency and found a two-thirds drop from normal. No wonder they were not interested. Even if they had been, they probably could not have done anything about it.

Now they substituted four new females for the original four. The males immediately regained their interest in sex and embarked on another orgy that lasted until the researchers took away the females and brought back the first four.

That did it. The males immediately lost interest in sex.

Boredom was obviously a factor here. The males' impotence was cured instantly when new females were brought in, but when the original females were brought back, the memory of past boredom was enough to turn off their newly rampant sexuality.

It would be reaching too far at this point to compare the human male to the male rhesus monkey, but it is possible to speculate, on the basis of reports in medical and psychiatric journals on masculine problems of impotency and lack of desire, that boredom is as much a sexual turnoff for men as for monkeys. There also seem to be grounds for believing that, while men have sex on their mind much more than women do, they become sexually sated sooner than women do. And there is no doubt at all but that the easiest way for a man to get back that old interest in sex is to find a new woman. (See How to Take the Ho-hum out of Sex, Chapter 26.)

This brings us back to the Seven-Year Itch. The single most dangerous aspect of the itch is that your husband is meeting someone who sees him as terrific, no matter how boring he may seem to you. It may be his secretary. It may be the woman behind the counter at the coffee shop. It may be someone who takes the same bus or train to work. It may be one of his customers, the girl at the self-serve gas station, your next-door neighbor. Anybody. And it does wonderful things for him. It makes him feel awfully good about himself. And awfully good about the woman who has made him feel good about himself. Just the way you feel special when you know that a man is turned on by you.

I remember early in our marriage I started saving up to get my teeth straightened. I had two protruding front teeth that made me look like Peter Rabbit's sister. My folks had thought I looked cute and never felt it necessary to do anything about them. But once I had managed to put aside the money, off I hopped to the orthodontist. To several orthodontists, in fact, because at that time orthodontia was considered out of the question for adults. I finally found a man who said it could be done and all of a sudden there I was wearing braces.

I felt I was the weirdest-looking person in the world. Then a doctor at Milt's hospital started paying attention to me. He was attracted to me! I could hardly believe it. Me with my mouth full of railroad tracks. I was thrilled!

Nothing ever developed. I was too much in love with my husband to look at another man. But just the same it made me feel good that this man thought I was special. If I had not been so crazy about Milt, who knows what might have happened? And all this was only a year or so after we had been married. Just think of the impact of having someone make it clear that he thinks you are terrific when you have been married six or seven years. It can be intoxicating.

This happens to almost every man. Including your very own husband. And even the most faithful of men may become unfaithful.

I remember talking with a European diplomat some years ago. He was in New York to attend a meeting of the United Nations. We met at a dinner party and he told me how much he missed his wife and children. It was hard, he said, to think that he would not see them for three long months.

We met again just before he was to leave. I remarked that he must be looking forward to getting home.

"Not really," he answered. After a little inconsequential chitchat, he said, "You're a psychologist. I wish you'd tell me what's wrong with me." And he told me his story.

A week after he arrived in New York, he met a young journalist at a cocktail party. He had thought her pretty. Quite charming. Nothing more. But she had thought him extremely attractive and brilliant and sophisticated—all of which he was. And she let him know it. He was flattered and then enchanted. The past three months had been a wonderful romantic fantasy.

"I feel like a boy again," he said. "I never thought one could recapture that kind of excitement, but Annette is everything I ever dreamed of in a woman—so desirable, so pretty, so amusing. At the same time, I can't believe this is me. I left home a happily married man. I adore my wife. I love my children. Now I'm dreading going home to my wife, to the same old life. What's come over me?"

I patted his hand. "In this country, Emile, we call it the Seven-Year Itch. How long have you been married?"

"Almost nine years."

"Close enough," I told him. "The Seven-Year Itch strikes a man—and a woman—when marriage has become routine. When sex has lost its spice and is no longer that heart-pounding breathless ecstasy. One day you meet a woman who thinks you are wonderful. No one has told you that you're wonderful for a long time. You think she is wonderful because she thinks you are and all of a sudden you are head over heels in a mad love affair."

"Exactly," said Emile, the diplomat. "But what am I to do? If I were to divorce my wife, she would be heartbroken. And I might never see my children again."

"Divorce?" I asked. "But you love your wife. What you must do is go home and take up your life again. This is a sentimental interlude that you will always remember—and never, never talk about. If you have a guilty conscience, get rid of it by working to make your marriage even better. After all, if you were vulnerable to a little change and admiration, your wife may be too."

He lifted an eyebrow. "I never thought of that."

"Men don't," I said, "but she is probably just as hungry for excitement and admiration as you were."

He nodded thoughtfully. "A romantic interlude, hmm? You may be right."

Several months later, I had a short note from him. "It was good to get home. I have learned that two of your folk sayings are absolutely correct. Absence makes the heart grow fonder. No doubt about it. I fell in love with my wife all over again. It is also true that out of sight is out of mind. I do think of Annette with tenderness, but, in truth, I rarely think of her."

Your husband may not be a diplomat. He may not be out of the country or out of town on business. But the same thing can happen to him. And it may not have such a happy ending for you. (For a further discussion of infidelity, see Chapter 27.)

I told the story of Emile to Trudy, who had been complaining that her husband, Loren, was so unutterably dull that she was thinking of getting a divorce. Or at the very least taking a lover.

"How would you feel if Loren were to fall for some other woman?" I asked. Trudy laughed. "Not Loren. He might fall for another woman, but no woman would ever take him seriously. He's such a drag. I'm safe in that direction."

"I'm not so sure you are," I said. "Did you ever consider that if you are bored, Loren may be even more bored?"

"Loren is a bore. Bores don't get bored," she said emphatically.

THE HUSBAND YOU DON'T KNOW

I let Trudy's comments go by for a moment. I was thinking of three letters that had come in that morning's mail. I can't tell you how many letters I get with this one theme. It is almost unbelievable. They come from women who tell me that their husbands are silent or cranky or depressed. That they are seldom affectionate. That they are not particularly interested in sex. That they are uncommunicative. And that they are boring. Then, in shocked amazement, they report their discovery that other women find their husbands fascinating.

"At the office Christmas party," one woman wrote, "his secretary came up to me and said she hoped she could find a husband just like mine. He was so thoughtful, so interesting, so attractive. I could not believe she was talking of the same man."

In the second letter, a wife had written, "My next-door neighbor, a divorcée, asked if my husband could fix her window for her. It was stuck. I almost hated to ask him I was so sure he would say no. He hates to be bothered. But I was wrong. 'Certainly,' he said. 'I'd be glad to help.' He went next door. I could hear him talking and joking with her. I could not believe it was my husband."

"When my husband comes home from work, he says 'Where's supper?'" the third wife wrote. "After supper he gets up without saying anything and turns on the TV. He's the original strong silent man. If I suggest having another couple over to play cards, he'll say that he doesn't want to listen to some idiots yak all night. If I suggest going to the movies, he'll ask why I want to waste his money. Yesterday I ran into his boss's wife at the shopping mall. She told me that her husband considered Max his most valuable employee, because he got along so well with everyone and knew how to get people to pull together. I felt like asking her if she hadn't gotten him mixed up with someone else."

I thought about these letters and then I asked Trudy, "Do you ever see Loren in his office? Is he the same there?"

"Funny you should ask," Trudy said. "I picked him up at the office last week. We were going to look at carpeting together. He was really very nice for a change. He asked the receptionist how much longer her father was going to be in the hospital and said he'd try to visit him. One of the men told me that Loren had won the darts championship. I hadn't even known he played darts. The elevator man thanked him for writing a letter of recommendation for his son. I couldn't believe this was the same man who comes home every night and falls asleep in front of the television."

"What you're telling me is that the people he works with don't think he's a bore. They see him as a warm and caring man, someone they respect. Perhaps you really don't know him as well as you think. He may have some surprises left for you."

She rolled her eyes. "Like what?" she asked scornfully.

I suggested that she take a little test I had devised. Every woman who thinks she knows her husband inside out would do well to take this test. You may be surprised at what you learn. It won't take you five minutes. Just jot down your answers to the following five questions.

1. If your husband won a contest in which the prize was one of the following, which would he choose?
   A. Two weeks at a tennis camp
   B. A week in Paris

    C. A season pass plus travel expenses to the games of his favorite major-league team

    D. A life membership in a health club

    E. Two months at a beach cottage

2. *Whom would your husband prefer to look like?*
    A. Prince Charles
    B. Tom Selleck
    C. Paul Newman
    D. Dustin Hoffman
    E. Tom Brokaw

3. *If your husband were not married to you, to whom would he like most to be married?*
    A. Jane Fonda
    B. Candice Bergen
    C. Elizabeth Taylor
    D. Brooke Shields
    E. Christie Brinkley

4. *What does your husband consider his best physical feature?*

5. *What is his favorite breakfast?*

Now ask your husband these questions and compare his answers with yours. How did you do? How close did you come to pinning down his fantasies? And how about breakfast? Did you get it right? If you got two out of the five right, congratulations. The truth is that we never really know another person. There are always hidden depths.

Trudy did not get any of the questions right, not even Loren's favorite breakfast. She admitted that perhaps she did not know her husband as well as she had thought, but "I'm still bored," she said. Trudy had a bad case of the Seven-Year Itch. She found sex more of a chore than a pleasure. Even worse, she felt her husband more of a bore than a treasure. She spent hours fantasizing about how great life would be without him. With almost anyone else.

There are marriages that are just not going to work no matter how hard one or both partners try, but I did not feel that Trudy's was doomed. Not unless she let herself be carried away by her fantasies. She had come this far in marriage. If she cared enough, I was sure she could cure the Seven-Year Itch, banish boredom and revitalize her marriage. It takes work, but work is the key to long-lasting marriages. When you think that a lifetime marriage today does not simply mean reaching your golden wedding anniversary together but most likely your diamond jubilee, you realize that life just has to be a never-ending series of adjustments.

The strength of marriage is that it does change. You grow. He grows. You develop new interests. You adjust to each other's new needs. And in the course of doing this, you weave a wonderfully rich fabric of love and understanding and companionship. Of crises conquered. Of sorrows and triumphs shared. This fabric is marriage. The longer you live together, the richer the marriage. But it does not come easy. It takes work, commitment, imagination and love.

THE WIDOW GAME

I wanted Trudy to understand this. I wanted to help her recognize how important Loren actually was to her. She had realized she did not know him as well as she had thought. The next step was to help her understand he meant more to her than she thought.

"Trudy, I want you to play a game. It is like Patience. Only one person can play. It takes a week and it is rather gruesome, but I think you will learn something about yourself that will surprise you."

"Okay," she agreed. "As long as you're not going to ask me to pretend that Loren is not a bore."

"No, no, this is quite different. You are to pretend that your husband is dead. As of this minute you are a widow. And you are going to be a widow for a full week.

"When you wake up tomorrow morning, pretend that he is not lying there beside you. You have no one to talk to. You drink your coffee alone. In the course of the day, you are to do all the things you usually depend on him to do. Take out the garbage. Put up a curtain rod. Call the garage to complain about the bill for tuning up the car. Bring in the logs for the fireplace. Stop by the liquor store on your way home from work. Whatever.

"If it is something that is not really practical for you to do, then imagine that you have to do it yourself or have to find someone to do it for you. As nearly as you can, lead the life you would lead if he were not there. But for heaven's sake, don't let Loren know what you are doing or thinking. He won't appreciate it.

"Pretend he is not coming home tonight. Or any other night. That you are cooking supper just for yourself and eating it alone. If you go out to a restaurant, imagine how you would feel if you were there by yourself. If friends ask you to dinner, ask yourself if they would have invited you without Loren.

"If he does not feel like having sex one night, imagine what it would be like not to have sex with him ever again. If you wake up in the middle of the night and feel comforted just to have him there beside you, think how you will feel all those nights when you wake up in the wee hours and there is no one there.

"If he pays you a compliment or thanks you for something or gives you a present, think how it is going to be without his thoughtfulness and appreciation the rest of your life. If he tells you something interesting that went on at work or a joke that he heard, think how it is going to be without his sharing his life with you.

"Don't cheat by telling yourself that if he were not in your life, there would be someone else, someone more stimulating, more attractive, someone sexier. Chances are that there will not be. Remember that without him, you join the ranks of those 7.3 million leftover women. If you should manage to find another man, you cannot be sure that he will be a better husband. Don't forget that you will eventually face another Seven-Year-Itch stage. It could be even worse than this.

"Once the week is over," I concluded, "let yourself rejoice that you are not a widow, that he is still there beside you sharing your life. Be grateful for all those things you don't have to do by yourself. And show your gratitude. You will see him through rosier spectacles."

Any woman who, like Trudy, feels that she could do better with someone else or simply without her husband, should make herself go through the Widow Game for a week. It is a very useful psychological exercise. It will not make waves and it should help you think much more clearly about your life and marriage. It helped Trudy change her attitude.

She called me when the week was over. "You were right," she said. "Living without Loren would be terrible. I kept crying at the idea that I would never see him again. He brought me coffee in bed Sunday morning, the way he always does, and I burst into tears. I was thinking that no one would ever love me enough to bring me coffee in bed again. Loren couldn't figure out what hit me. I was sniffling and telling him I was crying because I was so happy. That really baffled him. I wanted to tell him about the Widow Game, but I knew it would be a mistake. I could just imagine how it would make him feel."

"How do *you* feel?" I asked.

"The way you thought I would," she said. "I'm ready to work on our problems, but I don't know where to start. Or how."

Trudy had already started. She had changed the way she regarded her husband. She no longer thought she would be better off without him. And that was an enormous step forward. A lot of success in marriage depends upon your ability to see your husband through rose-colored spectacles. To feel, as Trudy had started to, that no one else could love her as much as Loren did. There is a certain amount of self-delusion in every happy marriage. It is the sweet deception of love and we should be grateful for it.

TWENTY-SIX

*How to use your memories to get close again . . . The
Ripple Effect . . . Adopting a critical approach . . . How a
New You pays dividends . . . Why you should start a
challenge list . . . How to take the ho-hum out of sex*

How do you go about eradicating the boredom that is causing
your Seven-Year Itch? The answer is slowly. The boredom
was not created overnight and the cure is not instant. You
have to adjust to the changes in yourself and your husband.
Many women tend to take a hopeless attitude when it comes
to change. "He'll never change," they say despondently. But
he will. He cannot help but do so. And neither can you. We
are in a perpetual state of change. There is not one cell in your
body today that was there seven years ago. What you have to
do is to adapt to the changes that have taken place and arrange
for more of them.

The first step is the hardest—accepting the need to change,
realizing, as Trudy did, that if your marriage is to last, you
have to change. You have to be the one who initiates it. I told
you at the very beginning of this book that woman have to
work harder at marriage because we have a bigger stake in it.

You have faced the problem—boredom. You understand
that stimulation is a basic human need. And now you are going

to provide that stimulation. How do you start?

Trudy and Loren started by looking backward.

"We don't talk to each other anymore," Trudy said. "We exchange service messages—'*I have to work late tonight,*'...'*Don't forget that your folks are coming over Sunday,*'...'*Harvey and Adele want us to come to dinner Friday*'— that kind of thing. But we never really talk and sex is purely mechanical. It's one-two-three and goodnight. I don't even start to get interested."

THE REMINISCENCE APPROACH

"Do you have snapshots of your honeymoon or vacation trips?" I asked.

Trudy was surprised. "Snapshots? Well, yes. We have whole albums full. We used to be really interested in photography. We spent a lot of money on lenses and stuff. I don't know why we stopped. We have hundreds of photographs of our honeymoon. Everything from our hotel room to me falling off a surfboard. My favorite is one I took of him brushing his teeth. Loren photographed the first meal I cooked in our apartment. I'd set the table with our wedding-present china and silver. He spent so much time shooting it that everything got cold. We used to have a lot of fun taking pictures."

"It might be a good idea," I said, "to get out those photograph albums and start looking through them tonight. Share your memories with Loren. Ask him 'Remember what happened the day you took this picture?' That kind of thing."

"What good is that going to do?" she asked.

"It may not do any good," I told her, "but it can't hurt. I think it may stir up pleasant memories. Remind the two of you of how much fun you used to have together. It might reawaken some of the romantic feelings you used to have for each other."

What I really expected would happen is that looking at their old photographs would help reopen communication between them, get them talking together. There is no pressure involved in looking back over good times. Reminiscing can be sweet.

And, as it turned out, it was. When Loren got home that evening, Trudy was sitting on the sofa, her shoes off, surrounded by their photograph albums. "Look," she said as he walked in. "Do you remember this?" It was a picture of him coming back from an all-day fishing trip with his catch—a deflated beach ball.

He laughed. "Yeah. And I remember the sunburn I picked up that day." He sat beside her and started flipping the pages of the album. An hour later, Trudy said, "You must be starving. I'll start supper."

"Oh, don't cook," he said. "This is fun. Why don't you call up and order a pizza." While she telephoned, he poured a couple of glasses of wine and they went back to reliving the early days of their marriage with the memories evoked by the photographs.

It was midnight when they closed the last album and smiled at each other. "We've come a long way," Loren said. "We were such kids seven years ago."

"Remember how we used to stay up until all hours," Trudy said. "Just talking, talking, talking."

"Like tonight," he said. He yawned. "I better get to bed if I'm going to function tomorrow." He hesitated a moment and then he said, "Maybe tomorrow night we can go to bed a little earlier." He held her face between his hands and looked at her. "You know I really do love you. A lot. How would you feel about sending out for another pizza tomorrow night? And eating it in bed?"

Trudy and Loren did not have a serious problem, even though Trudy had been ready to take a lover. It turned out to be easy for them to recapture the loving feelings they used to have. It would be a mistake to believe that their marriage was all moonlight and roses from that time on. It was not. But they managed to get in touch with each other—emotionally and sexually. They made an important change. They had spent one evening happily talking about the past and looking forward to the future. A big change from the uncommunicative evenings that had characterized their relationship in recent months.

This reminiscence approach is one that every woman can use as a means of restoring communication and a degree of empathy to a marriage. If you do not have a family album or snapshots to get you started down memory lane, there are other variations. Perhaps you had a favorite song when you were courting. You might find a recording of it and play it some evening, saying that it had been going through your head and made you feel sentimental. You can remind him of times when you listened to it or danced to it together.

You can simply say during supper some night, "Do you remember the time we did such and so? I don't know why, but it just popped into my head today. We really had a good time, didn't we?"

Courtship reminiscences seem to be most effective in triggering a response. If, when you talk about your courtship days, it seems impossible to strike even a spark of sentiment or tenderness, you can be fairly sure that your relationship is in a critical state. This is usually an indication that it is too late for self-help and that you should seek professional counseling. But don't go looking for a therapist on the basis of one night. He may have been tired or in a bad mood. Or he may be the kind of man whose reactions are a little delayed. The next time you remind him of something that happened on your honeymoon, he may come up with a memory of his own. With most couples, courtship reminiscences trigger romantic memories and help them see each other as lovingly as they used to—even if only briefly. That brief moment can be significant. It represents a change, a change that can trigger a host of other changes.

THE RIPPLE EFFECT

One change inevitably provokes another. In psychology we call this the Ripple Effect, a very graphic and appropriate term for the dynamics of change.

If you drop a pebble in a puddle of rainwater or in a pond, a series of ripples spreads out from the spot where the pebble hit. One after another after another. In the same way, if you change one element in a relationship, just one habit or attitude, this will trigger other changes in the relationship.

If mutual boredom has become a fact of marital life, the wise wife will make several small changes on her own without mentioning them to her husband. The first change I recommend is to become much more critical.

When I told Trudy that I wanted her to work at developing her critical faculties, she asked, "For heaven's sake, why? It's all I can do to stop criticizing Loren. My critical faculties are very highly developed."

"The point of this exercise is to make you less critical of Loren," I told her. "Instead of concentrating on Loren's shortcomings, I want you to be more aware of how other people measure up to your standards. And not only people, everything in your environment. I want you to start making value judgments about everything you see."

This is an exercise I recommend for every woman. Not because you may find your husband boring. You may not. But because it will heighten your appreciation of life. Make a conscious effort to expand your critical horizons. Start by using your critical judgment on every movie you see, every television program, every book or article you read. What did you really think of it? And why? How would you have changed it?

When you visit a friend's house, criticize her furniture and her decorating scheme (silently, of course). How would you change it? What do you particularly like in her house? How would you perhaps adapt it to your own home? When you go out to dinner, whether to a restaurant or to your best friend's house, criticize the meal. Be a bit of a gourmet. First of all, what do you think of the table setting? Do you approve of the china? The silver? And then the food. What about the salad? Did you like the dressing? And the main course. Was it overdone? Underdone? Could the seasoning have been improved? Rate every dish by your perfectionist standards.

And while you are doing this, observe how other husbands and wives relate to each other. What you see is not necessarily what goes on when they are alone. We all tend to put our best foot forward in public. But look at Stacey's husband, at Gail's new boyfriend. Do you think the couples are well suited?

As you do this, you will find that you have truly developed your critical faculties. You may raise or change your standards of what is good and what is acceptable. You will also find that you have helped your marriage, because as you criticize— favorably and unfavorably—the world around you, you are going to find that you are no longer as critical of your husband as you used to be. You can rate him more accurately now against other husbands. You may decide that you have a treasure, for as you take your critical look at the world, you no longer hold your husband up to perfectionist standards. You have learned to realize the limits of possibility.

A New You

While you are improving your critical judgment, you might also work to improve your appearance. Take a look at yourself. What about a new hair style? A different makeup? What about losing five or ten or fifteen pounds?

Take a look at your clothes closet. Are there things that you never wear? Do you have outfits that make you feel dowdy or fat or washed out? Get rid of them. Even if they are "too good to throw away." Give them to the hospital thrift shop or some other charitable organization that will allow you a tax deduction for your donation. Then gradually rebuild your wardrobe so that you feel good in everything you own.

Now let me tell you a secret. Your husband may not even notice that you've lost ten pounds or changed your hair. Your friends may marvel. Your coworkers may compliment you. Your husband probably won't say a word. This is because most men see their wives the way they were when they first met them, even if it was twenty years ago. That early you is the picture he has in his mind's eye. And we women should thank our lucky stars for this male idiosyncrasy.

So why go to all the bother? For your own sake. The better you look, the better you dress, the better you feel about yourself. And this makes real ripples. You stand up straighter. You have a little more sparkle about you. And a lot more assurance. And whether your husband recognizes the changes or not, it is going to affect the way he feels about you. You are going to seem more exciting to him, even if he can't seem to put his finger on the difference.

The changes you make in yourself are going to start changes in him too. You are going to feel more interest. More response. Little by little you will develop more respect for each other.

Incidentally, clinical studies have documented men's obliviousness to their wife's new makeup or even her hair color, but it is a bit of shock when you experience it for yourself. At one time I lost twenty pounds because I thought I was getting too pudgy for television. It wasn't easy, but the rewards were enormous. I felt better. I looked better. I was proud of my body again. I held my head higher and I felt a lot sexier. I experimented with a different look—very high-heeled shoes. Softer fabrics. Brighter colors. Clinging dresses rather than suits. I was really pleased with the way I looked. But my husband never said a word.

Then one day, a friend of Milt's said, "Joyce is really looking smashing these days. What is she up to?" And that made him take a real look at me. He was pleased. I could tell. He had the same smug look he used to have when he was a struggling medical student and people used to ask him what a pretty girl like me saw in him. All the same, it took a friend's remark to make him notice the exterior changes.

CREATING A CHALLENGE

Now it is time to toss another pebble or two into your domestic puddle and watch the ripples. You have to introduce some challenges into your marriage. The human animal becomes bored in the absence of a challenge. It is solving the problems that is fun. Once a problem is solved, we lose interest in it.

If you do not provide your husband with challenges, he may look for them elsewhere. Perhaps he will see if he can get that cute redhead to go to a motel with him. Or at least join him for a drink after work. Some men may turn to cocaine or another mood alterer for their challenges. It is up to you to put your imagination to work and find things you can do together that provide a challenge.

I have done this all my married life. When I convinced Milt we should buy our farm, it was an enormous challenge for the two of us. A big learning process. The first time we planted a garden, for instance, we took a stick and marked it at four-inch intervals. Then we laid it down on the ground and planted a seed at every four inches. When we got to the farm each weekend, we would take that stick, lay it on the ground again and weed everything that was not at a four-inch mark. When one of our neighbors discovered what we were doing, he laughed so hard Milt began to get worried. But we were city kids and knew nothing about gardens. We had to learn from scratch.

Later we decided to tap our own maple trees for syrup. This involved doing a lot of reading, asking questions at the county agricultural extension center and an awful lot of work. But I've rarely seen my husband as proud as when we have weekend guests and he lets them know that he boiled down the maple syrup, the syrup from our trees, that they are pouring on their pancakes.

A couple of years ago I bought an abandoned gold mine in Colorado. Not for the gold—there doesn't seem to be any—but for the view. It is breathtaking. It overlooks the Continental Divide. Milt thought I was insane when I said we should buy it. But I coaxed him to go see it. We went with Lisa and her husband. And we all had the best time. Milt fell in love with the place. Now he's busy studying gold-mining procedures and learning how to test for gold and all that sort of thing. He can't wait for summer so he can put his new learning to work. He's sure there's still gold to be mined. I'm not so sure. But we're both looking forward to finding out.

It's not just big things that provide challenges. Recently I bought a little pasta machine and we have a wonderful time making our own pasta. We went through a lot of yelling at each other at first, because we made the dough too wet or too dry. But eventually we got it down pat and now pasta of one kind or another is our favorite Sunday-night supper. Milt is not particularly interested in cooking, but it was the idea that you could make your own pasta that got him. And he enjoys playing with the machine.

We have always had a lot of fun together. We have a great number of things that we like to do together, that we laugh about together. He paid me the compliment I treasure most one night when I got home from a three-day trip. "It's more fun when you're home," Milt said as we were getting ready for bed. "Life is more interesting."

I have always tried to make it that way. I work at it. I plan ahead just the way I do for my television appearances. For television, I always have a whole list of topics prepared in advance so that I am never at a loss for something new and interesting to talk about. It is the same at home. I keep a list of things that I think will be fun for us to do.

I may read about some new gadget in the paper. Or I hear about something interesting someone else has done. One of the editors at *Good Housekeeping* told me that she and her husband had just built a tiny sailboat from a kit. This interested me, because I thought it was something Milt and I might build for our grandson. When he comes to visit us, he could learn to sail on our little pond. I just always keep my eyes and ears and mind open for things that will be fun for us.

Everyone has different interests and different budgets, but no matter what, there are challenges available. You can fix up your house. Refinish your old furniture. Learn how to wallpaper a bedroom. Make a playroom in the basement for the children. Join a square dance group. Get some language cassettes and learn French or Chinese or Hindustani together in preparation for a trip you hope to make some year. Buy a dog.

Pets open up a whole new world. There are obedience classes. Dog shows. Cat shows.

Often I have to talk Milt into getting started. The first time I coaxed him into doing something was just before we were married. We had decided we wanted a big wedding. We planned it all very carefully, but it was not until we were getting prices from various bands to play for the dancing at the reception that it dawned on us that we did not know how to dance. We had always both studied very hard, so we missed out on high school dances and that sort of occasion where youngsters teach each other how to dance.

I decided we should go to Arthur Murray's dance studio. He was offering a special rate for three lessons. Milt said he'd feel stupid, but I persisted. "Just three," I coaxed, "so we won't feel embarrassed at our own wedding." Well, we took the three lessons. And when it came time to step out on the dance floor at our wedding, we were very proud of ourselves. The steps we learned have stayed with us. We dance about every five years—the same steps we learned thirty-five years ago—but we enjoy it. The few dollars we spent on those three lessons have paid great dividends.

TAKING THE HO-HUM OUT OF SEX

The Ripple Effect works with sex too. You cannot separate emotional and sexual changes. They are too closely linked. The best sex comes when two people are emotionally and mentally stimulated by each other.

Changes in your sexual life must be as gradual as the changes that allow you to communicate more easily. And again you have to be the one to initiate them. If lovemaking has become ho-hum, it is partly because your mutual boredom prohibits sexual enjoyment and partly because you have become erotically desensitized. The caresses and positions that used to drive you crazy now leave you cold. It is up to you to let your husband know what you want now and what is good for you.

You may have become so disenchanted with sex that you

are out of touch with your body and don't really know what you want. It is easy enough to get into a body-aware state. A woman can almost always masturbate to a very satisfying orgasm. And this is the way to get clued in to your body's needs.

While you masturbate, be aware of your fantasies and your cravings. Do you pretend someone is doing this or that? Do you long for a certain touch? What would make your pleasure even keener? You will know.

Next time you make love, ask for one of the touches or strokes or rubbing that you wanted when you masturbated. Please, no more than one. You don't want him to feel pressured. On the other hand, if he shows that he loves your demands, go ahead. Ask for the moon. You may not just create ripples but waves.

We fall into bad sexual habits over the years. This is the time to change all that. Most couples tend to cut down on the time they devote to sex as the years go by. Oh, they may still make love three times a week, but it may only take six minutes a time. "Civilized sex requires time," says Dr. William Appleton, a psychiatrist at the Harvard Medical School, "as does haute cuisine and beautiful architecture. The work of the craftsman is loving and slow." A good lover, he says, is not judged by the number of partners he or she has had or the number of times orgasm is reached in an evening but by the care the lover takes with his or her partner.

This is the time to rethink your sexual habits. Do you spend enough time on sex? Do you devote prime time to sex? Too many couples postpone sex until bedtime. This is perfectly ridiculous. It puts it in the same category as brushing your teeth and taking off your eye makeup. Unless you have children, you might think of having sex before supper once or twice a week. If you have children, I suggest going to bed half an hour or so after they've gone to sleep.

Make these special nights. Clean sheets on the bed. Soft music. Candlelight. A glass of wine. (A locked door if you have children.) Then slowly, slowly enjoy making love. Play

a little. Talk a little. Have fun. Postpone the moment of penetration. Tantalize. Tease. Flirt. You are adults at play and
your bed is your playpen.

When the fireworks are over and you are lazy and relaxed,
don't fall asleep. Snuggle. Talk. Have something to eat. I love
ice cream on these occasions. Enjoy your closeness. You may
want to make love again before you go to sleep.

Some people recoil at the idea of setting aside a night or
two a week for leisurely sex. "There's no spontaneity in that,"
they object. "How do we know we'll feel like sex on a Tues-
day?"

This is not a valid objection. When you were courting and
had a date for Friday night, you looked forward to Friday.
You could hardly wait to go to bed together. Knowing that
sex was going to be part of your Friday night date made it
even more exciting. It can be the same in marriage.

Looking forward to sex is titillating. Whisper in his ear
when you kiss him goodbye in the morning that tonight is the
night. Flirt with him during supper, even though you have to
mop up your three-year-old's spilled milk and listen to your
five-year-old tell about what happened in kindergarten that
morning. You can still look and touch and let him know you're
thinking of what's ahead.

Be a little outrageous once in a while. Surprise him. If you
both work, why not telephone him some day when you know
he doesn't have a lunch date and tell him you have reserved
a hotel room and you have a picnic basket. Then enjoy love
at noon. If you are a stay-home wife with children, get a baby
sitter some night and whisk your husband off to a good meal
and a hotel room. So you'll have to leave at midnight to take
the sitter home. But he will love it.

Getting away from home every once in a while is important.
Just the two of you. Don't forget your MOMO account. You
might want to splurge on a weekend in Las Vegas or New
York or San Francisco. Someplace new and different where
you can have a good time together and no responsibilities.
Where you can make love before breakfast and after lunch.

Whenever you want. You will find that it does wonders for your spirits, your skin and your marriage.

Sex, after all, makes the marriage wheels go round. "People with a satisfying sexual relationship tend to overlook a lot of other dissatisfactions," states Dr. Arthur P. Bochner of Temple University, who has made a study of communications between husbands and wives. "Good sex may make them enjoy the rest of the relationship more. Women have the power to influence many areas of a relationship by enhancing the sexual part."

One more thing. Don't expect perfection. Aim for it. But it is not within human grasp. You have worked at banishing boredom. You have worked at making your sex life more erotically satisfying. And you have succeeded. But sometimes—sometimes you feel as if you're falling back into the old ways. You just don't feel like it. No matter what, you are simply not in the mood. Or he isn't. You are grumpy with each other. Even distant.

Where did you go wrong? You didn't.

Is the boredom going to come flooding back? Possibly, but not for long.

You are a human being, not a machine. Sometimes you long for sex. Sometimes you'd rather go to sleep. Sometimes you find your husband fascinating. Sometimes you wish he'd go for a long walk. Alone. Don't worry about it. "Like other powerful feelings, aphrodisia—the union of intense desire and excitement—comes to us in cycles," explains psychiatrist Avodah Offit. On the occasion when desire flags, don't panic. And don't decide the only way to recapture sexual excitement is to have an affair. It might work—for a time—but it is not the way to build a marriage that will last a lifetime.

Instead, concentrate on meeting your stimulation needs within marriage. What you are getting is an early warning signal that one area or another of your marriage is becoming desensitized. It is your cue to introduce more change and see that your stimulation needs are met. And his too.

TWENTY-SEVEN

What women ask me about infidelity... Why your
husband may not forgive your infidelity... Why a man's
affair may not affect his marriage... What to do if you
discover your husband is unfaithful... The one proof you
should demand from your husband... Why second
marriages are shaky... The best way to
keep a man faithful to you

Today, perhaps more than at any time in the past quarter century, women crave the emotional security of a stable marriage. I see this reflected in my lecture requests. Ten years ago, the topic most female audiences wanted me to talk about was "So His Business Is His Mistress." So many women are in the labor force now that most of them understand the seduction of a career only too well. What women want to hear about today is "How to Make Love Last a Lifetime." And in the question period that follows the lecture, they ask about infidelity.

Theirs are not idle questions. In an era when from 25 to 40 percent of married women and 50 to 66 percent of married men (depending on whose surveys you believe) have been unfaithful at least once, there is no escaping the fact that at least one partner in every other marriage is unfaithful. Add to this the fact that from 78 to 87 percent of divorces are triggered by infidelity. No wonder women want to know more.

IS INFIDELITY EVER JUSTIFIED?

Someone always asks this question and my answer is a flat no. This usually provokes a challenge along the lines of, "But, Dr. Brothers, I read your book* where you said a wife's affair would do wonders for a marriage. How can you say that an affair is never justified?"

I did say something along those lines. In 1975 I wrote, "Five years ago I would not have believed that I would ever consider that there could be any justification in the whole wide world for a woman to have an affair. Yet times have changed. And so have I. Where once I would have considered it immoral, unwise and dangerous, I now tend to question these rigid judgments."

I went on to say that in certain cases under certain circumstances, a short-term affair mght perk up the marriage of a woman over forty. I based this on the three effects a love affair produces in most women. The heightened sexuality a woman radiates when she is involved in an affair. The ego-bolstering effect of knowing that someone considers her exciting and desirable. And the guilt an affair engenders. The first two changes, I wrote, will affect her husband's response to her even though he may not be consciously aware of the changes. He will find her more exciting. And the guilt will make it difficult, after she has been with her lover all afternoon, to tell her husband she is not in the mood. Her ready acceptance will delight her husband and often inspire him to superior efforts.

Now I have reversed my position. The times have changed again. What worked in the early and mid-1970s for a handful of women is too dangerous for the woman today who wants a lifetime marriage. It is a case of the cure being more harmful than the disease.

In a time when 7.3 million women will never have a man of their own, the competition is too keen for a woman to risk an affair. And an affair is definitely no palliative for the Seven-

* *Better Than Ever.*

Year-Itch. It is more likely to be a greased slide right into the
divorce court.

Both husband and wife are going to be tempted during the
course of a marriage. It would be strange if they were not,
especially during the Seven-Year-Itch stage when boredom
breeds dissatisfaction. "To expect you and your husband to
have eyes only for each other all through life is to invest marriage with a large element of fantasy," says Dr. Laura J. Singer,
past president of the American Association for Marriage and
Family Therapy.

Being tempted is one thing. Succumbing to temptation is
another. The woman who wants a lifetime marriage should
remain faithful. The odds are against the woman who fools
around. If you need a challenge, give yourself the challenge
of making your marriage more exciting. It is easier to find
short-term excitement in an affair, but it is more rewarding
to create it in marriage.

SHOULD YOU TELL YOUR HUSBAND ABOUT YOUR AFFAIR?

This is another question that many women ask. The answer
is absolutely not. I cannot understand why a woman would
want to do this in the first place. Some women seem to feel
that confession is good for the soul and that it absolves them
of guilt. They say, "Darling, I had an affair and I'm sorry and
I'll never do it again." So what? All they have done is get their
husband upset. If you are ever tempted to be so inconsiderate,
think of how you would feel if your husband were to tell you
the same thing.

There is another, even stronger reason, for keeping your
mouth shut. And that is because men react much more violently to a wife's infidelity than women do to a husband's.

Anthropologists believe this may be a throwback to prehistoric times when a man had all he could do to protect and feed
his wife and offspring. Life was hard—and very short. If his
wife was unfaithful and presented him with a bastard who he

thought was his own child, the husband was at a genetic disadvantage. He might die or be killed before he had a child by his wife, which meant that he would have spent his short adult life caring for another man's child, ensuring that another man's genes would be passed on to future generations. Therefore the male went to great lengths to stop other men from mating with his wife.

Anthropologists believe this primitive fear of raising a bastard still lurks in some ancient part of the male brain. It is certainly true that men react to infidelity with an anger and outrage that is much more pronounced than a woman's.

"A woman will live with her husband's infidelity, even forgive it in time, but men have much greater trouble," says Dr. Selma Miller of the American Association of Marriage and Family Therapy. "Their egos are terribly, terribly damaged. They are not easily reconciled."

WHEN YOU LEARN THAT YOUR HUSBAND IS HAVING AN AFFAIR

"We have been married for seven years and my husband, I found out, is having an affair. I refuse to do anything about it because I do not want to risk losing him. My sister says I am wrong. Is she right?"

This is just one of hundreds of letters I received last year asking what to do when you discover that your husband is playing around. I had to tell this woman that she was the only person who could decide what was the right thing to do. Without knowing more about an individual situation, it would be improper and possibly harmful to give specific advice, but in general, as I told her, it is usually healthier to bring the problem out into the open than refuse to face it. I think that in most cases a woman should tell her husband that she knows he is having an affair.

If he admits it, what then?

It depends. On him. On you. On what you want. I am assuming that you want to preserve your marriage if at all possible. If so, the wisest thing to do may be to do absolutely nothing.

Even if you had known what the answer was going to be, you are shocked and hurt. Angry. Disoriented. You feel betrayed. Give yourself a chance to regain control. Tell your husband that you are too upset to talk at the moment and that you will discuss it with him the next day. Or the day after that.

Then spend that time trying to sort things out. Think about yourself. What does this really mean to you? Do you love him enough to forgive and forget? Does your marriage mean enough to you to work at making changes in it and in yourself if necessary?

And then think about him. Why did he get involved in this affair? Why was he vulnerable? What does it mean to him? What does he expect to happen now that you know? Does he want you to forgive and forget? Or is this something more serious than a short-term fling?

You will not know the answers to these questions at the moment, but you know your husband, and if you think back over the past weeks and months, you may have some insights you did not have before. These are the questions you need answered. And when you have the answers, you can think about your next step.

If he tells you that it was a one-night stand and meant nothing to him, you might simply say, "Well, don't have any more." Face the fact that it is not the end of the world. Try to understand the circumstances, but don't pry. Don't ask for details. If he was out of town on a business trip and picked her up at the hotel bar, that's all you need to know. Well, that is not quite correct. There is one other important thing you need to know before reestablishing marital relations, and I'll get to that in a moment.

What if he says that the affair has been going on for a couple of months, but means nothing? What if he promises to put an end to it? I would take him at his word. I would tell him something like, "All right, I will believe you that it means nothing to you. But you must promise me not to see her again. You have to understand that it means something to me. It hurts me. I feel betrayed. Don't ever do this to me again."

And then pick up your life and work at forgiving and forgetting. Forgiving is hard. Forgetting is next to impossible. But you will be surprised at your ability to put the incident behind you.

If your husband is really sorry, he will understand your hurt and sense of betrayal and make an effort to reassure you. He will understand that you are going to wonder about every night he works late and every overnight business trip he has to take. The two of you should work out ways of reassuring you without his feeling that you are checking up on him every minute.

If he has to work late, it might be a good idea, for instance, to have dinner together downtown and then you go to a movie while he works. If he has to go out of town on business, it would be a good idea for him to take you with him.

He must understand that it is up to him to convince you of his fidelity. It will be months before his affair stops gnawing at you, but you can't let it distort your life. You have to trust him. You can't turn into a jealous wife, forever questioning his every move.

You also have to work on restoring your own self-esteem. People tend to say things like, "Matt would never have strayed if there wasn't something wrong at home." This is hurtful nonsense. Studies have revealed that most unfaithful husbands rate their marriages as good. Or even very good. Your husband's little fling does not necessarily mean that he no longer loves you. He probably loves you as much as ever and is stomach-churningly dismayed at the marital crisis he has created.

Most men get involved in affairs, according to Dr. Alan Loy McGinnis, author of *The Romance Factor*, out of "boredom. No long-standing relationship can compete in excitement with a brand new affair with an attractive interesting person."

At the beginning of an affair, a man feels wonderful. He basks in the admiration of a woman who thinks he is terrific.

Sex has regained its old heart-banging excitement for him. And reality is far away. When he is with his lover, he does not have to worry about the bill for Jenny's allergy shots, the torn screen on the back door, the state of the septic tank or whatever. He is in a fantasy world. He is a little boy with a delicious secret.

This does not last long. The euphoria fades fast. In an affair, a couple has to sneak around. He can't take her out to dinner or the movies or even go for a walk with her. The only place where they are safe is the motel room.

In a motel, there is nothing to do after the main act. At the beginning, this does not matter. They tell each other how great it was. They make love again. But by the third or fourth time, there is a sense of emptiness. Perhaps they have another drink. Or he turns on the television. Finally with some relief, he says he has to get back to the office or that his wife will raise the roof if he isn't home by six-thirty.

As time passes, he becomes more and more anxious to leave right after sex. There is nothing but sex to hold them together. And it is not enough. The end of the affair is in sight. And this little adventure has not changed his feelings toward you or his marriage.

Think back to that romantic escapade my friend the diplomat had (Chapter 25). It lasted three months and he was in despair at the idea of having to leave Annette. But he had had the best of all illicit romances. He was in a foreign country, a strange city. He could take Annette out to dinner or go walking in the park with her without fear of seeing friends or neighbors. Still, once Emile was back home with his wife, he was snugly happy and, as he admitted, he very seldom thought of Annette.

If you understand this male approach to an affair, it is easier to forgive and forget, but before you forgive and forget, there is one demand you can—and should—make. And that is that your husband present you with a clean bill of health from the doctor.

This is sheer self-protection. The latest figures I have show that 14 million people contract a sexually transmitted disease every year. A sexually promiscuous man is hazardous to his wife's health. A study done at Oxford University in England shows that the risk of cervical cancer for a woman is 7.8 times higher if her husband is promiscuous.

Dr. Martin Vesey, an English researcher who was involved in the study, says, "It seems the husband actually picks up something that increases the wife's risk of cancer. No one knows what it might be, but it's most likely a virus such as the one that causes genital herpes.... The woman who has had only one sexual partner—her husband—could have a possible cancer-causing agent, which he acquired from another woman, transmitted to her."

Herpes is another one of the risks. One sexually active adult out of five gets herpes today. There are half a million new cases every year. Women who get herpes are ten times more likely to have cervical cancer than those who don't.

It is not only herpes that you may be given as a souvenir of your husband's affair. There are the old familiars—gonorrhea, syphilis, trichomoniasis, and so on. What you should understand is that women suffer more seriously than men from venereal diseases because the symptoms are often nonexistent or so slight at the beginning that they are ignored until the disease has a firm hold on a woman's body and is more difficult—or impossible—to cure.

If your husband is honestly contrite and sincere in wanting to be welcomed back into your heart and your bed, he should not get up on his hind legs and go into an indignation act when you request he give you a clean bill of health. It is as much for his own good health as yours.

WHEN HE CLAIMS IT IS A LOVE AFFAIR

What about the husband who says, "Yes, I have been having an affair. It has gone on for some time and I have been trying to get up my courage to talk to you about it. I am glad you forced my hand. I love her and want to marry her."

This is the hard one. You are faced with an intimate relationship that has existed for months and a man who wants a divorce. No matter how much you may want to preserve your marriage, it may be impossible. But you should try.

I suggest that you seek professional counseling as soon as possible. And that you ask your husband to go with you. Most marriage counselors prefer couple therapy, because if a marriage is to be saved, both partners must work at it.

Time may be your best ally. There are facts that your husband should know about second marriages. One is that second marriages break up more often than first marriages. The divorce rate is around 60 percent. And second marriages break up sooner.

A recent study of remarried couples pinpointed two severe stresses that seemed to precipitate divorce in a second marriage. Couples have a difficult time reaching the We Point because of conflicting expectations and life styles. Men and women do not approach a second marriage with the same idealism as their first. They are also more set in their ways. This makes it harder for them to adjust to each other. Their Make-or-Break stage frequently ends in Break.

Remarried couples also have the cast of their previous marriages to contend with. The former in-laws, the former spouses, the children do not disappear into thin air when one spouse remarries. They are part of his life forever. This gives rise to conflicting loyalties and places hard-to-handle stress on the marriage.

If your husband has time to consider what a divorce and remarriage will actually mean (and a therapist can help him understand the fragility of a second marriage), he may eventually decide it is better to repair what he has than to try to build a new relationship on a shaky foundation.

Is There Any Way to Ensure Your Husband's Fidelity?

This may be the question I am asked most often when I lecture on lasting love. It would be nice if there were a faithfulness vitamin we could give our husbands along with their morning fruit juice. But there isn't. If you follow the advice and suggestions in the previous chapters of this section, you will have gone a long way toward infidelity-proofing your husband, but you cannot count on 100 percent success. As a divorce lawyer told me, "You can have thirty years of monogamy, but there is no way of guaranteeing a thirty-first."

The best way to prevent infidelity is to make it unthinkable. You should make it clear how much faithfulness means to you. Heaven knows there are dozens of occasions in every woman's life when she can introduce the topic naturally. When the couple down the street puts their house on the market and announces they are divorcing. When your husband tells you he has seen a friend of his being very attentive to a woman who is not his wife. When your own beloved husband appears a little too bedazzled by another woman. In this latter case, don't play the jealous wife, but let him know you noticed his interest. Treat it lightly. He'll get the message.

When love is nurtured, when your husband knows he is the most important person in your world, when there is tenderness and openness in your relationship, when your sex life is not only passionate but playful and when you are each other's best friend, your husband will be so bound to you by love and comfort, delight and companionship and, yes, habit that it will be easy for him to resist temptation.

I wish I could promise you that if your marriage survives the Seven-Year-Itch stage, you will never have to worry about infidelity again. But I can't. It is a problem that may confront you at any future stage of your marriage. The divorce rate in the later years of marriage is increasing by leaps and bounds. I urge you to review the six chapters on the Seven-Year-Itch from time to time. They may just save your marriage.

PART EIGHT

THE DOLDRUMS

TWENTY-EIGHT

*The Doldrum years ... Blissful calms alternating with
squalls ... "Where is everybody?" ... A time of new
solutions for old problems ... Beware of
that comfortable familiarity*

I call the fourth vulnerable stage of marriage the Doldrums.
Webster's Third New International Dictionary defines the doldrums as "a region over the ocean near the equator abounding
in calms, squalls and light baffling winds." While the doldrums
are noted for their calms, they are also known as a place where
many hurricanes originate. There could hardly be a more apt
description of the period from the tenth to the twentieth year
of marriage.

So much is behind you. You survived the Make-or-Break
Years. You controlled the Baby Drift. You cured the Seven-
Year Itch. You deserve a period of happy calm. And this is
what you get most of the time in the Doldrums. It is the least
vulnerable of the five stages of marriage. There are long, lovely,
tranquil periods when your life is blissful.

Judith Viorst, the gifted writer on family and marriage,
published a little vignette of family life in *Redbook* magazine

a few years ago that captured the essence of the Doldrums stage.

"On a cold winter evening after ten years of marriage," one of her readers had written, "our three boys, two dogs, two cats and I were spread comfortably in the living room, watching television and awaiting my husband's arrival from work.

"I had left the group...for a moment when my husband entered. He surveyed the living room with its wall-to-wall kids and pets and noticed I was missing. His comment made me realize just how important I was to him....

"He said, 'Where is everybody?'"

Judith Viorst awarded this little story first prize in her Great Moments in Marriage Contest. And I agree it deserved it. The Doldrums are a time when everybody is happy and your husband thinks you are wonderful—most of the time.

The problems that do arise are usually light baffling winds or squalls rather than hurricanes. Most of them are easy enough to deal with. You have solved so many problems in your marriage by now that you have developed a constructive approach to new ones. Actually most of the problems are minor eruptions of old ones. Life changes, and the solution that worked two years ago may not work this year. You have to devise another. It is usually not difficult because you know each other so well.

The greatest danger of the Doldrums, however, is just that comfortable familiarity. In marriage, familiarity can breed carelessness. We go along as we have gone along for years. We think that life will always be this way. Then—bang! Something happens. We are confronted with one of those devastating hurricanes that breed in the Doldrums. All the rules of the game seem to have changed. Our lives are no longer characterized by happy contentment.

The commitment, love and trust that have been built up over the years of your marriage will usually help you navigate through your Doldrums hurricane. But you can't count on them. The sobering fact is that between 10 and 15 percent of divorces occur during the Doldrums. This reinforces the importance of continuing to work at marriage.

In the following chapters I discuss the most common squalls. These are usually the hurricane breeders. If you cope with them while they are in the squall stage, you may never have to live through a hurricane.

TWENTY-NINE

The Mule Syndrome . . . What's in it for him? . . . Family power versus financial power . . . Don't let yourself become smug about your marriage . . . Two rules for the Doldrums

There comes a time in many marriages when the husband feels that he is low man on the totem pole, a second-class citizen, a Mr. Nobody whose only role in life is to support the family.

I had been discussing this book with a friend of mine, a television producer in Los Angeles. I had remarked that women today could never feel relaxed in marriage because men were always scanning the horizon to see if there might be something better out there.

He had laughed rather bitterly. "Why don't you look at it from the man's point of view?" he asked. "I feel like I've got the Mule Syndrome."

This was a new one to me. "What do you mean?" I asked.

"My wife votes the kids' stock," he said. "Whenever there's a decision to be made, she makes it. Last night she told me that she couldn't go to San Francisco with me next week because our middle daughter is in the school play. I had been looking forward to the trip. I have to attend a couple of meetings, but most of the time I'll be free. I had thought we would go to a couple of good restaurants. Maybe drive down to Carmel or up to Sonoma. Gloria and I haven't had time by ourselves for years. And now she tells me she has to go to the school play."

"And that's the Mule Syndrome?" I asked.

"No, it's just a symptom. Here's what the Mule Syndrome is. I get up in the morning. I look in the mirror. I shave. I say to myself, 'I'm going to work. I'm going to pull that load all day long. I'm going to get a paycheck and I'm going to give it to Gloria. She is going to buy the kids all the things they need. She's going to buy whatever she needs for the house. She's going to pay the electric bill and the telephone bill and the mortgage.'

"And the next morning, I'm going to get up. I'm going to look in the mirror. I'm going to tell myself, 'I'm going to work. I'm going to pull that load.'

"But I've started thinking, 'Why am I doing this?' I'm not getting any gratitude from the kids. I'm not getting all that much attention from my wife. I'm not getting anything for myself. I'd like to have a suede jacket. I'd like to have a pair of those fancy leather boots. I'd like my wife to go to San Francisco with me.

"What I am is a mule," he said. "Pulling that load for the wife and the kids."

In a marriage, the one who has the final say on how money is spent is the boss. Traditionally it is the husband. But the husband's family power has always been limited, and this can weaken his financial power.

"The wife usually maintains considerable control. She is more deeply involved with interpersonal relationships in the family," explain psychiatrists David Keith and Carl Whitaker of the University of Wisconsin. "She appraises the family psychological condition and balances the emotional budget. The husband is outflanked emotionally."

This is a pattern in the first half of many marriages. The wife votes the children's stock, as my producer friend put it. She has the power because Mommy knows what's best. It's the three kids and Mommy against Daddy. But this state of affairs does not last. The time comes when the husband, like my friend, decides he wants something for himself. And, like a mule, he balks.

A recent study of two hundred married couples by researchers at Cleveland State University revealed that when wives were dominant, they usually were not really happy with their marriages. Nor were their husbands. When the situation was reversed and the husband was dominant, both spouses were happy.

So if the wife has taken over making the decisions about how to spend the husband's paycheck, there is great potential for trouble. But this was not the only hurricane breeder in my friend's marriage. He was not simply rebelling against being low man on the totem pole. The Baby Drift had resurfaced— or perhaps had simply gained momentum. So few women are aware of that very vulnerable stage of marriage that they do not take the necessary step to close the emotional split between husband and wife that starts when they become father and mother.

In this case, Gloria was putting her daughter ahead of her husband when she chose the school play over accompanying him to San Francisco. I know school plays are important. I hate to think of all the times I flew back to New York from Louisville or Muncie or Chicago to attend some school function—and two hours later flew right back to wherever I had been to finish my series of lectures or whatever.

But if it was a question of Milt wanting me to go with him to a medical convention and Lisa wanting me to go to a school play or a dance recital, I went to the medical convention every time. And Lisa survived. Not only survived but learned a valuable lesson that is helping her in her own marriage.

It is insensitive and unloving to put your daughter and a school play ahead of your husband and your marriage. And unwise. Gloria would have done well to consider that a man on his own in San Francisco may be exposed to all kinds of temptations. No woman should be so smug about her marriage that she fails to take preventive measures against infidelity. And surely a romantic weekend with your husband in San Francisco away from the children and household responsibilities is among the most delightful of preventive measures.

By the Doldrums stage, most women are halfway through the parenting years. This is a time to plan for the future. When the children leave home, there will be just the two of you. You want to be sure that you do not suddenly discover you are strangers at that time. There is a tendency for a woman to get so immersed in bringing up the children that she loses touch with her husband. He begins to feel he is a mule—working for nothing. He restructures his life. Since there is no appreciation or gratitude at home, he seeks his satisfactions elsewhere. The woman who wants her marriage to last will make a point of following two rules during the Doldrums. The first one—you have heard it before—applies to every stage of marriage.

1. Put your husband first.
2. Look to the future.

By looking to the future, I do not mean peering into a fortuneteller's crystal ball. I mean that you should share as many activities with your husband as you can. Otherwise you may find that you are sharing your bed with a stranger a few years from now when the children have left home. Too many women discover that all they have in common with their husband is the children—and the children aren't there anymore. This sets the scene for the Twenty-Year Ditch. And you don't want that to happen to you.

So stay in touch with your husband and keep adding to your challenge list so that you will never run out of interesting projects for the two of you. Even after thirty-five years of marriage, I keep adding to my list. I have a tattered little notebook in my handbag, and every time I hear of something that sounds interesting, I make a note of it. It takes seconds and it pays great dividends.

THIRTY

When the Doldrums wife becomes a career woman . . . Why your husband may not tell you the facts of business life . . . How your new self-assurance threatens your husband . . . The plus factors in a two-salary family . . . The companionship of two "working stiffs"

The Doldrums mark a turning point for many women. This is when they decide to enter or reenter the labor force. They want to get started on a career at last or pick up the threads of their old careers or simply find what a friend of mine calls a "job job," a paid position that broadens your horizons and makes life more interesting but does not demand the long hours and commitment of a career.

For most women, working is a positive step. Good for them and good for their marriage. But it is stressful, and until both you and your husband have adjusted to the changes your job triggers, your relationship can be stormy. So stormy that some marriages do not survive, but they are a small minority.

First of all there is the stress on you. It is hard to get a foothold in the business world. And once you have it, it is hard to hold onto it long enough to prove yourself. Many women have a hard time adjusting to the role change, from being Queen Bee of their household to being a trainee or an assistant's assistant. The thirty-seven-year-old tends to resent being told what to do by her twenty-four-year-old boss, especially if that boss is another woman. She argues that her way is better. She feels her ego is at stake.

Many women are surprised when they are not greeted with instant acceptance. "Mature women entering at the same level as college graduates may feel out of phase," says Cynthia Epstein, professor of sociology at the City University of New York. "While employers know how to treat junior recruits, they sometimes become confused when dealing with an older woman." And the young college graduates are often awkward in establishing a relationship with a woman some twenty years older than they who is on the same entry level and a competitor for promotion.

What does this have to do with your marriage? More than most wives—and husbands—realize at first. But think a minute. Who is it who gets to hear all your complaints, your criticisms of your coworkers and your boss, your insistence that the job could be done better if they would only listen to you? No matter how much your husband loves you, no matter how sympathetic and understanding he may be, chances are that he is on the other side of the fence. He has worked long enough to understand what a pest you may be making of yourself.

He can help you—if he dares. He can advise you that the way to get ahead is to be cooperative and not argumentative. He can warn you not to talk about what a hotshot you were as a trainee or researcher eighteen years ago. He can gently remind you that this is not the Do-Good Guild where effusive praise is the coin in which volunteers are paid. But he may not tell you these things. He may be afraid that he will hurt you with these blunt truths or even anger you. He is not quite sure he knows who you are any longer.

Your new life presents him with unexpected problems. While you are coping with the stress of your entry into the business world, he is coping with the reverberations of that stress in his domestic world. He is trying to adjust to what seems to him to be a new woman.

Just having paid employment makes a tremendous difference in a woman's self-esteem. According to one study, a woman's job is a more important factor in how well she thinks of herself than her education, her children or even her marriage.

Chester, an airline pilot, was really shaken when his wife went back to work after ten years out as a homemaker. "I didn't think anything was going to change," he said. "I had no idea how it would affect our marriage. I thought everything would be the way it always had been, except that we might be eating out more. I didn't anticipate that I would be having to adjust to her needs instead of her adjusting to mine." Most husbands tend to feel this way, like ostriches poking their heads in the sand, refusing to face reality. But reality forces itself on them.

Once the working wife feels in control of her job, she exudes a new assurance. She has a kind of polish and force that is new. She thinks of herself in a new way. "She is moving away from cleaning the toilet, scrubbing floors and doing the laundry," says Marjorie Shaevitz of the Institute for Family and Work Relationships in La Jolla, California. "She's moving toward a career— all the satisfactions and pleasures associated with having a career." She may still have to do the laundry and clean the toilet, but this is no longer part of her job description. And if she can afford to pay someone to do the unpleasant chores, she will.

This is disconcerting to her husband at the very least. In an article on how a wife's new career upsets the marriage balance in the Doldrum years, *The Wall Street Journal* reported that "men speak of a new-found sense of isolation: of an emotional separation from a preoccupied wife who now seems to be more involved with the world than with her husband, home and children." She takes her new responsibilities very seriously. She has new friends. New topics of conversation. She has a whole new nine-to-five life. No wonder her husband feels disoriented.

The Doldrums-stage husband is far more threatened by his wife's new job than the Make-or-Break husband. A major study, published in the *American Sociological Review* in 1982, established that having a working wife was associated with lowered self-esteem in men 30 years old and up but not among men in their twenties. There is nothing unsettling about a working wife for the younger man. What would be unsettling in today's economic climate would be if she did not work. But the man who is accustomed to his wife being at home finds her new job shakes the very foundations of his life.

"Husbands have been dependent on their wives—as listeners, consolers and ego builders—for their emotional sustenance," says social psychologist Zick Rubin, visiting research associate at the Wellesley College Center for Research on Women. "When the wife has a career of her own, however, the exchange is altered. She is less dependent on her husband for her self-esteem and she may also be less attentive to his needs and problems."

This is a new state of affairs in the history of marriage, and social scientists are just beginning to explore the effect of the housewife-turned-working-wife on the Doldrums-stage husband. "People talk about women's problems all the time," says Preston Munter, a psychiatric consultant to Itek Corporation, "but the adaptive stress men undergo when their wives take on a career has been virtually lost sight of."

"What we're seeing," says Elizabeth Douvan, director of the Family and Sex Roles Program at the University of Michigan, "is men expressing a lot more unhappiness and pain."

The life shock the Doldrums man experiences is exacerbated because he has no role models. His mother took care of the home, the children and her husband. So did his grandmother. And his great-grandmother. His colleagues' wives are homemakers and mothers. But his wife? She is something else. All of a sudden, his wife, who started out just like dear old Mom,

has become someone with a job of her own and a salary of her
own.

And there's the rub for many husbands. That salary of her
own. She is independent. What next?

What comes next can be wonderful. Your marriage can be
enriched tremendously. It can be more exciting and more comfortable at the same time. Your salary can be a more effective
anxiety dispeller than any drug. But it will take time for your
husband to adjust. And it will take great tact on your part as
well as megadoses of love and understanding.

Matthew, a friend of Milt's, who is in the textile business,
was deeply upset when his wife, an advertising copywriter,
went back to work when their youngest child was ten. She
had done some free-lance work during her years at home.
When she went back full-time, she was soon earning a very
substantial salary.

"I felt dispossessed," Matthew told my husband. "All these
years I'd been supporting the family, giving them everything
they needed. And more. Being happy to do it. Suddenly Cassie
was making enough money to support herself and the kids as
well as I could. I was desperately afraid that she might up and
leave me. I had no reason. It was just that I knew she didn't
need me.

"But after a while, I stopped being scared," he said. "Now
I know she really loves me and needs me. I'm not just a meal
ticket. She's making a bundle and I think that's great. I don't
have to worry anymore about what would happen to the kids
if anything happened to me. And it's certainly going to make
it easier when they go to college.

"The way I feel now is that we're really partners in every
way," he concluded happily.

And there was something else. Matthew did not tell Milt,
but Cassie told me. "Matthew feels very good about himself
these days," she confided. "He thinks he's pretty great stuff
if a woman who makes as much money as I do loves him. It
was kind of edgy between us for a while, but not any longer.

In fact, I think we're as happy as we've ever been."

One of my own friends summed up the marvelous companionship that can exist between a working wife and her working husband. She told me of one night last winter when the two of them were driving home from work, both dead tired after difficult days. Neither of them said a word. But when he had pulled into the driveway and turned off the ignition, her husband patted her knee and said, "I'm really glad to be married to another working stiff. Nobody else could understand the way I feel tonight."

(The Doldrums wife who has gone back to work may also find Chapters 17, 21, 23 and 24 helpful.)

THIRTY-ONE

If he wants sex more often than you do ... How to recharge your sexual batteries ... Can you recapture the early ecstasy? ... How a second honeymoon can make the Doldrums even sweeter

It is amazing how one of the great pleasures of life can turn into one of the great hassles. The commonest accusation hurled at wives during the Doldrums stage is "You never want to make love anymore."

Sex also may turn into one of the great disappointments of marriage. Both sexes lament that, "Sex isn't what it used to be. The rapture and the ecstasy have disappeared."

There is absolutely no doubt that there is a disparity of desire in most marriages, but this is no reason to make each other miserable. The solution is simple. Don't argue about it. Do it. It is a simple act of love and generosity. You have nothing to lose by making love—and a lot to lose if you don't.

You may not feel turned on or you may feel too tired. You may be convinced you will not climax. I do not consider these adequate excuses. I agree that it is hard to change gears after a hectic day at the office or at home and think sex, but it is one of the best things you can do for yourself. Women complain that their husbands don't communicate with them (see the following chapter), but then they balk at making love, the most intimate form of communication.

If you are tired, you don't have to make a big production of it. Just say that you're tired. If you have not fallen into the trap of faking orgasms, he will not feel inadequate if you don't have an orgasm. And he will love you for understanding and meeting his sexual needs and desires.

Most of the time, however, you can throw off your fatigue. What you probably need is a little time to yourself to recharge your sexual batteries. It is easier than you think.

If you leave work feeling utterly exhausted, it is not physical exhaustion as much as stress. You need to move your body. Consider taking an exercise class right after work before you go home. If you can't fit that in with your schedule, perhaps you can walk part of the way home. If that is impossible, change your clothes once you get home and get out and walk or bicycle for half an hour.

If you arrive home feeling exhausted and grouchy and it is raining or snowing or a brutal ninety-nine degrees outside, go straight to the bathtub. Spend half an hour in solitary peace soaking out the mental and physical kinks and then put on something comfortable and rejoin the human race.

My special friend is my jump rope. If I can't get out during the day to walk and I don't have time to swim, I jump rope for five minutes. That's enough to work up a good sweat and banish tension.

If you have been home all day with cranky children or working your head—and feet—off as a Pink Lady at the hospital, give yourself the same half-hour for recuperation that the working wife does.

Don't hesitate to ask your husband to man the decks while you get your second wind. If he knows that it means you will be in the mood for sex, you will find him quite cooperative.

•   •   •

Recapturing the early ecstasy is more difficult. This bothers men far more than it does women. Most women find that a blockbuster orgasm is rapture enough. But men, who in general have no difficulty in reaching orgasm, want more. All of us tend to be greedy about pleasure, and remembered pleasures are most tantalizing of all. If sex was rapture before, why can't it be the same now? Sometimes it can, but never as often as it was in those first giddy, toe-curling days of delight.

What happens is that we become desensitized (see Chapter 25). The more often you have sex together, the less exciting it becomes as the years go by. It almost seems like a case of damned if you do and damned if you don't. This does not mean that ecstasy is beyond your grasp forever. The truth is that it is in your head. If you do not bring those early emotions to bed with you, you cannot expect to reexperience that early ecstasy.

It was based on excitement and novelty and love. Every once in a while you may find yourselves carried away. That old leave-the-world-behind ecstasy is yours again. Usually because there is some extra excitement between you. You may have had a rip-roaring fight and are making up by making love. He may have had a big promotion and feel on top of the world. You may have won the lottery. Or you may simply have been exercising vigorously—running, playing tennis, cross-country skiing, swimming laps—and your heart is beating faster, your temperature is slightly elevated and your body is ready for love.

It is unrealistic to expect the heights every time. Unfortunately many men are unrealistic. They feel there is something wrong with their wives. That's why the rapture and ecstasy have disappeared. They look at other women and fantasize about having sex with them. No question about it, they tell themselves, the other woman would be more exciting. And so she would be. Simply because she would be a novelty.

You cannot block a man's fantasies, but you can usually prevent them from becoming more than fantasies by nurturing your sexual life. Don't take it for granted. Be receptive. Let him know that you find him exciting. Make time in your life for sex.

A 99 percent surefire way to help yourselves recapture that old magic is to go away for a weekend. "I don't need a new woman," one man said. "I just need my wife in a different bed in a different room. This business of making love at the same time in the same bed gets to be tedious. Like brushing your teeth. But I get really turned on when we're in a hotel or a motel." Almost any change—time of day, location, lighting, music, position—will add a little zip to sex that has dulled down. (You might also spend half an hour or so going back over Chapters 15, 25 and 26. A great deal of the information in those chapters also applies to this Doldrums-stage problem.)

The Doldrums are the perfect time for a second honeymoon, and every couple should treat themselves to one. Dip into your MOMO account (see Chapter 17) if you have to. It is worth it. You get a perspective on your marriage and the place of sex in your marriage from a second honeymoon I do not believe you can get any other way.

I would not have missed our second honeymoon for the world. It was glorious. We revisited the little cottage on the Gaspé Peninsula where we had spent our honeymoon. It brought back so many memories.

On our first honeymoon we had noticed that there were a lot of places called *auberge*. It was a word neither of us had learned in high school French. We had no idea it was the French word for "inn." We decided it was the name of an enormous chain of small hotels. The second time around, we relived that mistake, pointing out every little *auberge* that we saw to each other and laughing tenderly at that unsophisticated couple who had been so happy—and so very young.

And Milt took a second-honeymoon version of our favorite first-honeymoon snapshot, which he had captioned, "Joyce Standing on Her Hands." I was bending over with my hands tucked under my feet and looking up and grinning like an idiot. When we showed the second-honeymoon version to our daughter when we got home, I could tell she considered us rather quaint, not to say childish. And perhaps we were and are. But we loved it all. We were reliving a time when we had our whole life ahead of us and the world was our oyster.

Milt and I did a tremendous amount of reminiscing on our second honeymoon. We talked about the early years when we were both finishing our education. And about the crummy little apartment we lived in when Lisa was born and Milt was earning fifty dollars a month as an intern and we were poorer than church mice. We recalled the wonders of watching our daughter's first smile...her first step...her reaction to her first taste of ice cream. We marveled at how life had grown more interesting every year. How our love had grown.

The most wonderful thing—and I admit I cried from happiness the night we talked about it—was how completely realized we both felt, sexually and emotionally. From the perspective of this second honeymoon we could see just how far we had come and how much we had changed in our years together.

Our second honeymoon was not as full of sexual excitement as our first. But we had not expected it to be. Sex continued to be an enduring pleasure and a bond, but now it was just one of the multitude of pleasures we shared with each other.

And this brings us back to the problem of recapturing the early ecstasy. If you have a lot going on in your lives that you both find fun and interesting, sex is not likely to present a problem. It is when life gets dull—and maybe you get a little lazy—that he grumbles out loud about your never wanting to make love. And grumbles to himself about sex not being as good as it used to be. This is your cue to get out your challenge list (see Chapter 26) and start thinking of ways to make your lives fuller and more interesting. When you are having fun together, that zest and excitement will carry right over into your lovemaking.

THIRTY-TWO

*The communication gender gap... Are you
communicating?... How much do you really want to know
about your husband?... Learning to listen...
The most intimate communication*

While Doldrums-stage men complain that they don't get enough sex, their wives complain that their husbands don't talk to them enough. This is rarely a problem in the earlier years of marriage, but in the calm of the Doldrums, you may become aware that your husband rarely talks to you unless you count communications like "When's supper?... What did you do with my old blue sweater?... Who's got the car keys?... Tell Johnny that the next time he leaves his bike in the driveway I'm going to run over it" as talk. Few women do.

There is a real gender gap when it comes to communication. Women feel that men do not communicate enough. Men feel that they do. But no matter how silent they seem, men are almost as convinced as women of the vital importance of communication in marriage. In one study, a group of engaged couples was asked to list the most important ingredients in a happy marriage. The answers ranged from love to sex to children to companionship and back. Some time later the researchers asked the couples who were then married what they now considered most important. The second time around it was practically unanimous. For both men and women communication was far and away the most important factor in marriage. "The communication factor just overwhelmed everything else," a researcher reported.

If both sexes agree that communication is the key to a happy marriage, how is it that women are always complaining that their husbands never talk to them, never tell them what they are thinking and feeling? Most of the time it is because their husbands don't. "Men find it incredibly difficult to talk about feelings. They live lives of quiet desperation and isolation for the most part," says Marjorie Shaevitz of the Institute for Family and Work Relationships in La Jolla, California.

Women are socialized to talk. "Generally women's friendships with one another rest on shared intimacies, self-revelation and emotional support," Dr. Lillian Rubin wrote in her book *Intimate Strangers*. "Men's relationships, however, are marked by shared activities. Even when a man claims another man as his best friend, the two share little about their interior lives."

This is practically inevitable. All his life a man gets a subliminal message that "Real men don't talk." Feminist Kate Millett put it succinctly. "Women express, men repress," she said. And this seems to be the way we want it, no matter what we say.

We like our men to be strong and silent. One revealing study found that both men and women think more highly of a man and consider him better adjusted if he keeps his personal problems to himself. Quite the opposite is true of women. The woman who discusses her problems openly is considered better adjusted than the one who keeps them to herself.

Once you understand this, you will not expect your husband to confide in you the way you confide in him. Even so, no matter how reticent you may consider him, the fact probably is that he tells you more about his inner fears, his hopes and his state of mind than he does anyone else.

(I want to make it clear that I am not discussing that minority of husbands who refuse to even speak to their wives. Men who give their wives the silent treatment are as psychologically abusive as men who beat their wives are physically abusive. The man who gives his wife the silent treatment day after day, week after week, needs help, although he will undoubtedly resist any suggestions to this effect. If you cannot persuade such a man to seek professional help, do get some for yourself. A skilled and experienced therapist can help you keep your perspective and emotional equilibrium. He or she may even be able to suggest ways to break the silence.)

All this being said, most husbands communicate far more than their wives give them credit for. Because women find it so easy to talk, they often ignore the fact that talking is not the only means of communicating and that it may be more noise than communication as the following mini–case histories show.

ISABELLE AND SAM

"Sam is the original strong silent man," Isabelle complained. "Always has been. I tell him it is important that we talk. He just shrugs. But I make a point of communicating just the same.

"Like last night. I told him I didn't think the way they had remodeled the supermarket was any improvement. And I told him how one of the women in my aerobics class pulled a muscle. And that I thought the two gays who live on the next street are splitting up."

"At our house it's yakety-yakety-yak all the time," Sam said. "Isabelle likes to make noise. Most of the time I don't listen.

"Don't get me wrong. I love her. I'd rather be with her

than with anyone else in the world. But I do wish she didn't feel she had to tell me about every blessed thing that happens during the day. Lots of nights I'm just too tired to listen. And most of what she has to say is too trivial for me to make the effort."

SHARON AND PAUL

"I beg Paul to talk to me," Sharon said. "The other night I was knitting and Paul was reading. It was so quiet it got on my nerves.

"'Let's talk,' I said.

"'Okay,' he said. 'What about?'

"'Anything,' I said. 'We never talk.'

"'We're talking right now,' he said, 'but it doesn't seem to be going anywhere. If you've got something to talk about, let me know.'"

"Sharon's always after me to talk," Paul acknowledged, "but after fourteen years of marriage, I don't have much new left to say. I look forward to coming home to her and the kids. And having a couple of hours to myself to read or watch television before we go to bed means a lot to me. It's the only quiet time of my day. And I like to spend it with her.

"I didn't realize she felt so desperate about my silence. We talk more than you might think from what she said. We talk about the kids and what we want to do on vacation and what we want to plant in the garden next year. We've even started to discuss how we want to live after I retire—and that's a good twenty-five years in the future."

Both Sam and Paul were doing more communicating than their wives seemed to realize. Both of them showed that they loved their wives and children. Both were involved in family life. And both were convinced there was sufficient communication.

Just as there is often a disparity of sexual desire, there is also a disparity in the need for sharing, which is what communication is all about. A woman tends to want to share the minutiae of her day. Most men do not. The trivia of your day—or of their own—is simply trivia to them and not worth talking about.

There is something else to consider. How much, despite all your talk, are you really communicating about yourself? Take Isabelle. She told her husband about the remodeled supermarket, about the woman who pulled a muscle and about her suspicion that two of their neighbors were breaking up. A lot of talk, but nothing about her feelings or thoughts. And when you come right down to it, how many vital thoughts and feelings are left to communicate after twelve or fifteen or seventeen years of marriage. The law of diminishing returns sets in after a while.

Add to that the fact that we all have thoughts that we are better off not communicating. I am all for honesty in marriage, but I see no reason for a woman to tell her husband that she would love to know what John Neighbor is like in bed or that she has sometimes regretted not marrying Billy Boring, who surprised everyone by becoming president of his own company and now rides around in a chauffeur-driven limousine. These are thoughts better kept to yourself. Just as your husband is wise to keep to himself his observation that you look like something the cat dragged in just before your menstrual period or that he sometimes wishes he had not been in such a rush to get married.

We all have thoughts that are better not shared. If you keep after your husband to tell you what he's thinking, he may just blurt out one of these better-kept-silent thoughts. And what have you gained? Nothing but hurt feelings and grief. So give your husband room. Don't make him cross the t's and dot the i's of everything that crosses his mind.

THE ART OF LISTENING

Some husbands who started out by sharing their thoughts and feelings are uncommunicative by the time their marriage reaches the Doldrums. And in most cases, it is because they have discovered their wives don't listen.

"It's hopeless," Gordon said. "Heather never listens. A couple of nights ago I started to tell her about the memo headquarters sent out about the new vacation policy. All of a sudden, she interrupts me and says, 'The Costas are going to the Finger Lakes this summer.'

"It was totally irrelevant. I was trying to tell her that the new company policy was that one week of vacation had to be taken in the winter from now on. But she wasn't listening. Once she heard the word vacation, all she could think of was what the Costas were going to do. She's always like that. I didn't think I'd married a birdbrain, but sometimes I wonder."

Roger stopped sharing his concerns with Alison a couple of years ago after he had come home one night very worried about the future. "It looks like the men are going out on strike next week," he had told her. "That means I'll be working nights and weekends until it's settled."

"You can't," Alison said flatly. "We've got too much going on next week. Parents' night at school. The concert on Friday night. The Armstrongs' cookout on Saturday. And Jill is counting on you for the Dad and Daughter dinner. Tell them you have plans."

Roger's company had been hard hit by the recession. He was worried that the strike would prove to be a deathblow. The idea of being unemployed was frightening. He wanted to talk to Alison about it, but she seemed oblivious to what was at stake. Their social commitments seemed more important to her than his business career. So Roger held his tongue. His last thought before he fell asleep that night was, "She really isn't interested in me and how I feel."

Alison had listened to what Roger had said, but she had not heard the message behind his words, the message that he was deeply worried about the future.

Few husbands and wives really listen to each other, maintains Dr. Donald G. Ellise, associate professor of communication at Michigan State University. "Listening is an underdeveloped skill in most families," he says. Most of us listen only at about 25 percent efficiency.

Listening intelligently is a complicated process. "The listener is tracking incoming information, sorting it, organizing it and making decisions about its meaning," Dr. Ellise says. When you are really listening to what someone says, your temperature goes up a fraction of a degree, your heartbeat speeds up and your blood circulates faster. Listening is work. The woman who wants more and better communication in marriage should work to improve her listening skills.

If you follow three simple rules, you will find that you are a far more effective listener immediately. And the longer you follow these rules, the more sensitive a listener you will be. They are:

1. PAY ATTENTION.
Do not let your mind wander. Many people pretend to be listening, but their minds are a thousand miles away. They hear the words, but they do not really register. These people usually give themselves away because their expressions are either exaggeratedly attentive or blank.

If someone were to say, "You haven't been listening to a word I've been saying," the listener would protest self-righteously, "Of course I have," and parrot back the last few words the speaker had uttered. This means nothing. It is just automatic replay. It does not mean that the listener has absorbed what was said. If he or she were quizzed on the specifics, the listener would fail miserably.

2. DON'T INTERRUPT.
Be courteous enough to let the speaker have his or her say. Too often when someone says something we don't like or don't agree

with, we interrupt with a defense or a rebuttal. This is not only rude, it is not smart. If you listen until the speaker has finished, he or she will be more prepared to hear your comments. And what you have to say will be more pertinent because it will be based on the whole message and not just a fraction of it.

A sneaky form of interruption is to sit there and concentrate on what you are going to say when the speaker finishes. This means that you tune out most of what he or she has to say. Your response is bound to betray that you only listened to part of what the speaker was saying.

3. ANALYZE WHAT YOU HEAR.

This is the most important of the three rules. What is the speaker really saying? Is there another message behind those words? Ask yourself, "What does this mean to him (or her)? How does he feel about it?" It is important to respond to how the speaker feels about whatever it is before you respond to how it affects you. If Alison had done this, Roger probably would still be sharing his hopes and fears with her.

Women are usually very good at picking up these unspoken messages. We are much more gifted than men at sensing the difference between what people say and what they mean and picking up the nuances that reveal feelings. In marriage, however, especially in the Doldrums stage, we tend to take our husbands for granted and sometimes concentrate more on our own feelings than on his. This does not make for efficient listening—nor for good communication.

BETTER THAN WORDS

"The most powerful form of intimacy," says psychologist Stephen Thayer, "is touching." If a picture is worth a thousand words, a hug conveys volumes. When one man I know came home after a hard day at work, his wife opened the door and instead of giving him the customary peck on the cheek, she threw her arms around him and hugged him. "That's the nicest thing that's happened to me for ages," the happily surprised husband said. The unexpected gesture of loving welcome meant more to him that night than anything his wife could have said.

A pat on the hand or a stroke of the cheek may communicate more love and tenderness to a man than any number of words. And such loving touching often triggers reciprocal loving communication—with or without words.

Making love is one of our most basic forms of communication—not only the closeness of the sex act itself but the afterglow, that feeling of comfortable intimacy after sexual tension is released. It is a time when love and contentment make a couple realize how really close they are to each other.

By and large I have found that even the women who complain that their husbands seldom talk to them are very well tuned into his thoughts and feelings. They know when he is sad or happy, cranky or depressed without having to be told. They know how he feels about politics and religion and the people next door. They know when he wants to make love without his having to say a word. And they know when he needs to be alone. They know how he is going to react to most things, good or bad. They know how to comfort him—and how to hurt him.

When we live with someone we love day after day, year after year, we learn about them in all kinds of ways. We learn as much from the silences as from the words. So before you complain that your husband does not communicate, stop and think. Perhaps he communicates more than you give him credit for.

If there is a breakdown in communication, then start listening efficiently. And make sure you communicate love and tenderness and understanding. Above all, don't confuse talk with communication.

PART NINE

THE TWENTY-YEAR DITCH

THIRTY-THREE

*The disposable wife . . . Men's adolescent response to
middle-age panic . . . How Katina was ditched a week
after her twenty-first wedding anniversary . . . How no-fault
divorce discriminates against women over forty . . . The
gamble a wife can take to save her marriage—and why
the odds are against her*

Life is not fair. Neither is marriage. Especially today. Especially for women. Especially for women over forty. Earlier
in this book, I made the point that there is no time in marriage
when a woman can sit back and relax and say, "Well, this is
it. Now I'm married for life." There was a time when a woman
could, but no longer. Sociological projections suggest that a
woman in her twenties who marries today can expect to be
widowed or divorced by the time she is forty-four—and more
likely divorced than widowed.

I call the last vulnerable stage of marriage the Twenty-Year
Ditch. And with good reason. You may have been a devoted
and loving wife and mother. Your husband may have seemed
happy with you and the children, comfortable in his marriage.
He may have been considerate and emotionally supportive.
But when he reaches a certain age, there is a very real possibility that he will consider you of no more value than an empty
tube of toothpaste or a used Kleenex.

The Disposable Wife

We are back to savage time. Centuries ago when food for the tribe was scarce, the menopausal woman was set adrift on an ice floe to freeze to death or was abandoned to starve in the wilderness. Today wives are being abandoned for far less reason.

We have reentered the era of the disposable wife. The phenomenon is so new that few people are aware of its extent. A rather mild version of the Twenty-Year Ditch surfaced in the early 1960s. Dr. Alfred Messer, a psychoanalyst and family therapist in Atlanta, referred to it as the Twenty-Year Fracture.

Struck by the fact that the divorce rate among Georgia couples who had been married twenty years or more had started going up quite markedly, Dr. Messer studied forty-two couples who had sought professional help in preserving their marriage. He found that three-quarters of them filed divorce petitions within two years of their last child's departure from home.

"Marriages that were child centered," he concluded, "went through a stormy period during which the couples, instead of functioning primarily as father and mother, had to become comfortable once again in the roles of husband and wife." Not an easy task, it seems, since 75 percent of the couples in his study found it impossible. When the children grew up and left home, these couples discovered they had very little in common. They were miles apart emotionally and intellectually. The marriage had become a support system for the children and little else. Left alone in their empty nest, husband and wife discovered they had grown apart.

This pattern of divorce after twenty or more years of marriage was not confined to the state of Georgia. Twenty-Year Fractures were creating a new bulge in the divorce rate all over the country. These broken marriages were very much a minority, however. For most couples, the years after the children leave home represent a return to the freedom and romance of the early years before the first child arrived.

"It is my experience that healthy marriages are revitalized when the children grow up and leave," says Dr. Peter A. Martin, clinical professor of psychiatry at the University of Michigan Medical School. "By this time, healthy parents in good marriages have had it with putting their own interests aside for the sake of the children."

Nevertheless, the number of marriages that were breaking up after two, three and four decades kept increasing. Couples were divorcing years and years after the last child had left home. Childless couples were divorcing after twenty or thirty years of marriage. What was going on?

THE TWENTY-YEAR DITCH

What was going on was that the Twenty-Year Ditch, a far more virulent and destructive phenomenon, had appeared on the scene. The Twenty-Year Fracture is simply the final consequence of unstemmed Baby Drift in which both partners have lost touch with each other. But the Twenty-Year Ditch is a twentieth-century version of how primitive man abandoned women past their reproductive years to starve or freeze to death. It is a one-sided action. Women today are being ditched by their husbands. Dumped. Discarded. The woman in her forties or fifties or sixties or—yes, even her seventies—is considered disposable. And she is being ditched in increasing numbers every year.

What has happened? Why are these long-established marriages breaking up?

There is an old saying that, "Where there is a will, there is a way." In this case, the will has probably always existed to some extent, but the temptation has become greater. And the way has only become generally available during the last decade or so.

THE WILL AND THE TEMPTATION

To understand the Twenty-Year Ditch, one must understand the male midlife crisis. It is just as real as female menopause but is psychological rather than physical. By the time a man has been married for twenty years or so, he has reached middle age. This is not easy to accept. "Who? Me? Middle-aged? I don't feel middle-aged," he protests to his reflection in the bathroom mirror.

But he is. Middle age is not a state of mind or a feeling. It is the halfway point in our lives, bridging the gulf between youth and age. Men usually reach middle age before their wives, partly because of their shorter life expectancy, partly because they tend to marry women younger than themselves.

When a man first realizes he is middle-aged, he is scared silly—and depressed. It may be the advent of his first grandchild. Or the night he overhears his adolescent son's date describe him as "a dignified older man." Or the day he learns he will not get the promotion he had hoped for and understands he has gone as far up the career ladder as he can. Or, as novelist Charles Simmons put it, "It begins when you catch sight of yourself in the store window and wonder who that...*mature* man is. You look around, there is no one else, it is you."

Most men come to terms with the fact of advancing age after the initial shock. They make the necessary psychological readjustments. They gain a new perspective on their lives and achieve a new emotional depth. Their wives are fortunate, because these men become more committed to their marriages as the years go by. They recognize the values and rewards of the family. Their companionship becomes sweeter. Their love deeper.

Other men panic. They do everything they can to turn back the clock. They have a truly terrible sense of urgency. Researchers have found that nearly 40 percent of the men between the ages of forty and fifty feel unaccountably rushed. "They become aware of their mortality," says the Reverend Robert

Hoskins, a family counselor and Congregational pastor in Connecticut. "They feel the need for a last chance at life and so they act out like adolescents."

The acting out usually takes the form of infidelity. The husband who has always been faithful becomes a philanderer. He goes from affair to affair like a butterfly sampling meadow flowers. As time goes by, he begins to think quite highly of himself. He has never felt as alive and potent. He feels rejuvenated. "The affair serves to bolster his sagging feelings of self-worth, virility and physical attractiveness," says Professor Marcia Lasswell of the Marriage and Family Therapy Program of the University of Southern California. "There is no intent to threaten the marriage—only to feel better about himself."

He begins to think of himself as a valuable commodity. He may not know that there are 7.3 million women in this country who cannot hope to marry because there are not enough men to go around, but he is definitely aware that there are many younger women who are interested in him—and available.

As time goes by, he meets a young woman who makes him feel as young as she is and stimulates him to heights of lovemaking he has never achieved before. He decides to get a divorce and marry this wonderful young thing. Why should he be tied down to an old woman with graying hair and laugh lines? Why should he spend the rest of his life with this woman with the thickening waistline and the flabby thighs when youth can be his for the asking? He sees his present marriage as a wasteland. It holds nothing for him.

In days past when life expectancies were shorter, a man in his fifties could not look forward to much more than another five years of vigorous life, but today the man in his fifties can expect to enjoy another twenty to thirty vigorous years. He has a whole generation worth of time ahead of him, time to father a new family if he wants. And often he does. "If a wife with whom he has lived for twenty-five years is no longer attractive to a man, he has compelling motivation to leave," says Dr. Richard A. Kalish of the School of Public Health at the University of California. "Five years of a new relationship may not be worth a divorce, but the prospect of fifteen or more years makes it worthwhile."

And so this man who has been married for twenty or more years tells his wife he wants a divorce. There is nothing she can do to stop him, as I will explain later in this chapter. It usually comes as a brutal shock. Ann Landers, the columnist, who was divorced when she was in her fifties after thirty-six years of marriage, spoke for many when she told an interviewer that, "Yes, it was a shock...it was totally unexpected."

Most women have no idea of what has been going on. Yes, a woman will say, her husband had seemed distracted and impatient in recent months. Yes, he had been coming home later than usual, working more nights. But he had explained that they had been putting a lot of pressure on him at the office and she had believed him. Suspected nothing. And then, from one second to the next, her life was changed. She was ditched. That is what happened to Katina.

"Foster moved out one week after our twenty-first wedding anniversary," Katina said. "It was a quiet celebration. He seemed distracted, but that was nothing unusual. He had had a lot of business problems lately.

"We went to our favorite restaurant for dinner that night. I felt sentimental. I remember saying something about our having come full circle. Our daughter was married and our son had just enlisted in the army. It was just the two of us again. 'It's our turn now,' I told him. 'Now we can take that second honeymoon we've always dreamed of. We can turn in the old heap for a new car. Maybe get a new living room rug one of these days.' Foster didn't say anything. Just smiled. Rather weakly, as I think back on it.

"A week later, he came home from work looking simply exhausted. He was so pale I thought he might be coming down with something. He made himself a drink and came into the kitchen where I was getting supper. I had had to work late that night and it was going to be hamburgers again.

"I said something. I don't remember what. He didn't answer. I looked at him to see if he was all right. He put his drink down on the kitchen counter.

"'I want a divorce,' he said. Just like that. I couldn't believe what he was saying. 'Is there someone else?' I asked.

"He nodded. I started to cry. This could not be happening to me. Not in my own kitchen. 'Who?' I choked out.

"'Cheryl,' he said.

"Cheryl had been a year ahead of our daughter in school. I had heard she was working in an insurance office downtown.

"'Don't make supper for me,' he said. 'I'm moving out tonight. Cheryl and I have rented an apartment near my office.'

"That's when I threw half a pound of raw hamburger at him."

There are thousands of stories like this. Hundreds of thousands. Katina's is so typical that an army of women could exclaim, "But that's my story!" The anger, the hurt, the dismay, the grief and the feeling of rejection make the Twenty-Year Ditch sad and destructive, but it is nothing compared with the brutality of divorce in later years. The truth is that the Twenty-Year Ditch might just as well be called the Thirty-Year or the Forty-Year or even the Fifty-Year Ditch.

Late-life divorces, says Lester Wallman, chairman of the Family Law Section Committee of the New York State Bar Association, have increased by more than a third in the past decade. Even the wife who is on the verge of celebrating her golden wedding anniversary is not immune. The revered Dr. Benjamin Spock of baby book fame, for instance, divorced his wife after forty-eight years of marriage. He was seventy-three at the time and she was sixty-eight. After the divorce he married a much younger woman.

Jane Spock's life had revolved around her husband to such a degree that she suffered four years of depression after the divorce. She had no sense of her own identity. "I was raised in the New England tradition," she said, "where the husband is the center of his wife's life." She contributed so much to her husband's famous child-care book that the publisher had suggested she be named as coauthor. When Dr. Spock became active in the peace movement and campaigned against American involvement in Vietnam, Jane Spock became an activist too.

Her depression is long behind her now. In her late seventies, she is as vigorous and busy as many women half her age, involved in many projects, including a support group she started in New York City for divorcées fifty-five years and over—"women who thought they would grow old with their husbands" and discovered their husbands did not want to grow old with them.

Age, the fear of age and the age double standard that prevails in this country trigger the Twenty-Year Ditch. Age discrimination is insidious and women are more victimized by it than men. It is everywhere. More than 60 percent of the women in this country are over forty, but only 25 percent of the women in television commercials are over forty, while nearly half the men who appear in commercials are.

There is a sense that women over forty are not interesting or attractive. They are almost nonpersons. Oh, there are exceptions. There are even men who would rather have dinner with a charming, witty woman in her forties than with a young beauty, but they are a minority. When it comes to men over forty, that is something else. Out of 400 psychiatrists who participated in a survey by the professional journal *Medical Aspects of Human Sexuality*, 296 of them agreed that men keep their sex appeal longer than women. "Men are judged by what they have accomplished, while women are judged by their appearance," commented Dr. Anthony Pietropinto. "Since men's accomplishments and wealth tend to increase with age, their sex appeal may actually grow with the passing years."

Fear and age, then, are precipitating factors of the Twenty-Year Ditch, but there is another important factor. Temptation. There is that sobering figure of 7.3 million. The 7.3 million women who will not marry because there are not enough men.

As a man gets older, the number of available women becomes even higher, because men die earlier than their wives on the average.

The man who used to be Mr. Wimp in his twenties becomes Mr. Wonderful when he gets to be sixty-five. He walks into a party and all of a sudden every woman there is paying attention to him. Unless he is exceptionally levelheaded, he may be seduced by all the fluttering and flattering.

"I've got women fluttering around me like moths around a candle," he tells himself. "They think I'm terrific. What do I need with this wife who remembers all my idiocies in full thirty-five-year panoramic detail and reminds me of them too often? Who wants to be married to a grandmother?

"I want to start fresh," he decides. "I'm a hell of a guy and I deserve a hell of a woman to spend my last years with."

The next thing you know, another man has asked his wife of thirty, forty or more years of marriage for a divorce. And whether she wants it or not, he usually gets it. Remember earlier I quoted that old saying, "Where there's a will, there's a way"? There is a way indeed. It has only been available for the last fourteen or fifteen years. The increase in late-life divorces stems almost completely from this new enabling factor.

No-Fault Divorce

The precipitating factor behind the Twenty-Year Ditch is the no-fault divorce law. One California judge calls the no-fault laws "handy vehicles for the summary disposal of old and used wives." Some form of no-fault divorce law is in effect in all but two of the fifty states as I write this. Illinois and South Dakota are the only holdouts.

Before no-fault the spouse who wanted to continue the marriage and did not want a divorce had a considerable amount of leverage. The scorned wife had the bitter satisfaction of swearing, "I'll take that bastard for every penny he has if he wants a divorce," and being able to do just that—or very nearly that. And the discarded wife and mother could negotiate for adequate financial provisions for her children and herself as a condition for agreeing to the divorce. No longer. As sociologists Ruth Dixon of the University of California and Lenore Weitzman of Stanford University sum up their research on the consequences of this relatively new legislation, "No-fault divorce has reduced wives' bargaining power over whether or not there will be a divorce, when it will take place, and what the terms of the settlement will be."

The spouse who wants to end the marriage has the power to under the no-fault laws. And since 1970, hundreds of thousands of husbands have been exercising this power. The number of husbands filing for divorce has increased markedly in every state where the no-fault concept has been adopted.

In California, the first state to adopt no-fault, husbands had represented approximately one-fifth of the plaintiffs in divorce actions in the years before the no-fault law became effective. When it was adopted in 1970, their numbers increased strikingly. In Los Angeles County, for instance, well over a third of the plaintiffs were now men. In San Diego, almost 40 percent of the plaintiffs were men. The number of men filing for divorce had increased by 50 to 100 percent. This proved to be the pattern across the country. In Florida, nearly a third of the divorce actions in the Tampa area had been filed by husbands before no-fault. Afterward, three-quarters of the actions were filed by husbands.

It is important not to forget that a good many wives file for divorce against their wishes. They are blackmailed into it by husbands who say, "If you don't, I will, and then people will start gossiping. They will blame the divorce on you." And so the wife, to avoid being considered promiscuous or alcoholic or unfit in some embarrassing way, agrees to file for divorce.

Statistics show that men who file for divorce usually do so in order to marry younger women. They also show that these men are usually older than the women they divorce. Just another example of the age double standard.

The end result of this supposedly enlightened law, under which no one is saddled with the blame for the breakup of the marriage, is that a horrifying number of women who have been married twenty years or longer are being ditched by their husbands—because the law now makes it so easy for a man to get a divorce.

There is no question but that the divorced woman over forty is discriminated against. A divorced woman is a second-class citizen in most cases. She loses status. Even today a couple's status is derived from the husband and his job.

She also loses what financial security she had unless she has a good-paying job or money of her own. Most states require that the assets of the marriage be divided "equitably" between husband and wife in divorce. But in most states, "equitable" turns out to mean that a woman gets about a third of the couple's assets. Only in California and a handful of other states that have community property laws is there a fifty-fifty split between a husband and wife in divorce. And even then a wife cannot be sure she is getting half. Some men who plan divorce often try to conceal their assets beforehand.

The divorced woman does not start her new life on anywhere near an equal footing with her ex-husband. He has been working for twenty or thirty years; she may not have done anything but keep house and bring up the children. This means she starts from ground zero while he is exactly where he was at the time of the divorce. He has the same earning power. It is easy enough to say that the divorced woman should go out and get a job. But who is going to hire a fifty- or sixty-year old woman who has never done anything but take care of her home and do volunteer work in the community? Who is going to teach her skills? She is not worth anyone's investment. What happens is that figuratively she is back on that ice floe. Statistics show that one year after divorce a woman's standard of living has decreased by 73 percent on the average while a man's has increased by 42 percent.

The divorced woman also loses social status. She is seen as a competitor by other wives, a competitor for their husbands. The divorced man, on the other hand, becomes a social asset. If he does not remarry immediately, he is the extra man who is always in demand. If he remarries, he is the center of a new social life.

There is no need to go on reciting chapter and verse proving that the woman usually loses more by divorce than the man. It is obvious. It is also obvious that the woman should do everything she can to avoid the divorce. But there is very little she can do after her husband has informed her he wants a divorce. He has already put his marriage behind him.

The woman who holds her marriage together during these last vulnerable years is the woman who has been successful in making life interesting and exciting for her husband. She has kept boredom at bay. The divorce-proof woman is usually the woman who is her husband's best friend, the woman who has always made sure that they have a good time together, the woman whose husband laughs with her. Shared laughter can cement a marriage so firmly it will never break up.

It is too late, however, to start improving the quality of your life together the day your husband asks for divorce, but there is one thing you can try.

The Trial Separation

I suggest that women who are faced with a demand for divorce try to scale it down to a six-month trial separation. This is a situation where you have nothing to lose—and you might have a great deal to gain. If he agrees, you have bought time. And time is on your side.

First of all, time will help you get over the shock. No one can think rationally and make sensible plans for the future when she is reeling from the shock of being rejected and having her whole world come down around her ears. Six months will give the healing process a chance to begin.

It also gives your husband a chance to reconsider. Who knows how he will feel at the end of six months? If he still wants a divorce at that time, you will have had a kind of dress rehearsal for your new life. The transition will be a little easier.

If he agrees to a trial separation, the two of you should put it in writing. It does not need to be complicated. You do not have to cover every contingency. I suggest an agreement along these lines: "We, Jane and John, are separating on such and such a day. I, John, will continue to support Jane and the children, as I have in the past. We agree that I will see the children at such and such times. We further agree that we will meet in six months and consider our situation at that time and what we should do about it." This is not a legal contract but a contract of honor. You might want to ask a marriage counselor or psychologist or minister to help you with it, but there is no reason why the two of you should not do it on your own.

After six months on his own, he may decide he has made a mistake and want to give the marriage a second chance. More likely he will still want the divorce. Once habits are broken, they are hard to reestablish. He may find he likes the freedom of being able to do as he pleases. You may find the same thing. He may break up with the woman who triggered his demand for a divorce, but he may not want to move back home. Whatever the outcome, the two of you can discuss and negotiate more calmly when you get together after six months. If nothing else, you have gained a valuable breathing spell.

If it doesn't work? If he still wants out? All the woman of forty or fifty or more can do is pick herself up and get on with her new life. So many women are doing this and growing stronger in the process that one has to admire them—their courage, their accomplishments and their gallantry. But this is not the happy ending they had envisioned for their lives. It would be far better if they could grow in strength and accomplishments in marriage and enjoy the companionship, love and mutual support that marriage can provide. My strong hope is that this discussion of the vulnerable stages of marriage will help women avoid the Twenty-Year Ditch and have that happy-ever-after marriage they believed would be theirs on their wedding day.

THIRTY-FOUR

Is marriage worth the effort? ... How I put my own marriage ahead of my career ... Coping with football widowhood ... Meeting the marriage challenge ... The sweet triumph of a successful marriage

Is it worth it? Is it really worth the effort to keep a marriage strong, alive and interesting through all the vulnerable stages? Is it worth having to make the greater effort?

I say yes, Yes, YES! And I practice what I preach. It is not enough to be aware of the vulnerable stages of marriage and how to handle the problems that may arise at each stage. The woman who wants a forever-after marriage must work unceasingly to strengthen her marriage. She must always keep her goal in mind.

I do. Even after thirty-five years of marriage, I do everything I can to keep our marriage strong and vital. While I do not subordinate my career to my husband's, I do my best not to let it interfere with our marriage. And that takes some doing, especially since I travel thousands of miles every week to fulfill lecture and television commitments.

People are often surprised when they learn I get up before

seven every morning to make breakfast for Milt. While he is shaving and dressing, I'm in the kitchen grinding coffee beans for the coffee, squeezing fresh orange juice and scrambling eggs or setting out a choice of cold cereals. I am not superwoman. Let me confess that I eat breakfast in my wrapper, but my hair is combed, my face washed and I've taken the time to put on a tiny bit of makeup. We don't talk much at breakfast. We usually just sit there reading the newspaper and watching the news on television. Sometimes we don't even say boo between the time he kisses me good morning and then kisses me goodbye on his way out the door. Our conversation is usually along the lines of "Please pass the marmalade" and "Would you like a little more coffee?" But I know Milt feels better about life when I'm there to make breakfast and eat it with him. And I feel better too.

This is the reason I do not do extended lecture tours. It would make much more sense when I have a lecture date in Dallas, for instance, to accept engagements in Houston and Corpus Christi and Austin and spend four or five days at a time in Texas. But I don't. I do my lecture in Dallas and then I fly home. If I have a lecture in Houston the next day, I fly to Texas again. I often do the round trip between Los Angeles and New York three times a week just so I can be home at night and have breakfast with Milt in the morning.

It can be exhausting, but I feel it is worth the extra effort. If you stay away from home several days at a time week after week, you get out of the habit of marriage. So much goes on in each other's lives that you just don't get a chance to share. You find you are building up independent lives. This is why I think the new "commuter marriages" are so vulnerable.

This does not represent any particular sacrifice for me. Everything is so much more fun when Milt and I are together that I don't stay away from home one minute longer than I have to. Sometimes when I'm in Los Angeles and staying at the Beverly Hills Hotel, which, heaven knows, is one of the most comfortable places in the world, I am devastatingly lonely.

Especially if I have unavoidable commitments that keep me there over the weekend.

There are many things I enjoy doing by myself. I love to read. And I love to shop. Especially window shop. But there is a limit to what I can enjoy by myself. And when I come back to the hotel in the evening and I see couples setting off arm in arm, I feel terribly alone in the world. Even though Milt and I always talk on the telephone before we go to sleep when I'm away, it is not the same thing.

Milt feels the way I do. When I occasionally have to be away on the weekend and he goes to our farm, which is the place he loves more than any place else on earth, he says he just doesn't get anything done.

"I'm just moping around and wasting time," he told me on the telephone one recent weekend. "I'm not even doing any reading. I wish you'd hurry up and get back."

That made me feel good. I was sorry he was feeling lonely, but it was evidence that our marriage is very solid, that we both feel better when we are together than when we are apart.

I would not want to pretend to the world that our marriage is always sweetness and light. We squabble. We disagree. We fight. Fiercely sometimes. But we always make up.

And guess who takes the first step toward making up? Even when Milt is truly sorry, it is just impossible for him to be the first to say, "I'm sorry. I was wrong." So I do. This used to infuriate me when we were first married. It just was not fair that I always had to be the one to say "I'm sorry" first. But then I began to understand how hard it was for him to say, "I'm sorry. I was wrong." But once I've apologized, it is easier for him to say he is sorry too. It may not be fair, but that is the way it is. And it works just fine for us.

One of the hardest adjustments I had to make was to Milt's utter absorption in football. Football does not really interest me. But he is crazy about it. During football season, he is glued to the television set all weekend. I used to tell everyone I was a football widow, and I would go shopping or visit my folks while he was watching his games. But then he complained he was lonely. Why couldn't I stay home and watch football with him?

I kind of shrugged my shoulders when he said he was lonely. My feeling was that he didn't know whether I was there or not. I told a friend once that I could divorce Milt during football season and he would never be aware of it—unless it were announced on "ABC's Wide World of Sports."

Nevertheless, if Milt wanted me home with him, I was going to stay home with him. I was the one who had to make the adjustment. And I have. These days when he flicks on the set to watch football, I sit there with him, but I spend my time filing the recipes I clip from newspapers and magazines or I answer my mail. I plan our menus for the week and make out my grocery list. And I cook. If I am within the sound of his voice, that's almost as good as if I'm sitting there beside him. I've come to think of football weekends as very relaxing and peaceful.

Have I learned to love football? Not really. It is just not my game. Last fall when Milt excitedly yelled out to me in the kitchen, "It's 18 to 16!" I shouted back, "Who are we for? Eighteen?"

I could go on and on listing the ways I put extra effort into our marriage. I work harder at it than Milt does. As a matter of fact, I often think he does not work at it at all. He simply accepts it as an extremely pleasant arrangement for living. And I agree with him.

Life just does not seem right when we are not together. I feel completed when I am with Milt. Good things are better when we share them. And rotten things are not quite as rotten when we can share them.

When you feel hurt or frightened or disappointed or sad, if there is somebody who can hug you, things immediately seem a little bit better. When you have the blues, you tend to have tunnel vision. And everything you see down that tunnel is awful. Terrible. But when you can share your distress with your husband, he can point out things that lie beyond what you are able to see at the moment.

Milt always points out options that I had never even considered. Or he helps me look at things differently and think about them differently. And suddenly life is not so dismal after all.

There is no doubt in my mind that marriage is the most satisfactory way of life. And yes, I do work harder at it than my husband does. But marriage means more to a woman than to a man. So perhaps it is only right that I work harder. Besides—and this is important—there are those 7.3 million unmarried women out there who would just love to be in my shoes. That is enough to keep me working at our marriage.

It is a challenge. And the challenge is what makes it interesting. If you reach a point in marriage where you don't face a challenge in the relationship, life gets boring. And that means danger ahead. But there is no reason for life to get boring. The fact is that you will never know everything about your husband, just as you will never know everything about yourself. This means that life is full of surprises and challenges.

If you meet the challenges and you create a solid marriage that stands up to the crises and temptation of the years, it is a triumph. As William Attwood, the writer and former publisher, once asked, "Isn't there something triumphant about two people—so different in so many obvious and also subtle ways—staying together through decades of sickness, quarrels, hard times, obstreperous children, incompatibility, menopause, clashing egos, tiresome anecdotes, excessive proximity and deteriorating sex appeal? You bet there is!"

He is right. There really is. And it is just that sweet triumph that I wish for every woman.

THIRTY-FIVE

I keep telling people that marriage is not fair. And it never will be as long as the 7.3 million husband gap exists. But the time may come when the husband gap is replaced by the wife gap. Scientists believe that we will eventually have the capability of choosing the sex of our children. When and if this becomes possible, research indicates that there may be as many as 140 boys born for every 100 girls in this country. Even allowing for the greater fragility of the male and the higher death rate among male infants, this means that there will be a surplus of men. And then who is going to complain about marriage being unfair?